Prentice Hall

WORKBOOK

FOR WRITERS

FIFTH EDITION

Melinda G. Kramer
Purdue University

John W. Presley
Augusta College

Donald C. Rigg
Broward Community College

Prentice Hall, Englewood Cliffs, New Jersey 07632

Editorial/production supervision and
  interior design: *Maureen Lopez*
Manufacturing buyer: *Ray Keating*

Printed in the United States of America

10 9 8 7 6 5 4 3 2 1

ISBN 0-13-702763-X

Prentice-Hall International (UK) Limited, *London*
Prentice-Hall of Australia Pty. Limited, *Sydney*
Prentice-Hall Canada Inc., *Toronto*
Prentice-Hall Hispanoamericana, S.A., *Mexico*
Prentice-Hall of India Private Limited, *New Delhi*
Prentice-Hall of Japan, Inc., *Tokyo*
Simon & Schuster Southeast Asia Pte. Ltd., *Singapore*
Editora Prentice-Hall do Brasil, Ltda., *Rio de Janeiro*

CONTENTS

PREFACE

The *Prentice Hall Workbook for Writers,* 5th Edition, provides what users want most in a workbook. It contains new exercises in almost every section. In addition, the fifth edition preserves those teaching and learning aids from previous editions that suit the workbook for either classroom use or successful self-study.

The reason behind the new exercises is fairly simple: students learn better if the material is fresh and engaging. Since the ethnic heritage theme that proved so popular in the previous editions offers an almost limitless store of rich material for exercises and examples, we were delighted to continue that theme in this edition. As before, we have included a wide range of types of exercises and a large number of them. In areas where students frequently need extra work, the number of exercise sentences is especially plentiful.

Second, the *Workbook* has an extremely useful format. So that students will not lose the instructional material when they tear out the exercise pages, the exercises and the "teaching" portions are separated. This format allows for expanded instructional sections as well; students receive more complete explanations and examples before they work the exercises.

Also, a number of sections contain short "practices" to which answers are given at the end of the section. Thus, students can check their understanding of the subject matter and receive immediate feedback. Used in class, the practices enable instructors to identify and address problems that need further attention *before* students work the exercises rather than after the fact.

The *Workbook* has always had a dual purpose. It was conceived as a companion to the *Prentice Hall Handbook for Writers,* providing explanations and exercises to complement those in the *Handbook.* But it has also been effectively used alone in composition courses and is written as a totally self-sufficient text. The fifth edition continues to fulfill those two aims.

The fifth edition of the *Workbook* and the tenth edition of the *Handbook* follow the same order of presentation. Teachers wishing to refer students to the *Workbook* for supplementary exercises will have no trouble finding appropriately sequenced, matching material. References to corresponding *Handbook* sections are given in parentheses in the *Workbook's* section headings and in the table of contents.

Classes using the *Prentice Hall Diagnostic Test for Writers* will also find the *Workbook* to be a valuable aid. Its explanatory sections and exercises can give students additional instruction and practice in problem areas. The *Workbook* also contains review sections intended to familiarize students with the kinds of material in, and the format of, the *Diagnostic Test*.

Because we recognize that there are as many methods for teaching writing as there are writing teachers, we have used a variety of approaches in the *Workbook's* exercises while striving to keep the majority of them key-gradable. We advocate no one theory but acknowledge the best of our profession's pedagogy. We understand the concerns of traditionalists; at the same time, we value the innovations derived from recent research. Our constant goal has been to present what colleagues and students tell us is sensible—and what works.

We gratefully acknowledge the guidance and assistance of our acquisitions editor at Prentice Hall, Lynne Greenberg, and our production editor, Bob Pisillo. The worthiness of a book is due in no small part to the quality of the team supporting the authors; our support from Prentice Hall has been outstanding.

Finally, we wish to thank the students at Purdue University, Augusta College, and Broward Community College. It is our students, as always, who provide the essential challenge and inspiration.

MELINDA G. KRAMER

JOHN W. PRESLEY

DONALD C. RIGG

OUR COMMON LANGUAGE

This book is about language, particularly written English and specifically *standard* written English. Few of us always speak standard English; we frequently use slang, jargon, or dialects easily recognized by our families, friends, and coworkers. But when we pick up popular magazines or newspapers, open textbooks, or look at notices on bulletin boards, what we see—and *expect* to see—is standard English.

Because they are widely accepted and generally followed, the rules and conventions governing standard English ensure that the greatest number of people will understand a written message. We use standard English not necessarily because it is "good" or "right," but because it is the accepted norm; in fact, *standard* means "the norm." Of course that's the purpose of communication—to get the message across, to be easily understood by as many readers as possible.

Having a standard language is important to the development of a society. It enables people from different backgrounds and ethnic origins to communicate with one another. In a society as culturally mixed as the United States', standard English has been crucial. We are a nation of immigrants. You and I, or our relatives, came to this country from some place else. Even native Americans, the American Indians, immigrated to this continent from another land—from Asia, across the Bering Strait, so anthropologists tell us. The fact that our common language is English rather than Spanish, Swahili, French, or Vietnamese is much less important than the fact that we have a common language for communicating our present ideas and sharing our richly diverse pasts.

This book is also about sharing the past. Many of the exercises contain information about America's ethnic roots. Since we or our ancestors originally came from some place else, a book devoted to our common language is an appropriate place to learn a little about what we immigrants have contributed to American society.

*   *   *   *   *

My grandmother's family immigrated to America from Switzerland. As a child, Grandmother spoke only German. I remember asking her what she had wanted most when she was a little girl—assuming that, like me, she had wanted a pony or a new doll. I have never forgotten her answer: "I wanted most," she said, "to know English."

Melinda G. Kramer, coauthor

A WORKING VOCABULARY

One way people analyze a subject to find out how it works is to break that subject into categories, into its various parts, so they can more easily examine how the individual parts work together as a whole. They may also develop a special vocabulary or set of terms for naming the parts and their functions.

You have performed this kind of analysis and naming many times during your life. In order to know how to improve your car's performance, you must learn how the engine works. To do that, you have to learn the names for the parts: the carburetor, the pistons, the distributor. In order to understand the way the human body functions, you learn about its various systems—the cardiovascular system, the nervous system, the digestive system—and their parts, such as the heart, the brain, the stomach.

Learning about language is no different. It too is a system with parts and functions described by a vocabulary of terms. Just as you breathe without analyzing how to do it, so you write and speak without worrying much about the system or the terms for explaining how language is used. But in order to talk *about* language, about writing, important first steps are understanding the system and knowing the vocabulary.

The following paragraphs introduce some of the basic vocabulary used to describe how written language works, how individual words come together in larger groups that convey meaning. **Part** and **function** are key terms describing how English works. Both words and sentences can be classified by part (what they are called) and function (what they do).

We can categorize words by the parts of speech to which they belong—such as nouns or verbs. We can also categorize sentences by their parts—such as subjects, predicates, or objects. Word functions are naming, predicating, modifying, or connecting. Sentence functions are asserting (stating), interrogating (questioning), or exclaiming. For now we'll concern ourselves just with the categories for words.

TYPICAL WORD FUNCTIONS	PARTS OF SPEECH	EXAMPLES
naming	nouns, pronouns	grandmother, German, home, my
predicating (stating, asserting)	verbs	spoke, was
modifying	adjectives, adverbs	rapid, fluent, always
connecting	prepositions, conjunctions	at, and

That parts of speech can change their functions from sentence to sentence can sometimes be confusing. For example, a noun is always a noun, but it can modify as well as name.

NAMING NOUN   My *grandmother* always spoke rapid, fluent German at home.

MODIFYING NOUN   My *grandmother's* German was always rapid and fluent.

In the first sentence, *grandmother* is a straightforward noun telling us who spoke German. In the second sentence, however, *grandmother's* takes the possessive form and tells us whose German was rapid and fluent. In the second case, we say *grandmother's* is a noun functioning as a modifier. In fact, we can say that the noun functions as an adjective, describing or qualifying *German*, another noun.

Now you know why the preceding list used the heading ***Typical*** Word Functions. First you learn how a part of speech usually functions. In time, as you become familiar with the way language works, you will learn to recognize and become able to explain the variations.

NOUNS AND PRONOUNS (1a)

NOUNS

A **noun** names a person, place, or thing. A **concrete noun** names something that can be seen, heard, touched, smelled, or tasted, something that can be perceived by the senses; an **abstract noun** names an idea, quality, or concept, not a substance. A **proper noun** names a particular person, place, or thing and should be capitalized; a **common noun** is the general name of a person, place, or thing and is not capitalized. A **collective noun** uses the singular form to name a group of individuals in a unit.

CONCRETE NOUN	America is a *land* of *immigrants*.
ABSTRACT NOUN	Some people came here to escape *oppression*.
PROPER NOUN	Others, like my *Great-grandfather Kelly*, came to escape the famine in *Ireland*.
COMMON NOUN	Before 1820, no official immigration *records* were kept.
COLLECTIVE NOUN	But since 1820, the *population* has increased by nearly 50 million foreign-born men and women.

Practice A: Identifying Nouns   Underline all the words functioning as nouns in the following sentences. The answers are listed at the end of this section.

[1]More than the dollar, the cowboy hat, or the automobile, jeans have become a symbol of American culture throughout the world. [2]However, few people realize

5

that jeans are a very international product. [3]Jeans were invented by a Bavarian immigrant to the United States. [4]The cloth from which jeans are made is called "denim" as a shortened version of *serge de Nimes*—cloth from Nimes, France. [5]"Jeans" derives from *Genes*, the French word for Genoa, the city in which a competitive cloth was produced. [6]They're called blue jeans because they were typically dyed blue with indigo—a dye originally from India.

PRONOUNS

A **pronoun** is a word used in place of a noun. Pronouns (and other words that substitute for nouns) are sometimes called **substantives.** There are several types of pronouns:

PERSONAL	I, we, you, he, she, it, they, me, us, him, her, them, mine, our(s), your(s), his, hers, its, their(s)
RELATIVE	who, whose, whom, which, that
INTERROGATIVE	who, whose, whom, which, that
DEMONSTRATIVE	this, that, these, those
INDEFINITE	one, any, each, anyone, somebody, all, etc.
RECIPROCAL	each other, one another
INTENSIVE	myself, yourself, himself, etc.
REFLEXIVE	myself, yourself, herself, etc.

PERSONAL   RELATIVE   INTERROGATIVE
We   are a nation of immigrants   *who*   assumed (and   *who*   has

        DEMONSTRATIVE   INDEFINITE
not?) in   *this*   country new identities,   *each*   learning to call

RECIPROCAL   INTENSIVE   REFLEXIVE
one another American, just as we *ourselves* finally learned to think of *ourselves*

as Americans.

Practice B: Identifying Pronouns   Underline all the pronouns in the following sentences. The answers are listed at the end of this section.

[1]Blue jeans are loved especially by those whose access to them is difficult. [2]Though we all assume it is easy to find jeans, that is not the case for others. [3]Someone in iron curtain countries may have to pay a small fortune for a pair of jeans. [4]He or she may even risk jail to buy on the black market. [5]Russian police recently broke up a jeans gang which they had investigated for months. [6]Gang members sold their jeans on the black market for over two hundred dollars a pair. [7]We Americans are secure in our love affair with blue jeans, and it is contagious.

6

Answers to Practice A ¹dollar, hat, automobile, jeans, symbol, culture, world ²people, jeans, product ³Jeans, immigrant, United States ⁴cloth, jeans, denim, version, *serge, Nimes,* cloth, Nimes, France ⁵Jeans, *Genes,* word, Genoa, city, cloth ⁶jeans, indigo, dye, India

Answers to Practice B ¹those, whose, them, ²we, all, it, that, others ³Someone ⁴He, she ⁵which, they ⁶their ⁷We, our, it

EXERCISE (1a), NOUNS AND PRONOUNS

In the blanks, copy all of the nouns and pronouns in the following sentences. If a noun or pronoun is repeated in a sentence, write it out each time it appears.

Example   Denim jeans are an American symbol for many people.

_____ jeans, symbol, people _____

1. Jeans were invented by a Jew who was born in Bavaria.

   _____

2. Levi Strauss was born in Bad Ocheim, Germany, in 1829.

   _____

3. In 1848, Strauss decided to join his two brothers in New York.

   _____

4. For two years, Strauss sold yarn, buttons, and dry goods to housewives.

   _____

5. The stories his brothers told about their rich lives in America were lies.

   _____

6. He went west to San Francisco when his married sister offered to pay for his trip.

   _____

7. Strauss took two bolts of canvas to sell as tenting material in the gold fields.

   _____

8. His canvas was the wrong kind to use in tents, but Levi soon found a better use for it.

   _____

9. A miner told Strauss that it was almost impossible to find pants tough enough for digging in them.

   _____

10. Strauss measured the miner and had a pair of pants made for him from the canvas.

    _____

11. The first pair of Levis sold for six dollars, and the bill was paid in gold dust.

    _____

12. The pants were stiff but tough, and orders for "those pants of Levi's" soon were coming in by the hundreds.

_____

13. The original two bolts of canvas ran out, and Levi sent back East for more.

_____

14. His brothers sent him instead a brown cloth made in France.

_____

15. Strauss dyed the cloth blue with indigo, the cheapest blue dye then available.

_____

16. The Levi Strauss Company has been in business continually since that day in 1850.

_____

17. After twenty very successful years, its trademark, riveted pockets, was added by the company.

_____

18. A tailor in Nevada added them to satisfy a particularly nasty miner.

_____

19. Legend has it that this customer was named Alkali Ike.

_____

20. Alkali tore the pockets of his Levis by stuffing them with ore.

_____

21. His demands that the tailor repair them were difficult to ignore.

_____

22. To shut up Ike once and for all, the tailor had a blacksmith rivet the pockets.

_____

23. Word got around that one couldn't tear riveted pockets.

_____

24. Strauss quickly decided that the improvement would help his sales, and he added the feature.

_____

25. Strauss hired the tailor, Jacob Davis, and made him a regional manager.

_____

VERBS AND VERBALS (1a-1b)

VERBS

A **verb** provides the energy in a sentence. It usually expresses action, occurrence, or condition and indicates time relationships by its tense. For example, "My grandmother *spoke* German" expresses the action of speaking and places that action in the past. "My grandmother's English *improved* slowly" expresses an occurrence that took place in the past. "My grandmother's German *was* fluent" expresses a condition (fluency) that existed in the past.

Verbs may appear as single words or in groups called **verb phrases.** Verb phrases are composed of main verbs and auxiliaries, also known as helping verbs. The most common helping verbs are *have, had, is (am, are), was (were), does (do), did, will, would, can, could, shall, should, may, might,* and *must.*

We look at verbs in more detail in "Verbforms" and "Kinds of Verbs."

VERB PHRASE   VERB

Although I   *might have*   *learned* German from my grandmother, I *learned* it at

AUXILIARIES MAIN
VERB

school instead.

VERBALS

Verbals is the term used for verb forms that are not functioning as **predicators.** In other words, verbals do not assert, ask questions, or otherwise work like verbs.

Instead, they name or modify. Verbals act as noun substitutes, adjectives, or adverbs. The forms of the three types of verbals can help you distinguish them from verbs functioning as predicates.

TYPE OF VERBAL	FORM OF VERBAL	FUNCTION OF VERBAL
Infinitive	*to* + verb	naming or modifying: noun substitute, adjective, adverb
	to win	*To win* was very important. [Used as noun]
Participle	verb + *ing* (present form)	modifying: adjective only
	cooking	The soup smelled good *cooking*. [The participle *cooking* modifies *soup*.]
	verb + *ed* or *en* or internal vowel change (past form)	
	cooked, eaten, gone	*Cooked, eaten,* and *gone,* the soup had satisfied their hunger. [The participles modify *soup*.]
Gerund	verb + *ing*	naming: noun substitute only
	cooking	*Cooking* is hard work. [*Cooking* functions as a noun.]

Some predicating verb phrases are composed of participles and helping verbs (as in *Max was running*). To further add to the confusion, of the three types of verbals, both participles and gerunds can have the *-ing* form. You have to check the function of an *-ing* word to know which it is. Participles used alone (without helping verbs) function only as adjectives. Gerunds serve only as nouns. All verbals, however, use adverbs as modifiers, as do true verbs. For more practice with verbals, see "Phrases".

Practice: Identifying Verbs   Underline all the verbs and verb phrases in the following sentences. The answers are listed at the end of this section.

[1]The Levi Strauss Company has opened a museum in San Francisco. [2]It illustrates the rich history of Levis. [3]A railroad worker replaced a bad coupling with a pair of jeans, and the pants held a train together. [4]One pair was used instead of a towrope; they hauled a car out of a Wyoming ditch. [5]Several pairs, over sixty years old, were found in an abandoned mine; they were in perfect condition. [6]A construction worker wearing Levis once dangled fifty stories in the air. [7]All that held him was one belt loop of his Levis, through which he had hooked his safety rope.

Answers to Practice   [1]has opened [2]illustrates [3]replaced, held [4]was used, hauled [5]were found, were [6]dangled [7]held, was, had hooked

EXERCISE (1a-1b), VERBS

In the blanks, copy all of the verbs and verb phrases in the following sentences. Circle the main verb in each verb phrase that you write.

Example   New Year's Day always has been the most popular Chinese holiday.
_____ has (been) _____

1. On that day, the Chinese pour wine on the ground to honor their ancestors.

   _____

2. The date of celebration varies each year, because it falls on the day the new moon enters Aquarius.

   _____

3. The celebrations actually begin seven days earlier.

   _____

4. A full week is allowed for the more important parts of the festival.

   _____

5. These earlier activities are unknown to most outsiders who attend only the parades and fireworks displays.

   _____

6. Chinese housewives consider this to be a lucky week since it is devoted to purification of the home.

   _____

7. The Chinese identify dirt with evil influences, so physical and spiritual cleansing are equally important.

   _____

8. Other ceremonies are held to pay homage to the household gods that protect the house.

   _____

9. Old images are burned and new ones are brought home.

   _____

10. This continual replacement honors the household gods for protecting the home during the year.

_____

11. These customs vary among Chinese communities, reflecting the diversity of religious customs in China.

_____

12. Some Chinese-Americans fast on the last day of the year.

_____

13. For some, this has religious significance, but for others fasting simply helps them enjoy feasting the next day.

_____

14. Just as many Americans give gifts on Christmas, the Chinese give gifts on New Year's Day.

_____

15. In many communities, only unmarried people are given gifts on New Year's Day.

_____

16. Americans who follow Chinese customs number years differently than do most Americans.

_____

17. The Chinese year 4687 would be listed as 1989 on most calendars.

_____

18. The Chinese new year can be said to begin on approximately February 2.

_____

19. Each year is also named for one of twelve animals.

_____

20. In Chinese-American communities, 1984 was called "the year of the rat."

_____

21. A special celebration was called for that year.

_____

22. The year of the rat begins the cycle, since the rat has been first to report to the emperor of the universe.

_____

23. People born in the year of the rat are supposed to be spendthrifts and loners.

---

24. The years of the dragon and the monkey produce people who are most compatible with people born in the year of the rat.

---

25. People who were born in the year of the horse will be incompatible with people whose birthdays fall in the year of the rat.

MODIFYING WORDS: ADJECTIVES AND ADVERBS (1b)

ADJECTIVES

An **adjective** modifies a noun or pronoun. It describes, limits, or qualifies the meaning of the word it modifies, often telling *what kind, how many,* or *which one.* An adjective cannot modify an adverb or another adjective. There are several types of adjectives:

DESCRIPTIVE	To us, English is *ordinary,* the *common* language in North America.
POSSESSIVE	*Our* brand of English is somewhat different from the English in Great Britain or an Indian's English in New Delhi.
DEMONSTRATIVE	*That* variety of English is now called British English, whereas our language is called American English.
INTERROGATIVE	*What* differences are there between the two?
NUMERICAL	To cite just *one* example, Americans say a car has a "hood," but the British say it has a "bonnet."
ARTICLES	Whereas we refer to *a* car's "trunk," *an* English person calls *the* trunk *a* "boot."

Several words in the preceding examples also appeared in the previous list of pronouns. *That* is listed both as a demonstrative pronoun and as a demonstrative adjective. *What* shows up twice: once as an interrogative pronoun and once as an interrogative adjective. Remember that classifying a word by its part of speech sometimes depends on its function in a sentence. The appearance of *that* and *what* in two categories illustrates this point very well. In the examples here, *that* and *what* could be described as pronouns functioning as modifiers—that is, pronouns performing the function of adjectives.

Practice A: Identifying Adjectives   Underline all the words (including the articles) that function as adjectives in the following sentences. The answers are listed at the end of this section.

[1]In the early years of the Strauss company, Levi brought his immigrant brothers into the company. [2]By the time he had opened his third store, his two brothers-in-law were also part of the company. [3]In the later decades of the nineteenth century, Levi's company prospered in its local area. [4]Before his death in 1902, Levi Strauss had become one of the most prominent men in the whole state of California. [5]But even during the first three decades of the twentieth century, the business was small and profitable. [6]Its sales were to working people, mainly Westerners, people such as cowboys and rugged lumberjacks.

ADVERBS

An **adverb** modifies, describes, limits, or qualifies the meaning of a verb, an adjective, or another adverb. Besides modifying single words, adverbs can also modify whole sentences or parts of sentences. Adverbs frequently indicate time, place, manner, or degree, telling *when, where,* or *how.* Negatives such as *no, never,* and *not* may be used as adverbs. Some adverbs have a distinctive *-ly* ending, making them easy to spot in sentences. The following examples show the use of adverbs:

TIME	American English began to develop *soon* after English settlers arrived in the New World. [*Soon* modifies the verb phrase *began to develop,* telling when.]
PLACE	The settlers needed new words to describe the new experiences they found *here.* [*Here* modifies the verb *found,* telling where.]
MANNER	So they invented words or borrowed or adapted *suitably* descriptive words from other languages. [*Suitably* modifies the adjective *descriptive,* telling in what way.]
DEGREE	The settlers' vocabulary *very* quickly began to reflect their new surroundings. [*Very* modifies the adverb *quickly,* telling how.]
NUMBER	A new word spoken *once* or *twice* is just a novelty, but with repeated use it becomes part of the common language. [*Once* and *twice* modify the verb *spoken,* telling how many times.]

Practice B: Identifying Adverbs Underline all the words functioning as adverbs in the following sentences. The answers are listed at the end of this section.

[1]Apparently, Easterners first learned about jeans when people returned from vacations on dude ranches. [2]They had discovered some good-looking pants that were wonderfully rugged. [3]In World War II, blue jeans were declared essential to the war effort and sold only to defense workers. [4]This easily boosted their popularity. [5]In 1946, Levi Strauss Company had two efficiently run plants, only fifteen salespeople, and virtually no business east of the Mississippi. [6]The company grew rapidly after the 1950s. [7]They now have almost 23,000 salespeople and 50 plants in locations that even include 34 foreign countries. [8]Almost unbelievably, the company now sells over 250 million pieces of clothing every year—and that includes, stubbornly but proudly, 83 million pairs of riveted blue jeans.

Answers to Practice A [1]the, early, the, Strauss, his, immigrant, the [2]the, his, third, his, two, the [3]the, later, the, nineteenth, Levi's, its, local [4]his, the, prominent, the, whole [5]the, first, three, the, twentieth, the, small, profitable [6]Its, working, rugged

Answers to Practice B [1]apparently, first, when [2]wonderfully [3]only [4]easily [5]efficiently, only, virtually [6]rapidly [7]now, almost, even [8]almost, unbelievably, now, stubbornly, proudly

EXERCISE (1b), MODIFYING WORDS: ADJECTIVES AND ADVERBS

Each of the following sentences contains at least one adjective or adverb. Some sentences contain both. In the blanks, copy the adjectives and adverbs, labeling them *adj.* or *adv.* Write the words they modify in parentheses. Do not copy or label the articles *a, an,* or *the.*

Example   Chinese-Americans have contributed immensely to American business and culture.

immensely, adv. (contributed)   American, adj. (business, culture)

1. The first Chinese newspaper in America was published in San Francisco in 1854.

    _____

2. In 1940, the number of "Chinatowns" in the United States was conservatively reckoned to be twenty-eight.

    _____

3. Their number rapidly dwindled to sixteen by 1955.

    _____

4. Increasing Americanization of the Chinese-American population is illustrated by the decreasing number of separate Chinese communities.

    _____

5. The first Chinese-American who served as an elected official was Wing F. Ong.

    _____

6. Ong was elected, by popular vote, to the legislature of Arizona in 1946.

    _____

7. Hawaiian voters, not surprisingly, were the first U.S. voters to send a Chinese-American U.S. Senator to Washington.

    _____

8. One says "not surprisingly" because there is a large Chinese population in Hawaii.

    _____

9. However, Dr. Mary Stone was the first Chinese woman to graduate from an American medical school.

———————————————————————————

10. And, unexpectedly, she was trained at the University of Michigan.

———————————————————————————

11. Delbert E. Wong was an early judicial appointment of California governor Edmund Brown.

———————————————————————————

12. Wong's federal judgeship was the first held by a Chinese-American.

———————————————————————————

13. An Wang, an electronics specialist, started Wang Laboratories single-handedly in 1955.

———————————————————————————

14. A Chinese-American seat on the New York Stock Exchange was apparently first purchased in 1979.

———————————————————————————

15. Gerald Tsai started his mutual fund after emigrating to America from Shanghai.

———————————————————————————

16. The fund reportedly involves over 150,000 individual investors.

———————————————————————————

17. Optimistic investors happily put over $270 million into the fund.

———————————————————————————

18. Joe Shoong began a national network of discount stores in 1907.

———————————————————————————

19. Shoong originally owned one store and a warehouse.

———————————————————————————

20. He eventually developed his holdings into a network of fifty-three stores.

———————————————————————————

21. K. G. Li owns the world's largest tungsten refinery, Wah Chang Corporation.

———————————————————————————

22. Now he also has established the Li Foundation.

_____

23. The Li Foundation provides fellowships for advanced students.

_____

24. The Chinese student movement was initially a program to recruit Chinese students for American universities.

_____

25. The movement was begun by Yung Wing, who received naturalized American citizenship in 1849.

_____

CONNECTING WORDS:
PREPOSITIONS
AND CONJUNCTIONS (1b)

PREPOSITIONS

A **preposition** is a connecting word that typically indicates time, place, or move-ment. Some common prepositions are *about, above, across, after, around, at, before, behind, between, by, during, for, from, in, into, of, off, on, out, over, since, through, to, under, up, with.*

A preposition connects its object (a noun, pronoun, or noun substitute) with some other word in a sentence. Together the preposition, its object, and any words modifying the object form a prepositional phrase—for example, *on a sunny morning.*

PREPOSITIONAL PHRASE

VERB PHRASE   MODIFYING VERB

The words *succotash* and *skunk* were borrowed   from   the Algonquian Indians.

PREPOSITION   OBJECT OF

PREPOSITION

Prepositions and prepositional phrases can modify nouns, verbs, adjectives, or adverbs; they supply additional information about the words they modify.

USED AS ADJECTIVE   American English has borrowed many words *with In-dian origins.* [The prepositional phrase modifies the noun *words*, telling what kind.]

USED AS ADVERB	Algonquian words are alive *in our vocabulary today.* [The prepositional phrase modifies the adjective *alive,* telling where.]
USED AS ADVERB	We still use more than 100 words we owe *to the Algonquians.* [The prepositional phrase modifies the verb *owe,* telling whom.]
USED AS ADVERB	Once *upon a time* Algonquian was America's most widely spoken Indian language. [The prepositional phrase modifies the adverb *once,* telling exactly when.]

Practice A: Identifying Prepositions   Underline all the prepositions in the following sentences. The answers are listed at the end of this section.

[1]Armenians were invited to America by the early colonists in the New World. [2]In 1831, missionaries went to Turkey and encouraged another wave of immigration. [3]With a sultan's order to annihilate the Armenian Christians in 1894, the largest wave of immigrants left. [4]Many Armenians escaped to Greece, France, and England. [5]From these countries, which allowed immigration only under quota systems, many entered the United States at Ellis Island. [6]In 1975, Soviet Armenia began to allow its citizens to emigrate.

CONJUNCTIONS

A **conjunction** connects words, phrases, or clauses, and thus creates a relationship between sentence elements. Conjunctions can establish the following relationships between words or word groups:

Coordinating conjunctions show equal rank or importance. The coordinating conjunctions are *and, but, for, nor, or, so, yet.*

Many English words were adopted from their Indian inventors, *but* Indians did not invent "peace pipe" *and* "pale face." [The first half of the sentence tells a fact. The second half challenges a related misconception. The contrast between what is true and not true about Indian contributions to English is given equal grammatical emphasis by *but.* *And* connects *peace pipe* and *pale face* and establishes their equal status as examples of words Indians did not invent.]

Subordinating conjunctions create unequal rank or dependence. They join words, phrases, or clauses that depend on other parts of the sentence to complete their meanings. The subordinating conjunctions are *after, although, as, before, if, since, that, unless, until, when, where, whether, while, why.*

Although these words are associated with Indians, white settlers invented them. [The *although* clause depends upon, or is subordinated to, the second clause, because without the second clause the meaning of the first clause is incomplete.]

Practice B: Identifying Conjunctions   Underline all the conjunctions in the following sentences. The answers are listed at the end of this section.

[1]Before the Spanish Empire collapsed, hundreds of thousands of Basques entered America. [2]Although this early immigration accompanied French and Spanish colonial ventures, it was only briefly interrupted, and it began again in 1850. [3]The French Revolution, the Napoleonic wars, and the Carlist uprisings all made for more emigration, since the Basque homeland lies between Spain and France. [4]But the most important reason for emigration may have been the industrial revolution. [5]Because the Basques were farmers, they hated the idea of working in Europe's growing factory system.

Answers to Practice A   [1]to, by, in [2]In, to, of [3]With, in, of [4]to [5]From, under, at [6]In

Answers to Practice B   [1]Before [2]Although, and, and [3]and, since, and [4]But [5]Because

EXERCISE (1b), CONNECTING WORDS: PREPOSITIONS AND CONJUNCTIONS

Prepositional phrases function as modifiers, adding information to sentences. Expand each of the following sentences by supplying prepositional phrases that add modifying information.

Example   People have come to America.

People have come to America from other countries all over the world.

1. America has many ethnic groups.

    _____

2. Some are very interesting.

    _____

3. Each has a culture and tradition.

    _____

4. Some maintain their culture.

    _____

5. I am interested in studying one.

    _____

Conjunctions connect sentence elements, allowing us to combine information and ideas. Combine the sentences in each pair below, using coordinating conjunctions, subordinating conjunctions, or both.

Example   Many ethnic groups have distinctive dress. They also have distinctive foods.

Many ethnic groups have distinctive dress and distinctive foods.

1. Geographic patterns of immigration can be discovered. The patterns are not all-inclusive.

    _____

2. French-Canadians settled in New England. New England is close to Canada.

    _____

24

3. Cuba and Florida are only 90 miles apart. Many Cuban immigrants settled there.

_____

4. The Southwest has large Hispanic communities. It is close to Mexico. It was once owned by Mexico.

_____

5. California was once ruled by Spain. It has large Asian communities. It is directly east of Asia and the Pacific Islands.

_____

For each of the following sets of sentences, use prepositional phrases, conjunctions, or both to compose one sentence including all of the information given. You may have to rearrange or omit words to create a smooth sentence.

Example   I like French cooking. It is elegant. It is sophisticated.

I like French cooking because it is elegant and sophisticated.

1. I enjoy Mexican food. It is usually hot. It is usually spicy.

_____

2. I like tacos. I like burritos. I like chimichangas. I haven't developed a taste for guacamole yet.

_____

3. Some Mexican dishes are surprisingly mild. I enjoy quesadillas. A quesadilla is covered in a mild cheese sauce.

_____

4. Spanish food is milder than Mexican food. Good Spanish restaurants are difficult to find.

_____

5. There are many seafood dishes native to Spain. Mexican dishes do not emphasize seafood much. Paella is a mixture of seafood and pimiento-flavored rice.

_____

RECOGNIZING SENTENCES AND THEIR BASIC PARTS: PREDICATES, AND SENTENCE PATTERNS (1a)

All complete sentences have a **subject** and a **predicate.** The **subject** of a sentence is most often a noun, pronoun, or noun substitute that names someone or something. A subject with all its modifiers is called a **complete subject.** A subject without any modifiers is called a **simple subject.** The following sentences show various types of subjects. Each complete subject appears in italics; each simple subject is in boldface italics.

One of *the largest **groups** of immigrants to America* was the Germans. [Noun as subject]

They have accounted for more than 15 percent of the immigrants in the last century and a half. [Pronoun as subject]

Being *of German descent* is a source of pride for many people. [Verbal phrase substituted for noun subject]

*German **men** and **women*** made up 10 percent of America's total population in 1776. [Two nouns as subjects, called *compound subject*]

The **predicate** of a sentence gives information about the subject by making an assertion or asking a question. The most important part of the predicate is the **verb** or **verb phrase** that makes up the **simple predicate.** The simple predicate expresses action, occurrence, or condition (state of being). Other words in a **complete predicate** either are modifiers or receive the action of the predicate's verb. In the following sentences, the complete predicate is italicized and the simple predicate is in boldface italics.

The first wave of German immigrants *began* in 1683. The second wave *began arriving in 1825.* [Action]

In both cases, Germany *was suffering* from bad economic conditions. [Occurrence]

Most of the seventeenth-century immigrants *were* happy with their new lives. [Condition, state of being]

Practice: Identifying Subjects and Predicates   Underline the simple subject and simple predicate in the following sentences. Be sure not to overlook possible compound subjects or verbs. The answers are listed at the end of this section.

[1]Few immigrants from Austria came to America before 1870. [2]A small number of missionaries travelled to the early colonies. [3]In 1734, more than a hundred Protestant families left Salzburg to settle in Georgia. [4]A failed revolution in 1848 sent many political refugees to the United States. [5]But in 1870 the Austrian economy foundered and sank, and Austrian factories could not absorb the number of peasants moving to the cities. [6]Many of these workers eventually immigrated to America for work.

SENTENCE PATTERNS

Pattern 1   The simplest sentences contain only a subject and a verb, as in *Immigrants settled.* We can add information to these simple, or **core,** sentences by supplying modifiers: adjectives, adverbs, prepositional phrases.

SUBJECT   VERB
The Dutch immigrants settled quickly in their new homes.

Besides the pattern shown in a core sentence, English sentences can follow four other patterns that provide additional information in the predicate. The pattern variations all occur in the predicate—in the verb and what follows it.

Pattern 2   The predicate may contain a **direct object,** a noun, pronoun, or noun substitute that receives the action of the verb and answers "what" or "whom."

SUBJECT   VERB   DIRECT OBJECT
A German immigrant built the Brooklyn Bridge.

Pattern 3   The predicate may contain a direct object followed by an **object complement,** a noun or modifier that renames or describes the direct object.

SUBJECT   VERB   DIRECT OBJECT   OBJECT COMPLEMENT (NOUN)
People   called the Brooklyn Bridge the Eighth Wonder of the World.

SUBJECT   VERB   DIRECT OBJECT   OBJECT COMPLEMENT (ADJECTIVE)
The   bridge   helped make   Brooklyn   famous.

Pattern 4 The predicate may contain a direct object preceded by an **indirect object,** a noun or pronoun that identifies the receiver of whatever is named in the direct object.

SUBJECT	VERB	INDIRECT OBJECT	DIRECT OBJECT
A con artist	tried to sell	me	the Brooklyn Bridge.

Indirect objects function rather like prepositional phrases with the *to* or *for* left out: *A con artist tried to sell [to] me the Brooklyn Bridge.*

Pattern 5 The predicate may contain a linking verb followed by a **complement**— either a **predicate noun** or a **predicate adjective.** Linking verbs are discussed in "Kinds of Verbs." Some common linking verbs are *is, are, was, were, has, been, might be, see, appear, become;* sometimes *feel, act, look, taste, smell,* and *sound* function as linking verbs. You will be able to spot predicate nouns if you remember that they rename the subject of the sentence. Predicate adjectives modify the subject.

		COMPLEMENT	
SUBJECT	VERB	PRED. NOUN	PRED. ADJ.
The builder of the Brooklyn Bridge	was	a German.	
His name	was	John Roebling.	
Roebling's death	appears		tragic.
The bridge	may have been		responsible.

These patterns form the basis for all English sentences. All of their elements can be compounded without changing the basic sentence pattern. That is, a sentence may have two or more subjects, verbs, indirect objects, direct objects, and/ or complements. *Someone tried to sell my friend and me the Brooklyn Bridge.* has a compound indirect object (*friend, me*), but the basic sentence pattern remains unchanged.

Other sentence variations are created by rearranging or recombining the elements in these patterns. One variation is worth special notice because it can be confusing. Certain sentences use *there* plus a verb as something called an **expletive.** Such a phrase is never the subject of a sentence. For instance, in *There were two deaths in his family last year.*, *there were* is an expletive. The verb makes a statement about *deaths*, not about *there*. *Deaths* is the subject. The sense of the sentence is "Two deaths occurred in his family last year."

Answers to Practice [1]immigrants, came [2]number, travelled [3]families, left [4]revolution, sent [5]economy, foundered, sank; factories, could absorb [6]Many, immigrated

EXERCISE (1b), SUBJECTS AND PREDICATES

Underline and label the subjects (*s*), verbs (*v*), direct objects (*do*), indirect objects (*io*), and complements (*c*) in the following sentences.

(s)   (v)

Example   Early Armenian <u>settlers</u> <u>moved</u> to the Atlantic Coast states.

1. All fifty states currently have Armenian-American citizens.

2. Many Armenian farmers travelled to California and bought and worked farmland in the San Joaquin Valley.

3. More than half a million Armenians are citizens of the United States, Mexico, or Canada.

4. The first to arrive in America was Martin the Armenian.

5. Martin grew and sold tobacco.

6. His fellow Armenians traded silk and ornaments to Indians.

7. Armenian farmers imported seeds from Armenia and grew familiar crops.

8. They introduced many new varieties in this way.

9. Figs, apricots, Persian melons, and grapes are some of these new crops.

10. Many Armenian-Americans remain loyal to their language and religion.

11. The Armenian Gregorian Church actually has gained members during these migrations.

12. Armenian private schools teach their students Armenian history.

13. No such unity exists among descendants of Austrian immigrants.

14. This is a result, of course, of Austrian political history.

15. Austria was not a separate independent nation until 1918.

16. Until then, "Austria" had referred to various geographical areas.

17. Early Austrian immigrants were clerks or metalsmiths.

18. Many of these immigrants settled in New York and its border states.

19. Cincinnati, St. Louis, and Milwaukee received many of the 1848 immigrants.

20. By 1900, over 87 percent of these Austrians, however, lived in the northeastern and north central states.

21. In 1938, the last great wave of Austrian immigrants arrived.

22. These last Austrian immigrants were refugees from the Nazi takeover.

23. Many statistics about Austrian immigrants are unreliable.

24. Austrians were considered Germans by the United States Immigration Commission.

25. The United States has a long history of sympathy for political refugees.

RECOGNIZING PHRASES   (1c)

If you have read the sections in this book on verbs and prepositions, you already have a working knowledge of phrases. A **phrase** is a group of related words that differs from a clause in that a phrase lacks either a subject or a verb. A phrase may contain a subject or a verb but never both. For example, the following sentence is constructed of a **noun phrase** containing a subject and a **verb phrase** composed of a finite verb and its auxiliary:

> The old man   has died.

The sentence *The old man has lived a long life.* contains two noun phrases (*the old man* and *a long life*), each having its own subject (*man* and *life*) and a verb phrase (*has lived*).

Keep in mind that even though a phrase may contain its own subject or verb, these do not necessarily function as the subject or predicate of the entire sentence. For example, although *life* is the subject of its noun phrase in the example sentence, it is also the direct object of the verb and is thus a part of the predicate in the sentence as a whole.

Other types of phrases usually consist of a **preposition** and its object or a **verbal** and its object.

PREPOSITIONAL PHRASES	*In the forest, down the road*
PARTICIPIAL PHRASE	The man *picking the flowers* was in love.
GERUND PHRASE	*Driving the stake* caused her to sweat.
INFINITIVE PHRASE	He wanted *to leave home.*

31

You also know, if you have read the previous sections about verbals and prepositions, that phrases frequently function as modifiers. They act as adjectives when they modify nouns or noun substitutes. They act as adverbs when they modify verbs, adjectives, or other adverbs. Some verbal phrases and, occasionally, prepositional phrases can also function as nouns. The following examples show how phrases (in this case, prepositional phrases) can function as adjectives, adverbs, and nouns:

ADJECTIVE MODIFYING NOUN	She likes pastry *with cherry filling*. [Modifies *pastry*]
ADVERB MODIFYING VERB	The recipe came *from Vienna, Austria*. [Modifies *came*]
ADVERB MODIFYING ADJECTIVE	Viennese pastries are full *of calories*. [Modifies *full*]
ADVERB MODIFYING ADVERB	Viennese pastries should be eaten slowly *for the most satisfaction*. [Modifies *slowly*]
NOUN SUBSTITUTE	*"Without guilt"* is my motto when eating fattening, luscious pastry. [Acts as subject of sentence]

Phrases are among a writer's most versatile tools. They enable you, as a writer, to elaborate, to amplify, and to qualify the core of a sentence—its subject and its verb. With a few well-chosen phrases, you can give your readers a wealth of information and thus add substantially to their understanding of a sentence's meaning.

For example, suppose you have written the simple sentence *Pastries tempt me.* Most people will read the sentence sympathetically and will agree, "Me too." Each reader will also supply his or her own mental picture of a tempting pastry. Perhaps this is the reaction you want, but you've left a lot of "detail work" up to each reader's imagination. In fact, you haven't really exerted very much control over the writer-reader relationship because the sentence is so bare. Chances are that you, too, have a specific mental image of a tempting pastry, and chances are that you really want the reader to see *your* image. Using phrases to expand the core sentence is an appropriate means for providing the reader with a more complete understanding of just what *you* mean.

PARTICIPIAL PHRASE
PREPOSITIONAL PHRASE
Covered   in thick, sugar icing,

PARTICIPIAL PHRASE
PREPOSITIONAL PHRASES
scenting the bakery shop with their aroma of yeast and fruit filling,
CORE
pastries tempt me

to stop and spend my money on short-lived delights but long-lived pounds.

Two participial phrases, an infinitive phrase, and four prepositional phrases have expanded the three-word core sentence *Pastries tempt me.* into a richly detailed sensory experience for the reader. Of course, you will not always need so much information in your sentences, but phrases do give you the tools for building detail and adding information when you want it.

Practice: Expanding a sentence with phrases Write a brief core sentence; then expand your sentence with details, using at least one participial or gerund phrase, at least one infinitive phrase, and at least two prepositional phrases. Be sure that the final sentence is grammatically correct and that it is logical. Revise your sentence until you feel satisfied with it.

EXERCISE (1c), RECOGNIZING PHRASES

Write sentences with prepositional phrases using the given prepositions.

Example   with ___*Here she comes with the keys.*___

1. in _____
2. of _____
3. behind _____
4. for _____
5. by _____
6. between _____
7. on _____
8. under _____
9. above _____
10. with _____
11. through _____
12. before _____
13. upon _____
14. across _____
15. during _____

Form participles, gerunds, and infinitives from the following verbs; and write sentences using them as participial, gerund, and infinitive phrases. Review the end of the section on verbals if you need a refresher.

Example   search

(participial) *Searching the grounds, we exhausted ourselves.*

(gerund) *Searching for the keys was exhausting work.*

(infinitive) *Since I have spares, we don't have to search anymore.*

16. travel

(participial) _____

(gerund) _____

(infinitive) _____

17. hope

(participial) _____

(gerund) _____

(infinitive) _____

18. lament

(participial) _____

(gerund) _____

(infinitive) _____

For each of the following sentences, indicate whether the italicized phrase functions as a noun (*n*), an adjective (*adj*), or an adverb (*adv*) by writing the appropriate abbreviation over it.

Example   America's sheep industry was developed *with the help* of Basques.

19. Basques learned about raising sheep *on a large scale* in Argentina.

20. The open range there is similar to the grasslands *of the American West.*

21. *Adapting Argentinian practice* to America's industry was simple.

22. *In the 1940s*, immigration quotas threatened the supply of Basque shepherds.

23. Range associations asked *for more Basque immigration.*

24. Ranchers began *to sponsor* Basque shepherds.

25. These ranchers, *motivated by economic concern*, substantially added to the number of Basques in America.

RECOGNIZING CLAUSES   (1d)

INDEPENDENT CLAUSES

An **independent clause,** often called a **main clause,** has both a subject and a verb. It makes a complete, independent statement, and it is not introduced by a subordinating word.

A sentence may have one main clause, or it may have several. When two or more main clauses are present in a sentence, they are usually joined by **coordinating conjunctions.** The most common coordinating conjunctions are *and, but, or, nor, for,* and sometimes *so* and *yet.* Ordinarily, a comma is used before a coordinating conjunction that joins independent clauses.

My Danish mother is a fantastic cook, *and* she is proud of it.

She prepares delicious meals, *yet* she makes it look easy.

Conjunctive adverbs are another group of words used to connect independent clauses. When a conjunctive adverb is used between independent clauses, it is preceded by a semicolon and followed by a comma. The principal conjunctive adverbs are these:

accordingly	consequently	hence	moreover	then
also	else	however	nevertheless	therefore
besides	furthermore	likewise	otherwise	thus

The following sentences use conjunctive adverbs between independent clauses:

> The Danes love Danish bacon; *however,* they cannot buy it in Denmark.

> Danish bacon is exported only; *consequently,* Danes buy it abroad when they travel and bring it home.

SUBORDINATE CLAUSES

A **subordinate** or **dependent clause,** like an independent clause, has both a subject and a verb. However, it functions as an adjective, adverb, or noun and thus cannot stand alone as a complete sentence. Whenever a group of words contains a subordinate clause, the group must also contain an independent clause in order to qualify as a sentence.

> When I arrived [Subordinate clause is not a sentence; the meaning is incomplete.]

> When I arrived in Denmark, my mother asked if I had brought home any bacon. [Subordinate clause is joined to an independent clause which completes its meaning; the construction is a sentence.]

A subordinate clause is always preceded by a **subordinating conjunction** or a **relative pronoun.** Some of the most widely used subordinating conjunctions follow:

after	how	though	when
although	if	unless	where
as	since	until	whether
because	then	whatever	why

Relative pronouns often introduce subordinate clauses. When used in this way, a relative pronoun may also be referred to as a conjunctive pronoun. Common relative pronouns are the following:

that	which	who	whom	whose

A subordinate clause can function as an adjective, an adverb, or a noun. An **adjective clause** modifies either a noun or a noun substitute.

> Anyone who has seen Victor Borge loves this humorous Danish immigrant. [The subordinate clause *who has seen Victor Borge* modifies the pronoun *anyone.*]

The **adverb clause** modifies either a verb, an adjective, or an adverb.

People laugh when he plays the piano. [The subordinate clause *when he plays the piano* modifies the verb *laugh.*]

Borge is especially funny because he mixes jokes and music. [The subordinate clause *because he mixes jokes and music* modifies the adjective *funny.*]

He can play seriously if he wants to. [The subordinate clause *if he wants to* modifies the adverb *seriously.*]

The **noun clause** may serve as either a subject, a complement renaming the subject, an indirect object, a direct object of a verb, or an object of a preposition.

Whoever Borge entertains is made happier. [The subordinate clause *Whoever Borge entertains* serves as the subject.]

His infectious humor is what audiences like. [The subordinate clause *what audiences like* serves as the complement, the predicate noun, of the sentence.]

Borge brings whoever listens moments of delight. [The subordinate clause *whoever listens* serves as the indirect object of the verb *brings.*]

Audiences frequently request that he play certain songs. [The subordinate clause *that he play certain songs* serves as the direct object of the verb *request.*]

They are always curious about when he will give another concert. [The subordinate clause *when he will give another concert* serves as the object of the preposition *about.*]

USING CLAUSES TO COMBINE IDEAS

Clauses enable a writer to combine several related ideas into a single sentence, instead of having to use a separate sentence for each thought. In elementary school you may have learned this definition of a sentence: A sentence is a complete statement expressing a single thought. Although that definition is true in a very general way, sentences containing several clauses allow for the expression of complex, or multifaceted thoughts.

Consider, for example, the following sentences:

Lego toys are plastic bricks. They interlock. Children build houses, cars, and towers with them. Lego toys were invented by Ole Christiansen during the Depression. Christiansen was a Danish cabinetmaker. He could not find work. He made the Lego toys from wood. He then exchanged them for food.

Notice how short and choppy many of these sentences sound. As you read them, you probably began combining some of the related thoughts in your mind to smooth out the bumps. The practice with phrases in "Recognizing Phrases" gave you some tools for expanding sentences with details. By using clauses to form additional relationships, you can also coordinate and subordinate ideas:

SUBORDINATE CLAUSE
The Lego toys that children use to build houses, cars,

CLAUSE

INDEPENDENT

and towers are interlocking, plastic bricks. They were invented by Ole Christiansen

INDEPENDENT

CLAUSE   SUBORDINATE CLAUSE
during the Depression. Christiansen, who was a Danish cabinetmaker, could not

CLAUSE

INDEPENDENT CLAUSE   SUBORDINATE CLAUSE
find work, so he made wooden Lego toys which he then exchanged for food.

In place of the choppy statements, we now have three sentences that combine ideas from the original eight. Besides being smoother, these three sentences establish relationships between ideas by means of their interlocking clauses.

CONFUSING PHRASE AND CLAUSE CONNECTIVES

Certain words that can be either prepositions or conjunctions sometimes cause students to confuse phrases with clauses. This confusion can occur if you try to identify a word group on the basis of the connective alone instead of examining the entire word group. For example, the following sentences use the same connective; but in the first sentence the connective introduces a phrase, and in the second it introduces a clause:

George has not practiced the piano *since* his accident.

Since he broke his arm, he has been unable to play.

Rather than rely on the connective alone, examine the entire word group it introduces. Remember that a preposition introduces a phrase—the noun, pronoun, or substantive that is the object of the preposition, and any words that modify that object. A conjunction, on the other hand, introduces a clause—a group of words containing a subject and a verb. A phrase never contains both a subject and a verb.

Some of the words that may be either prepositions or conjunctions are *after, before, for, until,* and *since.*

Practice: Using Clauses to Combine Ideas   Revise the following sentences, using subordinate clauses to combine the original ten sentences into no more than five sentences expressing the same ideas. One possible answer is listed at the end of this section.

American Basques have a name for themselves. The name is "Amerikanuak." Many American Basques are from the Spanish province of Navarre. They joined French Basques in southern California in the 1850s. The two groups then migrated eastward into Nevada, Arizona, Colorado and Wyoming. Another group of American Basques is also from Spain. They call themselves "Vizcayans." The Bay of Biscay is one boundary of their homeland. They migrated to northern Nevada, Oregon, and Idaho. San Francisco is a social center for French Basques, and Reno is a social center for the Vizcayans.

Answer to the Practice   Many answers are possible; the following revision shows one representative type.

American Basques have a name for themselves, which is "Amerikanuak." Many American Basques who are from the Spanish province of Navarre joined French Basques in southern California in the 1850s, after which the two groups migrated eastward into Nevada, Arizona, Colorado, and Wyoming. Another group of American Basques, who call themselves "Vizcayans" because the Bay of Biscay is one border of their homeland, migrated to northern Nevada, Oregon, and Idaho. San Francisco is a social center for French Basques, and Reno is a social center for the Vizcayans.

EXERCISE (1d)-1, INDEPENDENT AND SUBORDINATE CLAUSES

Write sentences with two independent clauses joined by the listed coordinating conjunctions and conjunctive adverbs. Be sure to punctuate your sentences correctly.

Example   accordingly *My name is first; accordingly, I should be first in line.*
            thus *I'm afraid I'm ill; thus, I must be absent tonight.*

1. meanwhile ————————————————————————————

2. nor ——————————————————————————————

3. furthermore ————————————————————————————

4. hence ————————————————————————————————

5. or ———————————————————————————————————

6. moreover ——————————————————————————————

7. otherwise ——————————————————————————————

8. for ——————————————————————————————————

9. likewise ——————————————————————————————

10. and ——————————————————————————————————

11. consequently ————————————————————————————

12. but ——————————————————————————————————

13. then ——————————————————————————————————

14. so ———————————————————————————————————

15. also ——————————————————————————————————

16. besides ——————————————————————————————

17. nevertheless ————————————————————————————

18. however ——————————————————————————————

19. therefore ——————————————————————————————

20. else ——————————————————————————————————

Write sentences, each with an independent clause and a subordinate clause. Begin the subordinate clause with the given subordinating conjunction or relative pronoun.

Example   until   _Until I finish my notes, I won't be able to leave._

that   _I thought that I would help you transcribe them._

21.   since _____

22.   than _____

23.   whatever _____

24.   why _____

25.   whoever _____

26.   whether _____

27.   whose _____

28.   where _____

29.   when _____

30.   until _____

31.   who _____

32.   unless _____

33.   which _____

34.   though _____

35.   if _____

36.   how _____

37.   because _____

38.   after _____

39.   as _____

40.   although _____

EXERCISE (1d)-2, FUNCTIONS OF SUBORDINATE CLAUSES

In the following sentences, underline main clauses once and subordinate clauses twice. Indicate whether a subordinate clause functions as an an adjective (*adj*), adverb (*adv*), or noun (*n*) by writing the appropriate abbreviation above the clause.

Example   When news of the California gold rush reached China, economic and political troubles had engulfed southeast China.

1. The 1840 Opium War and the Taiping Rebellion, both of which caused economic havoc, were the immediate causes of the unrest.

2. Rumors that spread throughout China were exaggerated claims of "mountains of gold" in California.

3. Most Chinese immigrants, who faced a 7,000-mile journey, planned to stay in America only briefly.

4. They intended to return to China as soon as they made their fortunes.

5. Because the gold rush was such an attractive lure, 99 percent of the Chinese in America in 1870 lived in California.

Underline the subordinate clause twice in each of the following sentences. Indicate its function by writing *adj, adv,* or *n* above it. Then underline once the word the clause modifies, complements, or serves as subject or object.

Example   Before World War II, almost all the Chinese who immigrated to Write sentences containing subordinate clauses that perform the functions

6. As political refugees fled Communist China, this pattern has changed radically.

7. A quota system that was only relaxed in 1965 discouraged Chinese emigration.

8. The year that saw passage of the first Chinese Exclusion Act was 1882.

9. When the acts were repealed in 1943, they were simply replaced by a quota system.

10. The only real change was that exclusion was changed to restriction.

Write the sentences containing subordinate clauses that perform the functions stated in parentheses.

Example   (adverb clause modifying verb)

I couldn't hear you while the water was running.

11. (subordinate adjective clause modifying noun)

_____

12. (subordinate adjective clause modifying pronoun)

_____

13. (subordinate adverb clause modifying verb)

_____

14. (subordinate adverb clause modifying adjective)

_____

15. (subordinate adverb clause modifying adverb)

_____

16. (subordinate noun clause, subject)

_____

17. (subordinate noun clause, complement)

_____

18. (subordinate noun clause, direct object)

_____

19. (subordinate noun clause, object of verb)

_____

20. (subordinate noun clause, object of preposition)

_____

EXERCISE (1d)-3, CONFUSING PHRASE AND CLAUSE CONNECTIVES

A few connectives may be either prepositions or conjunctions and can thus introduce both phrases and clauses. These connectives are *after, before, until, for,* and *since.* In the following sentences, carefully examine the word groups introduced by the italicized connectives. Then write *P* above the connective if it is a preposition (introducing a phrase) or *C* if it is a conjunction (introducing a clause).

Example   The Depression continued *until* the industrial boom caused by World War II gained strength.

1. *Since* the country was fighting fascism in Europe, it could hardly continue segregationist policies at home.

2. The income gap between whites and blacks narrowed *after* industrial production speeded up.

3. Blacks became bitter, *for* they were assigned menial tasks in the segregated army or defense industries.

4. *Until* June 1941, this policy conflicted with all the war idealism abroad in the country.

5. A. Philip Randolph, a union president, planned a march on Washington *until* Roosevelt issued Executive Order 8802.

6. *After* this order took effect, all discrimination in hiring by defense industries was illegal.

7. The Fair Employment Practices Commission worked constantly *for* greater job opportunities for blacks.

8. The commission's work was easier than it might have been, *since* labor was in short supply during the war.

9. *Since* the military needed personnel equally desperately, the desegregation of the armed services was rapid.

10. Not *until* the 1960s, however, were civilian facilities desegregated to any great extent.

In each of the following sentences, word groups are italicized. Write *P* above the word group if it is a phrase, or *C* if it is a clause.

Example   *Until the Depression*, blacks had been largely neglected by politicians.

11. *Since blacks traditionally voted for Republicans*, even Republican politicians ignored them.

12. *Since the days of Reconstruction*, blacks had been victims of economic neglect.

13. The black was, *until Roosevelt's New Deal*, "the last hired and the first fired."

14. *Before Roosevelt*, black leaders had referred to "the lily-White House."

15. *After Roosevelt took office*, Washington began to demonstrate sympathy for the problems of blacks.

16. New Deal agencies such as the CCC created new opportunities *for blacks*.

17. Many able blacks were nominated *for senior jobs in these agencies*.

18. *After taking office*, these blacks initiated programs that helped their fellow blacks.

19. These agency administrators symbolized new opportunities that had been unavailable before the Depression spurred political change.

20. By 1936, black voters were shifting to Democratic candidates, *since these opportunities were seen as Roosevelt's creation.*

Write sentences using the listed connectives to head a phrase or clause, as indicated.

21. (*before*, phrase) _____

22. (*before*, clause) _____

23. (*until*, phrase) _____

24. (*until*, clause) _____

25. (*after*, phrase) _____

26. (*after*, clause) _____

27. (*since*, phrase) _____

28. (*since*, clause) _____

29. (*for*, phrase) _____

30. (*for*, clause) _____

SENTENCE CLASSIFICATION   (1d)

Since you began studying the parts of speech in the first section of this book, you have been increasing your knowledge of the way words function individually and in groups. You have been learning to analyze sentences and to describe how their components work together. Beginning with words and progressing through phrases to clauses, the relationships of the components have grown more and more complex.

Being able to analyze the components in a sentence is likely to make you a better writer. When you understand how sentences work, you have better control over the ones you write. When things go wrong, you can figure out why. When you want to achieve a certain effect, you can take sentence structures apart and put them back together in new, planned ways.

For example, if a paragraph you have written sounds monotonous because all the sentences seem the same, you have probably used only one or two sentence patterns. Your knowledge of sentence patterns, clauses, and phrases will enable you to vary those sentences, creating a much more pleasing paragraph.

Now we are ready to examine the broadest category in our analysis of word groups: sentence types. There are four. A **simple sentence** is composed of a single independent clause. A **compound sentence** is composed of two or more independent clauses. A **complex sentence** has an independent clause and one or more subordinate clauses. A **compound-complex sentence** contains two or more independent clauses and one or more subordinate clauses. Examples of each type of sentence follow:

	INDEPENDENT CLAUSE
SIMPLE SENTENCE	It is raining outside.

	INDEPENDENT CLAUSE INDEPENDENT CLAUSE
COMPOUND SENTENCE	It is raining outside, and it is quite chilly.

	SUBORDINATE CLAUSE
COMPLEX SENTENCE	The bike trip that we planned

SUBORDINATE CLAUSE
will have to be postponed because we'll get soaked

SUBORDINATE CLAUSE
if we go now.   [*The bike trip will have to be postponed* is the independent clause.]

	SUBORDINATE CLAUSE
COMPOUND-COMPLEX SENTENCE	Although I was looking forward to the trip,

INDEPENDENT CLAUSE
the rain will make my cold worse, so

INDEPENDENT CLAUSE
I'd better stay home.

Practice: Identifying Sentence Types   Examine the following sentences and decide whether each is a simple, compound, complex, or compound-complex sentence. The answers are listed at the end of this section.

[1]While it remained basically English, Colonial America was already a melting pot. [2]The Scotch-Irish were really Scots Lowlanders who had come to America from Northern Ireland, and they made up about seven percent of the colonial population. [3]Their economic life was severely affected by English restrictions on the linen and wool trade. [4]Upon their arrival in America, the Scotch-Irish found the best lands already occupied, so they immediately moved to claim new ground further west. [5]The "Pennsylvania Dutch" were really Germans, who comprised about six percent of the population. [6]Another five percent of the colonial population were French, Dutch, Swedes, Jews, Irish, Swiss, and Scots Highlanders. [7]Approximately one-fifth of the population was Black and constituted easily the largest non-English element in the Colonies.

Answers to the Practice   [1]complex [2]compound-complex [3]simple [4]compound [5]complex [6]simple [7]simple

EXERCISE (1d), SENTENCE CLASSIFICATION

Using subordinate and independent clauses, expand the following simple sentences into the sentence types indicated in parentheses.

Example   Levi Strauss was an immigrant from Bavaria.

(compound) Levi Strauss was an immigrant, and he was from Bavaria.

(complex) Levi Strauss was an immigrant who was from Bavaria.

(compound-complex) Levi Strauss, who invented blue jeans, was an immigrant, and he was from Bavaria.

1. The Chinese New Year celebration is complex.

(compound) _____

(complex) _____

(compound-complex) _____

2. Chinese-Americans are an interesting ethnic group.

(compound) _____

(complex) _____

(compound-complex) _____

3. Armenians helped develop America's sheepherding industry.

(compound) _____

(complex) _____

(compound-complex) _____

4. Many new crops were introduced into California by Armenian farmers.

(compound) _____

(complex) _____

(compound-complex) _____

5. Austria was not a separate country before 1918.

(compound) _____

(complex) _____

(compound-complex) _____

6. The California Gold Rush lured many people to this country.

(compound) _____

(complex) _____

(compound-complex) _____

7. Franklin Roosevelt began opening opportunities for blacks.

(compound) _____

(complex) _____

(compound-complex) _____

8. World War II also created opportunities.

(compound) _____

(complex) _____

(compound-complex) _____

9. Labor was in short supply during the war.

(compound) _____

(complex) _____

(compound-complex) _____

10. Discrimination in defense industries was illegal.

(compound) _____

(complex) _____

(compound-complex) _____

CASE   (2)

The function of nouns and pronouns within clauses and sentences is indicated by their **case.** There are three cases in English: the **subjective case,** used for the subject of a verb or for a pronoun serving as a predicate complement; the **possessive case,** used to show ownership; and the **objective case,** used for the object of a verb, verbal, or preposition.

Nouns and pronouns change form to show their case. Nouns have a **common form,** such as *ancestor,* and a possessive form, such as *ancestor's.* Personal pronouns and relative or interrogative pronouns are **inflected**—that is, they have different forms for the subjective, possessive, and objective cases. The following table shows these various pronoun forms:

	PERSONAL PRONOUNS			RELATIVE PRONOUNS		
	Subjective	Possessive	Objective	Subjective	Possessive	Objective
		Singular			*Singular*	
First Person	I	my, mine	me	who	whose	whom
Second Person	you	your, yours	you			
Third Person	he, she, it	his, her, hers, its	him, her, it			
		Plural			*Plural*	
First Person	we	our, ours	us	who	whose	whom
Second Person	you	your, yours	you			
Third Person	they	their, theirs	them			

Using the correct case and form to indicate a particular function requires a little care.

51

SUBJECTIVE AND OBJECTIVE CASES

All parts of a compound subject should be in the subjective case. All parts of a compound object should be in the objective case.

SUBJECT   My *brother Sam* and *I* wanted to trace our ancestors.

OBJECT   Dad sent *him* and *me* to look in the family Bible.

After the conjunctions *as* and *than,* use the subjective case if a pronoun is the subject of an understood verb. Use the objective case if it is the object of an understood verb.

SUBJECT   The old Bible seemed to weigh more than *I* (weigh).

OBJECT   When it fell off the shelf, it hit my brother as well as (it hit) *me.*

An **appositive** is a word or phrase following a noun or pronoun that identifies or explains the noun or pronoun by renaming it. A pronoun in an appositive describing a subject or complement should be in the subjective case. A pronoun in an appositive describing an object should be in the objective case.

SUBJECT   *We* three—Sam, the Bible, and *I*—lay on the floor in a heap.

OBJECT   The big old book had claimed two *victims—me* and my brother.

Relative pronouns should be in the subjective case when they function as subjects: *who, whoever.* They should be in the objective case when they function as objects: *whom, whomever.* Remember that the case of the relative pronoun depends upon its function within the clause and not upon the function of the whole clause within the sentence.

SUBJECT   Sam, *who* got to his feet first, lifted the book to the desk. [*Who* is the subject of the subordinate clause modifying *Sam.*]

OBJECT   *Whom* we should look up first was the major question. [*Whom* is the object of the verb *look,* even though the whole clause *whom we should look up first* functions as the subject of the sentence.]

Pronouns following forms of the verb *be* (*is, are, was, were,* etc.) should be written in the subjective case because they function as complements renaming the subject.

It was *I* who decided that first we had to locate the family tree.

Similarly, the possessive case of *who* and *you* is *whose* and *your,* not *who's* and *you're.* *Who's* and *you're* are the contractions for *who is* and *you are.*

POSSESSIVE CASE

Be careful when forming the possessive case of personal pronouns. For most nouns, the 's possessive shows ownership. But personal pronouns show possession through inflection: *my, your, his, hers, its, theirs,* and so on. No apostrophe is used. Be particularly careful with the possessive form of *it.* The possessive is *its,* not *it's. It's* is the contraction for *it is.*

It's [It is] between the Old and New Testaments of the Bible, near *its* center.

The 's possessive is generally used for nouns naming living things. Conventionally, the *of* phrase is preferred for referring to inanimate objects.

ANIMATE   Sam's question, my children's birthdays

INANIMATE   the top of the desk, the pride of possession

There are many exceptions, including a number of familiar expressions: *a dollar's worth; for pity's sake; yesterday's news; heart's desire; last year's fashions.*
Nouns and pronouns preceding gerunds should be in the possessive case.

What was the reason for *my* falling on the floor?

My *brother's* tripping over the chair is a good one!

EXERCISE (2), CASE

In the following sentences, decide which of the pronouns in parentheses is correct and cross out the incorrect one.

Example   Martha told (we/us) about the game of darts.

1. She asked me to go with (her/she) to a darts game.
2. (She/Her) and her family play darts almost every evening.
3. The game earned (its/it's) popularity in England.
4. It was popular with American colonists, (who/whom) played at taverns.
5. (They/Them) developed an American version of the game.
6. In the last century, tavern games lost (they/them/their) popularity.
7. Northeasterners, (whom/who) kept the game alive, make the best players.
8. Martha said (she/her) and (her/hers) family have watched international matches.
9. Almost everyone (who/whom) is English is at least familiar with darts.
10. American players, many of (who/whom) learned the English version abroad, can now compete internationally.

In the following sentences, cross out any incorrect cases and write the correct form above the error. Write *Correct* after correct sentences.

Example   Martha and me are learning the English version of darts.

11. I found brass darts and bought six for Martha and she.
12. Those whom can afford it prefer brass.
13. Brass is the favored material for their competition darts.
14. All those players practice to better theirselves.
15. Martha, in fact, practices more than me.
16. It was her whom bought me my first serious dart.
17. Each dart has it's weight carefully balanced.
18. Competition darts have their weights carefully regulated.
19. Its weight should be between eleven and forty-five grams.

20. Whomever organized the contest chose the wrong dartboard.

21. Us serious players must use the "English clock" dartboard.

22. It has it's face divided, like a pie, into twenty numbered sections.

23. The workers who make the boards consider theirselves artisans.

24. Bristle keeps its consistency longer.

25. Anyone whom buys a cardboard dartboard is wasting him or hers money.

26. Whomever wants to take up the game must know its history.

27. You and me could waste time and money.

28. There are dozens of versions of darts for we to learn.

29. Whose going to teach us to play?

30. Who has the time to teach you and I?

ADJECTIVES AND ADVERBS   (3)

In "Modifying Words: Adjectives & Adverbs" we examined adjectives and adverbs as parts of speech with a particular function—modifying. **Adjectives** modify nouns, pronouns, or other noun substitutes. **Adverbs** modify verbs, adjectives, or other adverbs, and occasionally whole sentences. Both adjectives and adverbs limit or qualify the meaning of the words they modify, thus adding information to a sentence.

Now that you are familiar with sentence patterns and types (Sections 1a and 1d(4)), as well as all the parts of speech, we can examine some other characteristics of adjectives and adverbs.

Some words, such as *fast, much, late,* and *well,* can function as **either adjectives or adverbs.**

ADJECTIVE   She is a *fast* runner. [*Fast* modifies the noun, *runner.*]

ADVERB   She ran *fast.* [*Fast* modifies the verb *ran,* telling how she ran.]

Linking verbs such as forms of the verb *be* (*is, are, was, were, become,* etc.) and verbs such as *seem, remain, prove,* and *stand,* as well as such verbs relating to the senses as *feel, look, smell, taste,* and *sound,* are followed by **predicate adjectives** that describe the subject of the sentence or clause.

You must be careful when you use such verbs since they may or may not be linking. *That soup tasted good* uses a linking verb and hence requires an adjective after the verb. However, in *I tasted the soup* the verb *tasted* takes an object and hence is not a linking verb. In *She looked tired, looked* is a linking verb followed by the adjective *tired.* In *She looked away tiredly, looked* is not a linking verb. The modifiers *away* and *tiredly* do not describe the subject, *she,* but rather provide information about the verb and thus are adverbs.

Most adverbs are distinguished from their corresponding adjectives by the *-ly* ending: *grateful, gratefully; free, freely; pleasing, pleasingly.* However, an *-ly* ending does not automatically mean a word is an adverb. Some adjectives, such as *friendly, slovenly,* and *cowardly,* also end in *-ly.* Furthermore, some adverbs have two forms, one with *-ly* and one without: *quick, quickly; slow, slowly.* The key, as always, is to see what part of speech a word modifies or what role it plays in a sentence pattern when deciding whether it is an adverb or an adjective.

Adjectives and adverbs show degrees of quality or quantity by means of their **comparative and superlative forms.**

For the **comparative** form, which permits a comparison of two, *-er* is added to the adjective, or the adverb *more* is placed before it (*pretty, prettier; rapid, more rapid*). For the **superlative** form, which involves a comparison among three or more, *-est* is added to the adjective, or *most* is placed before it (*pretty, prettiest; rapid, most rapid*).

Most adjectives and a few adverbs of one syllable form the comparative and superlative with *-er* and *-est.* Adjectives of two syllables often offer a choice (*lovelier, loveliest* and *more lovely, most lovely*). Adjectives of three or more syllables and most adverbs usually use *more* and *most* in making their comparisons (*more industrious,* not *industriouser; more sadly,* not *sadlier*).

The comparative and superlative forms of the adjectives *good* and *bad* are irregular:

good	bad
better	worse
best	worst

Some adjectives and adverbs are absolute in their meaning and thus cannot logically be compared. Examples of such words include the following:

complete	final
dead	perfect
empty	unique

Practice: Identifying Adjectives and Adverbs   Underline once all the words that function as adjectives in the following sentences. (Do not underline the articles.) Underline twice all the words that function as adverbs. The answers are listed at the end of this section.

[1]The classic game of English darts, played mainly in pubs, is called "301." [2]Each player starts with an initial score of 301 points. [3]Each player takes three throws at the board, and the colored sections of the board double or triple the score for that throw. [4]The score for each successive throw is subtracted from 301. [5]The first player to eventually reach zero wins the game. [6]A further complication is the really dif-

ficult requirement that the players must begin and end the game by hitting a double zone. [7]The English version of darts makes the American version, in which points are simply added up, seem awfully simple. [8]That may be the reason that the English still dominate the game at the international level.

Answers to the Practice   Adjectives: [1]classic, English [2]Each, initial, 301 [3]Each, three, colored [4]each, successive [5]first [6]further, difficult, double [7]English, American, simple [8]international
Adverbs: [1]mainly [5]eventually [6]really [7]simply, up, awfully [8]still

EXERCISE (3a-d), ADJECTIVES AND ADVERBS

In the blanks, indicate with the appropriate abbreviation whether the adjective (*adj*) or the adverbial (*adv*) form of the given word should be used.

Example   original   Charles Atlas's ——*adj*—— name was Angelo Siciliano.

1. *weak*   Angelo began to grow —————— after emigrating from Italy.

2. *fair*   He was a —————— strong boy in Italy.

3. *approximate*   His troubles began when he was —————— eleven.

4. *quick*   He —————— lost interest in school.

5. *difficult*   Angelo found climbing the stairs to the family apartment —————— .

6. *nervous*   He became pale and even —————— .

7. *actual*   He was once —————— beaten by another boy who used a sock.

8. *obvious*   He was —————— in trouble.

9. *thorough*   Angelo found himself becoming —————— depressed about life.

10. *final*   He was —————— inspired by a statue of Hercules.

11. *natural*   Angelo, —————— enough, joined the YMCA a week later.

12. *strict*   He began lifting weights in a —————— regimen.

13. *dedicated*   He spent —————— hours with weights, stretchers, and medicine balls.

14. *intense*   He became —————— interested in home strength courses.

15. *famous*   Two courses that were —————— in his day were the Swoboda Course and Strongfortism.

16. *simple*   For use at home, Angelo built a —————— barbell with a broomstick and rocks.

17. *complete*   His family at first worried that Angelo was —————— obsessed with developing strength.

18. *serious* One day, as he toured the zoo, Angelo's most _____ discovery came to him.

19. *superb* A tiger was stretching when Angelo asked himself, "What keeps a tiger so _____ fit?"

20. *original* Angelo's realization that tigers exercise one muscle against another was a completely _____ idea.

Write your own sentences, using the adjectival or adverbial form of the italicized word, as indicated.

Example (*probable*, adjective) Your story doesn't sound probable.

21. (*virtual*, adverb) _____

22. (*total*, adjective) _____

23. (*slow*, adverb) _____

24. (*eventual*, adverb) _____

25. (*usual*, adverb) _____

26. (*sure*, adverb) _____

27. (*real*, adverb) _____

28. (*continual*, adjective) _____

29. (*basic*, adjective) _____

30. (*logical*, adverb) _____

31. (*ordinary*, adverb) _____

32. (*original*, adjective) _____

33. (*typical*, adverb) _____

34. (*frequent*, adjective) _____

35. (*excellent*, adverb) _____

36. (*late*, adverb) _____

37. (*relative*, adverb) _____

38. (*primary*, adverb) _____

39. (*heavy*, adverb) _____

40. (*fair*, adverb) _____

EXERCISE (3e-f), COMPARATIVE AND SUPERLATIVE FORMS

In each blank, write the appropriate comparative or superlative form of the modifier given in italics to complete the sentence correctly.

Example *famous*   Angelo Siciliano became the <u>most famous</u> strongman in history.

1. *strong*   Angelo may not have been the _____ man who ever lived.

2. *frequent*   Nevertheless his name is linked _____ with "physical culture" than is the name of anyone else.

3. *common*   "Dynamic tension," now _____ called isometric exercise, was Angelo's great discovery.

4. *important*   It eventually became _____ than anything else in his life.

5. *effective*   Isometrics is now considered _____ than many other forms of exercise.

6. *good*   Aerobics may be _____ for the cardiopulmonary system.

7. *good*   Some forms of weight training may be _____ than isometrics for adding bulk to muscles.

8. *bad*   But weight training is the _____ thing to undertake if one has joint problems.

9. *perfect*   For people with sore joints, isometrics is the _____ answer.

10. *efficient* Angelo developed a _____ series of exercises for himself.

11. *careful*   He was _____ than Swoboda to involve almost every muscle.

12. *small*   The exercises Angelo developed involved even the _____ muscles.

13. *good*   The _____ way to describe "dynamic tension" is as a tug of war staged between different sets of muscles.

14. *likely*   Since it involves only the body, it is _____ to be done every day than exercise using heavy, specialized equipment.

15. *impressive*   Using his exercises, Angelo developed a _____ form, doubling his weight.

16. *large*   His 17-inch biceps and 55-inch chest were _____ than those of anyone else training at his gym.

17. *wide*   Of all the methods of body-building, Angelo's was destined to become _____ known.

18. *important*   The _____ cause of its popularity lay in the name of its founder.

19. *similar*   His friends at the gym said Angelo's new body looked _____ to the statue of Atlas, on the bank across the street, than anyone who had ever worked in that gym.

20. *commercial*   Angelo changed his name to Charles Atlas, by far the _____ of the two.

Write sentences using the proper form—comparative or superlative—of the listed modifiers.

21. (*low*, superlative)

_____

22. (*less*, superlative)

_____

23. (*bad*, comparative)

_____

24. (*bad*, superlative)

_____

25. (*well*, superlative)

_____

26. (*badly*, superlative)

_____

27. (*good*, superlative)

_____

28. (*good*, comparative)

_____

29. (*obnoxious*, comparative)

_____

30. (*speedy*, comparative)

_____

VERB FORMS
AND TENSES   (4–5)

The section "Verbs and Verbals" sketches the general role verbs play, but it only begins to suggest the amount of information a verb actually conveys. The single word comprising a verb (or the few words of a verb phrase) tells us not only the exact nature of an action or condition but also

1. the time when it occurs and whether the action is completed or continuing (**tense**);

2. whether or not the verb passes its action to an object (is **transitive, intransitive,** or **linking**);

3. whether the subject is performing or receiving the action (**voice**);

4. the attitude of the speaker or writer (**mood**).

TENSES

Verbs show present, past, and future time by means of their three tenses. Each of these tenses is further subdivided into categories, according to whether the action or condition is continuing (in progress) or completed at the time indicated. The following table lists, explains, and gives examples of the categories of tense. Notice which helping verbs are used to form each of the tenses.

TENSE	TIME	EXAMPLE
Present	Present or habitual action	I *call* my parents.
Present perfect	Action completed at an indefinite time in the past or extending up to the present time	I *have called* my parents every Sunday.
Present progressive	Present action continuing or in progress	I *am calling* my parents now.
Present perfect progressive	Continuing action occurring up to but not including the present	I *have been calling* my parents.
Past	Past action	I *called* my parents.
Past perfect	Past action completed before another past action	I *had called* my parents before lunch.
Past progressive	Continuing action that occurred in the past	I *was calling* my parents.
Past perfect progressive	Continuing past action that occurred before another past action	I *had been calling* my parents when you arrived.
Future	Future action	I *shall/will call* them later.
Future perfect	Future action that will be completed before another future action	I *will have called* them before I see you again.
Future progressive	Continuing action that will occur in the future	I *will be calling* them again next Sunday.
Future perfect progressive	Continuing action that leads up to a point in the future	If I arrive late, the reason is I *will have been calling* my parents.

REGULAR AND IRREGULAR VERBS

The verb previously used to illustrate tenses, *call,* is a **regular verb.** Most verbs are regular—that is, the past tense and past participle (the combining form used with many helping verbs) are formed by adding *-ed* to the present tense form: for example, *help* + *ed* and *show* + *ed* yield *helped* and *showed.* If the present tense form of a regular verb ends in *e,* the past tense and past participle are formed by simply adding *d: hoped, filed.*

Irregular verbs, as the term suggests, follow another pattern. Of the more than 200 irregular English verbs, about twenty have the same form for the present tense, past tense, and past participle: *cut, cut, cut.* Many change an internal vowel for the past tense and past participle: *keep, kept, kept.* Some irregular verbs have three distinct forms, a different one for each of the tenses, present, past tense, and past participle: *forgive, forgave, forgiven; do, did, done.* The following list shows the three forms for the most commonly used irregular verbs:

PRESENT INFINITIVE	PAST	PAST PARTICIPLE
awake	awoke, awaked	awaked
arise	arose	arisen
bear (carry)	bore	borne
bear (give birth to)	bore	borne, born
beat	beaten	beaten
become	became	become
begin	began	begun
bet	bet	bet
bid	bade, bid	bidden, bid
bite	bit	bitten
blow	blew	blown
break	broke	broken
bring	brought	brought
burst	burst	burst
buy	bought	bought
catch	caught	caught
choose	chose	chosen
come	came	come
cut	cut	cut
dig	dug	dug
dive	dived, dove	dived
do	did	done
draw	drew	drawn
drink	drank	drunk
drive	drove	driven
eat	ate	eaten
fall	fell	fallen
feel	felt	felt
find	found	found
fly	flew	flown
forget	forgot	forgotten, forgot
forgive	forgave	forgiven
freeze	froze	frozen
get	got	got, gotten

PRESENT INFINITIVE	PAST	PAST PARTICIPLE
give	gave	given
go	went	gone
grow	grew	grown
hang (suspend)	hung	hung
hang	hanged	hung
hid	hid	hidden
hit	hit	hit
hurt	hurt	hurt
keep	kept	kept
know	knew	known
lay (place)	laid	laid
lead	led	led
leave	left	left
let	let	let
lie (recline)	lay	lain
lose	lost	lost
make	made	made
mean	meant	meant
pay	paid	paid
read	read	read
ride	rode	ridden
ring	rang	rung
rise	rose	risen
run	ran	run
see	saw	seen
set	set	set
shake	shook	shaken
shine	shone	shone
shrink	shrank, shrunk	shrunk
sink	sank, sunk	sunk
speak	spoke	spoken
spin	spun	spun
spring	sprang, sprung	sprung
stand	stood	stood
steal	stole	stolen
stink	stank	stunk
strike	struck	struck
swear	swore	sworn

PRESENT INFINITIVE	PAST	PAST PARTICIPLE
swim	swam	swum
swing	swung	swung
take	took	taken
teach	taught	taught
tear	tore	torn
tell	told	told
think	thought	thought
throw	threw	thrown
wake	woke, waked	woken, waked
wear	wore	worn
weave	wove, weaved	woven, weaved
weep	wept	wept
win	won	won
wind	wound	wound
wring	wrung	wrung
write	wrote	written

The verb *be* is also an irregular verb. It appears often in many forms, and it is used frequently with the combining forms of other verbs. Study it carefully.

SINGULAR	PLURAL	SINGULAR	PLURAL
Present Tense		*Present Perfect Tense*	
I am	we are	I have been	we have been
you are	you are	you have been	you have been
he, she, it is	they are	he, she, it has been	they have been
Past Tense		*Past Perfect Tense*	
I was	we were	I had been	we had been
you were	you were	you had been	you had been
he, she, it was	they were	he, she, it had been	they had been
Future Tense		*Future Perfect Tense*	
I will be	we will be	I will have been	we will have been
you will be	you will be	you will have been	you will have been
he, she, it will be	they will be	he, she, it will have been	they will have been

Practice: Identifying Verb Tenses   Name the tenses of the verbs in the following sentences. The answers are listed at the end of this section.

¹Several Balkan states lost their independent existence in 1918 when a commission created Yugoslavia. ²The Hapsburg family had ruled these small states for generations before 1918. ³All these countries—Serbia, Croatia, Montenegro—have merged into the larger, modern Yugoslavia. ⁴The first Croatian immigrants came to America in 1698. ⁵Oddly, many of the Croatians had been silkworm farmers before they settled in Georgia. ⁶Unfortunately, an early Civil War battle had destroyed their settlement. ⁷Before World War I, almost 700,000 Croatians had emigrated to the United States; they lived and worked in our large industrial cities. ⁸They had been waiting only for peace in their homeland, since after the commission formed Yugoslavia, over 200,000 Croatians returned to Yugoslavia.

SPECIAL PROBLEMS WITH VERB TENSES

Problems writers face in using verbs correctly sometimes arise from difficulties with tense forms. Several of the most common problems are discussed next.

Writers sometimes omit necessary verb endings, especially if they do not audibly pronounce these endings when speaking. The two most frequently omitted endings are *-s* and *-ed*. The *-s* form is required for present tense verbs used with singular nouns, third person singular pronouns (*he, she, it*), and indefinite pronouns such as *each, someone,* and *everybody*.

He *likes* the sweaters that his Scottish aunt *knits*.

For the present tense verbs ending in *o*, the form is *-es: goes*. For the verbs *be* and *have*, the *-s* forms are *is* and *has*.

He *is* very fond of the last sweater she sent him, because it *goes* with the tweed jacket he *has*.

The *-ed* form is required for the past tense and past participle of all regular verbs. When the next word following the verb in a sentence begins with a similar sound, the *-ed* can be hard to hear and may be difficult to remember when you write. Be particularly careful to include it when you write the past tense for constructions such as *used to* and *supposed to*.

He was *supposed* to write her a thank-you note. [Not *He was **suppose** to write*.]

Writers sometimes use nonstandard forms of irregular verbs. Remember that although most English verbs are regular, a great many are irregular. *See* is an irregular verb, so you should not write *I seed him yesterday* instead of *I saw him yesterday*.

Also, the principal parts of an irregular verb are not interchangeable—that is, you need to select the correct tense for the time you wish to indicate. *I done my homework* is incorrect because *done* is the past participle form (*do, did done*); it requires a helping verb and cannot be used for the past tense. *I did my homework* is correct.

Writers sometimes have trouble choosing the appropriate tense sequence for verbs in main and subordinate clauses in complex sentences. When the verb in the main clause is in any tense except the past or past perfect tense, the verb in the subordinate clause should be in whatever tense the meaning requires.

> Because our old refrigerator *broke,* we *need* a new one. [The need is in the present but is the result of a past event.]

> The sales clerk *promises* they *will deliver* the new refrigerator on Tuesday. [The promise occurs in the present but refers to a future event.]

When the verb in the main clause is in the past or past perfect tense, the verb in the subordinate clause should usually be in the past or past perfect tense, too—unless the subordinate clause states a general truth.

> The clerk *said* that he *had checked* the delivery schedule. [He checked before he made the statement.]

BUT

> We *learned* later that clerks *promise* quickly, but stores *deliver* slowly. [Here the subordinate clause is offered as a general truth and so is in the present tense.]

Answers to the Practice ¹past, past ²past perfect ³present perfect ⁴past ⁵past perfect, past ⁶past perfect ⁷past perfect, past, past ⁸past perfect progressive, past, past

EXERCISE (4a–b), VERB TENSES

Change the present tense verbs in each of the following sentences to past tense, rewriting the sentence with past tense verbs in the blank provided. Be sure to choose the correct form for irregular verbs.

Example   Bing cherries are the sweetest cherries grown in America.

Bing cherries were the sweetest cherries grown in America.

1. The cherry has been developed by a Chinese immigrant.

    _____

2. He is known only by the single name of Bing.

    _____

3. Thus, he remains a mysterious figure, even to historians.

    _____

4. The cherry is an ancient crop, first born in China.

    _____

5. It has been grown by Bing's ancestors for centuries.

    _____

6. Henderson Luelling brings the first cherries west of the Rockies.

    _____

7. The first wagonload of stock provides the ancestors of the Bing cherry.

    _____

8. The Bing cherry has sweet, firm, juicy characteristics.

    _____

9. Its skin ranges from deep red to black.

    _____

10. The Dutch introduce the waffle to America.

    _____

11. The waffle has to be served dripping with butter.

    _____

12. The Dutch contribution to the American diet represents a roll call of fattening food.

_____

13. And for some reason, most Dutch foods in America are eaten at breakfast.

_____

14. The list includes crullers, hot cocoa, buckwheat cakes, and chocolate bars.

_____

15. Buckwheat cakes make many a cold morning bearable.

_____

16. Crullers seem to be first cousins to the doughnut.

_____

17. Doughnut lovers claim that their favorite breakfast is a Dutch invention, too.

_____

18. The Dutch call doughnuts "oilycake."

_____

19. Historians think the recipe was brought to America by the Pilgrims.

_____

20. It takes an American, of course, to think of putting a hole in the middle.

_____

21. A Pilgrim oilycake resembles a little round wad of dough that is the size of a walnut.

_____

22. It's obvious why the Pilgrims were the first to call them "doughnuts."

_____

23. The difficulty is that a doughnut shaped this way can't cook thoroughly.

_____

24. Even when the outside is cooked crisp, the inside stays cool.

_____

25. The Pilgrim doughnut is plagued by a soggy middle.

_____

26. Hanson Gregory comes to the rescue with a novel idea.

_____

27. Gregory, a sailor, decides to punch out the middle of the doughnut.

_____

28. He reasons that if the middle is removed the rest of the doughnut cooks more evenly.

_____

29. A plaque in Rockport, Maine, honors Gregory for his invention.

_____

30. Of course, a later entrepreneur has an even better idea—selling the hole.

_____

EXERCISE (5a–5b), SPECIAL PROBLEMS WITH VERB TENSES

In the blank in each sentence, write the correct form of the listed verb in the tense indicated.

Example   (*have*, present)
The hamburger _____**has**_____ a long and colorful history.

1. (*begin*, past)
The hamburger's history probably _____ with Tartar steak.

2. (*cover*, present progressive)
Tartar steak is raw egg that _____ raw beef.

3. (*introduce*, past perfect)
Russian sailors _____ the dish to the German city, Hamburg.

4. (*improve*, past)
German cooks _____ the dish immensely by cooking it.

5. (*find*, present perfect)
Imagine a diner who _____ the raw dish disgusting.

6. (*send*, present progressive)
He _____ the dish back to be cooked.

7. (*cook*, present)
After the cook _____ it, it is irresistible.

8. (*see*, past perfect)
Such a popular dish must have a name, since it never _____ the light of day before.

9. (*exist*, future perfect)
It _____ under the name of its city of origin for hundreds of years by now.

10. (*serve*, past)
German immigrants first _____ hamburger in America.

11. (*serve*, past perfect progressive)
In 1904, a St. Louis vendor _____ so many hamburgers that he ran out of plates.

12. (*offer*, past progressive)
Before long, he _____ the hamburger on buns.

13. (*decide*, past)
    Everyone at the St. Louis Exposition _____ to have their hamburger on rolls, too.

14. (*begin*, past)
    In this way, the dish _____ to resemble its modern form.

15. (*take*, past)
    It _____ an accident, a miscalculation of vendors' supplies, to make the hamburger a sandwich.

For each of the following sentences, select the appropriate verb for the tense sequence from the choices in parentheses, and cross out the incorrect choice.

16. Other German foods that became popular in America (were/are) convenient, casual foods.

17. Pretzels, sausage, and beer are from Germany; so (had been/are/were) noodles and sauerkraut.

18. Frankfurters were from Germany; the people in Frankfurt (have been making/were making) them since 1852.

19. All the specialty sausages (become/became) as popular here as they (were/are) in Germany.

20. Two German immigrants (claimed/had claimed) to have invented the frankfurter sandwich.

21. They (hoped/had hoped) to make the sausage more popular by making it more portable.

22. A Bavarian, Arnold Feuchtwanger, (said/had said/had been saying) he invented the frankfurter in the 1880s in St. Louis.

23. Charles Feltman said he (sold/had been selling) the same sandwich at Coney Island in the 1890s for a price he (established/establishes) at a dime.

24. Feltman's story (has seemed/seems) more likely to me.

25. Americans called frankfurter sandwiches "Coney Islands" and "dime red hots" before they (had called/called/will have called/will have been calling) the sandwiches "hotdogs."

KINDS OF VERBS:
TRANSITIVE, INTRANSITIVE,
AND LINKING VERBS   (4)

A **transitive verb** transmits or passes action from a subject to an object.

> She *bought* a ticket.

An **intransitive verb** does not transmit action and has no object or complement.

> The train *arrived* on time.

Some verbs can be either transitive or intransitive. For example, in the sentence *She watched the train.*, the verb *watched* is transitive; it is followed by the direct object *train.* However, if the sentence is changed to *She watched carefully.*, the verb becomes intransitive; it has no object.

Two pairs of verbs that are often confusing and used incorrectly as a consequence are *lie, lay* and *sit, set.* If you remember that *lie* and *sit* are intransitive but *lay* and *set* are transitive, it will be easier to use them correctly. To help you distinguish their uses, the principal parts of the four verbs are illustrated here:

	PRESENT	PAST	PAST PARTICIPLE
INTRANSITIVE	I *lie* down.	I *lay* down.	I *have lain* down.
TRANSITIVE	I *lay* the book down.	I *laid* the book down.	I *have laid* the book down.
INTRANSITIVE	I *sit* down.	I *sat* down.	I *have sat* down.
TRANSITIVE	I *set* my watch.	I *set* my watch.	I *have set* my watch.

Practice A: Identifying Transitive and Intransitive Verbs   In each of the following sentences, underline transitive verbs once and intransitive verbs twice. The answers are listed at the end of this section.

[1]The Swiss are the smallest ethnic group in America; they appear in Census reports as only 0.7 percent of the American population descended from foreign ancestors. [2]Yet they have made outstanding contributions to American culture and history. [3]Swiss immigrants gave America Swiss chard, the leafy green vegetable. [4]They brought to America a curtain and dress fabric, dotted Swiss, and they introduced the Brown Swiss cow, a dairy breed that is raised in New England. [5]Swiss descendants developed Hershey's mild chocolate, Chevrolets, Waldorf salad, and the Lincoln Tunnel. [6]Presidents Hoover and Eisenhower claimed Swiss ancestry. [7]Swiss mercenaries served in the New World in the armies of Spain, the first Swiss colony was located near Charleston, and William Penn promised religious freedom to Swiss who settled in Pennsylvania.

A **linking verb** joins the subject of a sentence to its complement, the predicate adjective that describes the subject or the predicate noun that renames the subject. A linking verb expresses a condition and frequently acts as an equal sign. For example, *the apples are ripe* means the same as *apples = ripe*. Because a linking verb does not convey action from a subject to an object, it can never have an object.

The most common linking verbs are forms of *be, become, seem, appear, feel, look, smell, taste,* and *sound*. Verbs pertaining to the five senses can be either linking or transitive, depending on how they are used. Remember that a linking verb states a condition, but a transitive verb passes action to an object.

TRANSITIVE VERB	LINKING VERB
The cat *smells* a mouse.	The cat *smells* terrible since its fight with a skunk.
She *looked* her opponent straight in the eye.	Her opponent *looked* nervous.
He *sounds* the alarm.	His voice *sounds* hoarse.
Mother *felt* my forehead.	I *felt* faint and dizzy.
Taste the stew.	Does the stew *taste* too salty?

Practice B: Identifying Linking Verbs   In each of the following sentences, underline the transitive verbs once and the linking verbs twice. The answers are listed at the end of this section.

[1]Swiss-Americans are famous for their contributions to America's restaurant menus. [2]Peter and John Delmonico were two Swiss brothers who opened their famous restaurant in New York, in 1827. [3]It was at Delmonico's that Americans first tasted elegant European dishes. [4]Lobster Newburg became their most famous dish, but it was Lobster Wenburg when a Delmonico descendant first prepared it in 1876. [5]He invented it in honor of Ben Wenburg, who first conceived the idea that lobster would taste better with egg yolks, heavy cream, sherry, and cognac. [6]After an ar-

gument with Ben, Delmonico changed the menu so Ben could claim no credit for inspiring Lobster Newburg.

Answers to Practice A Transitive: [2]have made [3]gave [4]brought, introduced [5]developed [6]claimed [7]promised
Intransitive: [1]are, appear, descended [4]is raised [7]served, was located, settled

Answers to Practice B Transitive: [2]opened [3]tasted [4]prepared [5]invented, conceived [6]changed, claim
Linking: [1]are [2]were [3]was [4]became, was [5]taste

EXERCISE (4c)-1, TRANSITIVE AND INTRANSITIVE VERBS

For each of the listed verbs, first write a sentence using it as a transitive verb and then another sentence using it as an intransitive verb. You may use the verb in any tense you wish.

Example   *drink*

(transitive) _I drank the whole pitcher, I'm afraid._

(intransitive) _I drank quickly and thirstily._

1. *wind*

    (transitive) ————————————————————————

    (intransitive) ————————————————————————

2. *begin*

    (transitive) ————————————————————————

    (intransitive) ————————————————————————

3. *flip*

    (transitive) ————————————————————————

    (intransitive) ————————————————————————

4. *draw*

    (transitive) ————————————————————————

    (intransitive) ————————————————————————

5. *do*

    (transitive) ————————————————————————

    (intransitive) ————————————————————————

6. *burst*

    (transitive) ————————————————————————

    (intransitive) ————————————————————————

7. *blow*

    (transitive) ————————————————————————

    (intransitive) ————————————————————————

8. *freeze*

(transitive) _____

(intransitive) _____

9. *grow*

(transitive) _____

(intransitive) _____

10. *know*

(transitive) _____

(intransitive) _____

11. *lay*

(transitive) _____

(intransitive) _____

12. *lead*

(transitive) _____

(intransitive) _____

13. *return*

(transitive) _____

(intransitive) _____

14. *run*

(transitive) _____

(intransitive) _____

15. *swim*

(transitive) _____

(intransitive) _____

EXERCISE (4c)-2, TRANSITIVE, INTRANSITIVE, AND LINKING VERBS

In each of the following sentences, select the correct verb from the choices in parentheses, and cross out the incorrect choice.

Example   I believe I'll (sit/set) to work recording our old family recipes.

1.   Have you (set/sat) as a goal recording your family's recipes?

2.   Many community organizations have (set/sit) themselves to work collecting recipes on a large scale.

3.   It is amazing where many of these old recipes (lie/lay).

4.   First, (sit/set) down with all the older members of your family.

5.   (Sit/Set) yourself the objective of learning all the recipes they know.

6.   It does no good to (lie/lay) around and wonder.

7.   (Sit/Set) a schedule for yourself so you can interview each relative.

8.   Many of our family's recipes (lie/lay/laid) forgotten in my uncle's attic.

9.   If you (sit/set) enough value on finding these old recipes, you may even have to travel.

10.   In this kind of research, you don't just (sit/set) and study old records.

For each of the listed verbs, first write a sentence using it as a linking verb, and then write a sentence using it as a transitive verb. You may use the verb in any tense you wish.

Example   *feel*

(linking)   I feel happy today.

(transitive)   I could feel the rust on the bars.

11.   *become*

(linking) _____

(transitive) _____

12.   *grow*

(linking) _____

(transitive) _____

13. *act*

(linking) _____

(transitive) _____

14. *taste*

(linking) _____

(transitive) _____

15. *smell*

(linking) _____

(transitive) _____

16. *prove*

(linking) _____

(transitive) _____

17. *watch*

(linking) _____

(transitive) _____

18. *turn*

(linking) _____

(transitive) _____

19. *look*

(linking) _____

(transitive) _____

20. *sound*

(linking) _____

(transitive) _____

VOICE: ACTIVE AND PASSIVE VOICE VERBS (5)

Transitive verbs can either be active voice or passive voice verbs. An **active voice verb** indicates that the subject performs the action and transmits it to an object: *Carla called her cousin in Mexico City.* A **passive voice verb** indicates that the subject receives the action performed by someone or something else: *Carla was called by her cousin from Mexico City.*

Passive voice verbs enable us to emphasize the receiver of the action rather than the performer, or agent, of the action. For example, in the sentence *Carla packed her suitcase.*, the subject is *Carla*. The emphasis is on what she is doing. In the sentence *The suitcase was packed by Carla.*, however, the subject is *suitcase*. The emphasis is not on Carla, the agent, but on what happened to the suitcase. Sometimes the agent in a passive voice sentence is not even identified: *The suitcase was packed.*

The passive voice is formed by using the past participle of the main verb with the appropriate form of the verb *be* to indicate tenses. Like active voice verbs, passive voice verbs also have perfect and progressive forms. The following table lists, explains, and illustrates the various passive voice verb forms:

TENSE	TIME	EXAMPLE
Present	Present or habitual action	I *am called* to the telephone.
Present perfect	Completed action in the immediate past	I *have been called* to the telephone.
Present progressive	Present action continuing or in progress	I *am being called* to the telephone now.

TENSE	TIME	EXAMPLE
Present perfect progressive	Continuing action occurring up to but not including the present	I *have been being called* to the telephone all morning.
Past	Completed past action	I *was called* to the telephone.
Past perfect	Past action completed before another past action	I *had been called* to the telephone, so I ran down the stairs.
Past progressive	Continuing action that occurred in the past	I *was being called* to the telephone when I tripped.
Past perfect progressive	Continuing past action that occurred before another past action	I *had been being* urgently *called* to the telephone, until I shouted that I had fallen down.
Future	Future action	I *shall/will be called* to the telephone no more.
Future perfect	Future action completed before another future time	I *shall/will have been called* at home by my boss tomorrow, however.
Future progressive	Action in progress at a future time	In fact, I *shall/will be being called* daily for progress reports.
Future perfect progressive	Continuing future action that leads up to another future time	I *shall/will have been being called* for weeks by the time my broken leg heals.

Obviously, we do not often need to write sentences using passive voice perfect progressive verb forms. Nevertheless, the other passive voice forms are widely used in writing, particularly for technical and scientific subjects in which the receiver of an action is more important than the agent: *The results of the survey were tabulated, and the findings were reported to the review board.*

Keep in mind, however, that a passive voice sentence is longer and less forceful than an active voice sentence. Passive voice requires the addition of at least one helping verb, and a prepositional phrase if you identify the agent of the action. Active voice sentences are more direct, more economical, and more forceful, as the following comparison shows:

PASSIVE VOICE   The meeting was called to order by the president.

ACTIVE VOICE   The president called the meeting to order.

When you write, be aware of verb voice so that you select verbs in the voice that best achieves the emphasis you want.

Practice: Identifying Passive Voice Verbs   Underline all the passive voice verb phrases in the following sentences. The answers are listed at the end of this section.

[1]The current American interest in cultural and historical roots was encouraged by Alex Haley. [2]Haley's *Roots* appeared first as a best-selling book and then was developed into a television miniseries. [3]On television, *Roots* drew one of the largest audiences in history. [4]In addition, *Roots* was published as a series in several national magazines. [5]Haley was led to the discovery of his African ancestors only after intricate research, and he published articles on his research methods, as well. [6]Haley was born in New York; he was six generations away from his ancestors, who were taken to Tennessee. [7]He not only rekindled all Americans' interest in their roots; his story dramatically recounts Black America's emergence from slavery.

Answers to the Practice   [1]was encouraged [2]was developed [4]was published [5]was led [6]were taken

EXERCISE (5d-e), ACTIVE AND PASSIVE VOICE VERBS

Rewrite the following sentences, changing the passive voice verbs to active voice verbs. Try to retain the verb tense of the original sentence. If an agent is not supplied in the original sentence, provide an appropriate one in your revision.

Example   Three African words were remembered by Haley's grandmother.

Haley's grandmother remembered three African words.

1. The vaguest memories were all that could be assembled by Haley.

   _____

2. Even the three African words had been forgotten by most family members.

   _____

3. The origin of the words could not be determined by Haley.

   _____

4. Haley was reminded of Africa by the words.

   _____

5. His older relatives were interviewed as quickly as possible.

   _____

6. The researcher was afraid that their knowledge would be allowed to disappear.

   _____

7. The origin of the three words was located in Gambia, West Africa.

   _____

8. The oldest known ancestor of the Haley family was discovered to be a Gambian.

   _____

9. Haley was aided in this first task by a linguist.

   _____

10. The task that had once seemed impossible had been begun in earnest.

   _____

11. The details of his ancestors' lives were now being gathered.

_____

12. Census records, wills, and plantation records were searched.

_____

13. Cargo invoices and tax records were found to be equally useful.

_____

14. Haley was allowed to reconstruct the daily lives of his ancestors from these facts.

_____

15. One of the African words was discovered to be a name.

_____

16. "Kunta Kinte" was recognized as the name of Haley's African ancestor.

_____

17. He was referred to as "The African" by Haley's oldest relatives.

_____

18. Haley's roots were traced to 1750.

_____

19. The Moslem religion was practiced by Kunta Kinte, who was a Mandinka tribesman.

_____

20. The Arabic language and the Koran were known by all Mandinkas.

_____

21. Their livelihood had been derived from harvesting rice and cotton.

_____

22. The village of Juffure was called home by Kunta Kinte.

_____

23. His basic education in Arabic, history, and mathematics had been completed at the age of ten.

_____

24. West Africans often were victimized by slave traders.

_____

25. At seventeen, Kunta was kidnapped and was sent to America.

_____

26. After having been sold to a plantation owner, Kunta was renamed "Toby."

_____

27. The lives of Kunta Kinte and his descendants were fashioned into a gripping story by Haley.

_____

28. Talent, inner strength, and resilience were demonstrated by each generation born in America.

_____

29. After they had been emancipated by the Civil War, Kunta's descendants moved to Tennessee.

_____

30. Haley's grandmother was born in Tennessee, and the three African words had been remembered by her.

_____

MOOD (5f–h)

English has three moods. The **indicative mood** expresses a statement: *I will go.* The **imperative mood** expresses a direct command or request: *Go do what I told you.* In sentences in the imperative mood, the understood subject is always *you.* The **subjunctive mood** is now mainly used to express wishes and conditions contrary to fact: *I wish that I were at home. If I were you, I would leave now.* The subjunctive should also be used in *that* clauses that express formal demands, resolutions, recommendations, requests, or motions: *He moved that the motion be tabled.*

The subjunctive mood uses special forms in several tenses, persons, and numbers of the verb *be* and in the third person singular, present, and present perfect tenses of all verbs. The following tables pinpoint these variations:

Subjunctive Mood: *To Be*

	SINGULAR	PLURAL
PRESENT TENSE	I *be* [not *am*] you *be* [not *are*] he, she, it *be* [not *is*]	we *be* [not *are*] you *be* [not *are*] they *be* [not *are*]
PAST TENSE	I *were* [not *was*] you were he, she, it *were* [not *was*]	we were you were they were
PRESENT PERFECT TENSE	I have been you have been he, she, it *have* been [not *has*]	we have been you have been they have been
PAST PERFECT TENSE	had been (all persons and numbers)	

Subjunctive Mood: *To Speak*

	SINGULAR	PLURAL
PRESENT TENSE	I speak you speak he, she, it *speak* [not *speaks*]	we speak you speak they speak
PAST TENSE	I spoke you spoke he, she, it spoke	we spoke you spoke they spoke
PRESENT PERFECT TENSE	I have spoken you have spoken he, she, it *have* spoken [not *has* spoken]	we have spoken you have spoken they have spoken
PAST PERFECT TENSE	had spoken (all persons and numbers)	

The following sentences illustrate the correct use of the subjunctive:

I demand that this defendant *be found* guilty.

My lawyer has insisted that the judge *have delivered* her opinion by tomorrow morning.

If this woman *be* a citizen, as she claims, why have we found no public record of her existence?

They would not have asked that we *be* consulted if they *were* not interested in our opinions.

If Fargo *were* a Republican, he could not have been elected.

The subjunctive mood also survives in a few idiomatic expressions:

Far be it from me . . .

Suffice it to say . . .

Heaven help us!

The devil take the hindmost.

Long live the king!

Come what may . . .

Be that as it may . . .

Glory be to God!

EXERCISE (5f–h), MOOD

Select the correct verb from the choices in parentheses, and cross out each incorrect choice.

Example   I wish I (was/were) in that class.

1. If a person (is/be) teaching a class on ethnic history, should that person be a member of an ethnic minority?

2. If such a person (was/were) well trained, why complain?

3. A knowledge of the subject (is/be) really all that is required.

4. Such a person (read/reads) and (perform/performs) research in ethnic history.

5. (Be it/It is) resolved that the student union (requires/require) that all ethnic studies courses be taught by minorities.

6. Such a demand (was/were) frequent not too long ago.

7. We think it impossible that all such courses (be/are) taught by minorities.

8. Ethnic studies instructors (are/be) in great demand.

9. The requirement that such instructors (are/be) the only instructors involved in these programs is misguided, in many people's opinion.

10. Is it essential that Elizabethan history (is/be) taught by an Elizabethan?

11. The two examples (are/be) not similar.

12. I prefer that such a course (is/be) taught by someone who can speak about the psychological dimensions of life in a minority group.

13. Students prefer that such a perspective (is/be) given by a student.

14. Most important is the necessity that all information included in the course (is/be) accurate.

15. I wish that this issue (was/were) resolved.

Write sentences using the mood indicated for each of the verbs listed below.

Example   (*be*, formal demand, subjunctive) I demand that the vote be secret.

(*be*, condition, subjunctive) If that be the case, we're doomed.

(*give*, imperative) Give me the book.

(*be*, wishes, subjunctive) I wish I weren't so tired.

16. (*jump*, imperative) _____

17. (*love*, indicative) _____

18. (*succeed*, subjunctive) _____

19. (*meet*, formal demand, subjunctive) _____

20. (*watch*, imperative) _____

21. (*discover*, condition, subjunctive) _____

22. (*complete*, formal demand, subjunctive) _____

23. (*finish*, imperative) _____

24. (*see*, condition, subjunctive) _____

25. (*choose*, wishes, subjunctive) _____

The following sentences are in the indicative mood. Rewrite them, using the subjunctive or imperative mood appropriately.

Example   What if the student government wants no ethnic studies at all?

What if the student government were to want no ethnic studies at all?

26. We asked the director to explain the ethnic studies program.

_____

27. The school expects her to be responsible for the entire program.

_____

28. She ensures that all courses taught in the program are taught professionally.

_____

29. She requires that all instructors have the appropriate degrees and training.

_____

30. She prefers that each of her instructors has taught the class previously.

_____

BASIC GRAMMAR REVIEW (1–5)

For each of the following sentences, write in the blank the correct form of the word listed at the left. Notice that verbs may require a change in tense, voice, or mood or the addition of auxiliaries to be correct.

Example   *be*   Everyone assumes that the Pilgrims ___were___ a singular group of people with a single purpose.

1. *who/whom* These people, _____ were the first immigrants to America, were themselves a pluralistic society.

2. *They/Their* _____ immigrating to America demonstrated their radical view of society.

3. *quiet/quietly* They were not a people to remain _____ wherever they were.

4. *separated* Years before, they _____ from the Church of England.

5. *live* Many of them _____ in Holland before immigrating to America.

6. *actual* But only about one-third of the 102 people on board the *Mayflower* _____ were Pilgrims.

7. *be* The rest of the passengers _____ volunteers or recruits.

8. *themselves/theirselves* The Pilgrims called _____ "Saints."

9. *They/Their* _____ calling the others "Strangers" was no accident.

10. *different/differently* These people must have seemed _____ to the religious Pilgrims.

11. *be* Many Stranger families _____ whole families of drunkards or criminals.

12. *place* Both men and women _____ in the stocks frequently for public drunkenness.

13. *cause* At least two early problems _____ by Stranger children.

14. *blow*   On the voyage, one child almost _____ up the *Mayflower* while he played near the powder supply.

15. *become*   This same child's brother _____ lost and had the entire colony searching for him for days.

16. *charge*   Their mother _____ with being "a common gossip."

17. *hang*   Ten years after the landing, their father _____ for murder.

18. *come*   Thus, whole families of rather unwholesome people _____ along.

19. *recruit*   The Strangers _____ by the merchants who backed the colony.

20. *illiterate* Most were _____ , of course.

21. *lie/lay*   Imagine the shock that _____ ahead for them.

22. *who/whom*   All the settlers had agreed to send goods back to the merchants, _____ would sell the goods at a profit.

23. *plentiful*   Opportunity must have been _____ in America than in England, in order to tempt the Pilgrims to attempt the crossing.

24. *take*   The crossing _____ nine weeks.

25. *kill*   One sailor _____ during the crossing.

26. *quick*   Since he had not been sympathetic to the Pilgrims, they _____ decided his death was a good omen.

27. *become*   Strangers and Saints immediately _____ accustomed to hard work.

28. *near*   During the first year, _____ half the settlers died.

29. *drink; who/whom* Since they feared the water, the settlers _____ more beer per person than any other group for _____ we have figures.

30. *real*   Even the first Thanksgiving was _____ not a religious festival, as we sometimes think.

31. *involve*   The "harvest festival" _____ games, dancing, singing, feasting, and drinking.

32. *complete*   The usual image of the Pilgrims may be _____ false.

33. *more/most*   They were less religious and _____ radical than most people believe.

34. *remember*   _____ that "ancestors who came over on the *Mayflower*" were immigrants, too.

35. *have*   And even the 102 Pilgrims _____ their minority groups among them.

SENTENCE FRAGMENT   (6)

A **sentence fragment** lacks either a subject or a predicate or both and is not a complete statement. Usually, a fragment occurs because the writer has mistaken a phrase or subordinate clause (see Sections 1c and 1d (1–3) for a complete sentence. Consequently, fragments can often be corrected by attaching them to an adjacent sentence.

COMPLETE STATEMENT: INDEPENDENT CLAUSE
American music offers something for everybody.

FRAGMENT: SUBORDINATE CLAUSE
Because it has borrowed something from everybody.

COMPLETE STATEMENT: COMPLEX SENTENCE
American music offers something for everybody because it has borrowed something from everybody.

Sometimes a comma is required to attach the fragment to an adjacent sentence.

Our music owes a lot to ethnic groups. *Particularly black song writers and musicians.*

Our music owes a lot to ethnic groups, *particularly black song writers and musicians.*

Denied the opportunity to learn to read and write. Enslaved blacks recorded their history in song.

Denied the opportunity to learn to read and write, enslaved blacks recorded their history in song.

By reading a sentence aloud, you can usually tell if a comma is needed or not.

Another way to correct a sentence fragment is to rewrite the fragment as a complete sentence containing both a subject and a verb.

The blues originated in the black community. *Eventually becoming popular throughout the country.*

The blues originated in the black community. *It eventually became popular throughout the country.*

Remember, to be a sentence a group of words must have a subject and a predicate and must not be introduced by a subordinating conjunction. Prepositional phrases, verbal phrases, appositives renaming or explaining nouns or noun substitutes, and other word groups lacking a subject or a verb are not sentences. The following examples show these types of fragments and suitable revisions:

PREPOSITIONAL PHRASE	Bessie Smith was a great blues singer. *With a powerful style.*
REVISION	Bessie Smith was a great blues singer *with a powerful style.*
VERBAL PHRASE	Her style became a legend. *To inspire generations of singers.*
REVISION	Her style became a legend *to inspire generations of singers.*
SUBORDINATE CLAUSE	Bessie's music lived on in Billie Holiday and others. *Even after she died in 1937.*
REVISION	*Even after she died in 1937,* Bessie's music lived on in Billie Holiday and others.
APPOSITIVE	Bessie Smith's blues style influenced Janis Joplin. *A young pop singer of the 1970's.*
REVISION	Bessie Smith's blues style influenced Janis Joplin, *a young pop singer of the 1970's.*
COMPOUND PREDICATE	People who heard Bessie sing called her "the Empress of the Blues." *And never forgot her.*
REVISION	People who heard Bessie sing called her "the Empress of the Blues" *and never forgot her.*

Practice: Identifying Sentence Fragments   Underline all the sentence fragments in the following paragraph. The answers are listed at the end of this section.

[1]Polish sailors, according to legend, on board Columbus's ships. [2]Certainly no legend that many early settlers in America were Polish. [3]Pulaski who was an immigrant from Poland. [4]He was a hero of the American Revolution. [5]Pulaski created an Amer-

ican cavalry force at just the right time. ⁶When Washington himself was becoming discouraged. ⁷He was probably the major military strategist for the entire American army. ⁸Count Pulaski was a titled nobleman from Poland when he arrived in America. ⁹He was, quite simply, an idealist who believed in the Revolution. ¹⁰And who volunteered to fight.

Answers to the Practice   The following items are fragments: 1, 2, 3, 6, 10

EXERCISE (6), SENTENCE FRAGMENT

Revise the following word groups, eliminating fragments in two ways: (a) by joining the groups to form one complete sentence, and (b) by rewording them as
necessary to form two separate sentences.

Example   General Kosciuszko helped Washington and his army.
                In different ways.

    a. *General Kosciuszko helped Washington and his army in different ways.*

    b. *General Kosciuszko helped Washington and his army. He did so in different ways.*

1. Kosciuszko was an engineer. Who built forts and fortifications.

    a. _____

    b. _____

2. Kosciuszko was considered a genius. At using natural terrain as a defense.

    a. _____

    b. _____

3. To fortify all of Washington's camps. He dug trenches, cut trees, and used
   natural barriers.

    a. _____

    b. _____

4. His advice at Saratoga probably won this battle. Which convinced the French
   to become an ally of the American revolutionaries.

    a. _____

    b. _____

5. A steady stream of Poles immigrated to America. Mostly in the nineteenth
   century.

    a. _____

    b. _____

6. By the early years of the twentieth century. Almost three million Polish
   peasants had come to America.

    a. _____

    b. _____

7. They often were a source of cheap labor. And forced to live in ethnic "neighborhoods."

   a. _____

   b. _____

8. Poles began to excel in the professions, the arts, and the sciences. Within less than just one generation.

   a. _____

   b. _____

9. Madame Curie, who discovered radium. She was actually Marie Curie-Sklo-dowska.

   a. _____

   b. _____

10. Originally from Poland. Madame Curie had married a French physicist. And came to America to establish Polish-American schools.

   a. _____

   b. _____

Revise the following paragraph, eliminating sentence fragments. You may join groups of words to form a complete sentence, or you may reword fragments adding missing subjects and predicates to form complete sentences. Write out your revision on your own paper.

One area in which Polish-Americans have been excelling for generations, theater. At the turn of this century, for example. Helen Modjeska was probably the finest Shakesperean actress in the world. Arthur Rubenstein, Charles Bronson, and Jack Palance are all creative artists. Who are of Polish lineage. Matuszak, Yastrzemski, and Strain are some Polish names. That are familiar to sports fans. Goldwater, Muskie, and Brzezinski are names of great politicians. Who illustrate the continuing influence of Poles in American politics. The intermingling of Polish and American history as thorough as ever.

COMMA SPLICE; RUN-TOGETHER OR FUSED SENTENCE (7)

A **comma splice** occurs when two main clauses are joined by a comma without a coordinating conjunction. A **fused sentence** (also called a **run-on sentence**) occurs when two main clauses are run together without any punctuation.

COMMA SPLICE	Immigrants change the nation, they are also changed by it.
FUSED SENTENCE	Immigrants change the nation they are also changed by it.

Comma splices and fused sentences are similar types of errors, and they have similar solutions. In both cases, the independent clauses require clear signals to tell the readers where one complete thought stops and another begins.

The conventions of written English provide only two such signals: the period and the semicolon. Two other alternatives are also acceptable. The thoughts may be coordinated, joined by a comma and a coordinating conjunction (*and, but, or, nor, for, so, yet*), or one thought may be subordinated to the other and joined by a subordinating conjunction. The following sentences illustrate these four solutions for the comma splice and fused sentence:

PERIOD	Immigrants change the nation. They are also changed by it.
SEMICOLON	Immigrants change the nation; they are also changed by it.

COORDINATION	Immigrants change the nation, but they are also changed by it.
SUBORDINATION	Even though immigrants change the nation, they are also changed by it.

Notice that when the subordinate clause precedes the main clause, a comma joins the two. You may be wondering why a comma is acceptable in the middle of *Even though immigrants change the nation, they are also changed by it.* but not in *Immigrants change the nation, they are also changed by it.* Remember, the issue is not where the comma appears as much as it is *why* it appears. In the first instance, one idea is subordinate and functions as a modifier of the main clause. The comma helps to signal the subordinate relationship and marks the beginning of the main clause. In the second instance, the ideas are not subordinate, and, consequently, they are expressed in independent clauses. A comma used between them would be a false signal, indicating a connection that does not grammatically exist.

Why is the comma in *Immigrants change the nation, but they are also changed by it.* acceptable? The coordinating conjunction *but* grammatically establishes the connection between the two complete thoughts. The comma signals that relationship.

Practice: Identifying Comma Splices and Fused Sentences Decide which of the following sentences contain comma splices and which are fused. The answers are listed at the end of this section.

[1]North America was "discovered" and claimed by many different ethnic groups. [2]We all know the story of its discovery by Christopher Columbus, he claimed it in the name of Queen Isabella of Spain. [3]He was followed by English and Portugese explorers, each of whom claimed an area for his country. [4]All of these explorers may have been preceded by others, though, it is generally accepted that Leif Ericson and his Viking sailors were in North America before Columbus. [5]Even the Vikings may have discovered America after someone else there is evidence that this country was visited centuries earlier by Chinese sailors. [6]Who knows what evidence we may eventually discover ourselves about the early "discoverers" of America?

REVISING SENTENCES WITH MULTIPLE ERRORS

When a sentence contains more than two fused independent clauses, more than one comma splice, or both comma splices and fused independent clauses, a combination of remedies is usually needed. Rewriting a sentence using only periods, only semicolons, or only coordinating conjunctions is likely to result in a choppy, awkward, and illogical or unfocused revision.

FAULTY SENTENCE	Our town holds its ethnic festival everybody turns out, the food and entertainment are wonderful.

POOR REVISION	Our town holds its ethnic festival; everybody turns out; the food and entertainment are wonderful.
BETTER REVISION	When our town holds its ethnic festival, everybody turns out because the food and entertainment are wonderful.

Unless fused or spliced sentence elements are parallel—that is, of equal rank and therefore expressed in parallel grammatical form—repeating the same punctuation or conjunction does not create an effective revision. Notice that the preceding final revision focuses the ideas and clarifies the time sequence and the cause-effect logic by means of the subordinating conjunctions *when* and *because.*

Similarly, in the revision of the following example, a relative pronoun is used to subordinate less important information. To avoid awkward length and to handle two relatively independent ideas, the clauses have been divided into two separate sentences.

FAULTY SENTENCE	The ethnic festival has been held every July for the past twenty years it attracts huge crowds, they get bigger every year.
EFFECTIVE REVISION	The ethnic festival, which attracts huge crowds, has been held every July for the past twenty years. The crowds get bigger every year.

Answers to the Practice ²comma splice ⁴comma splice ⁵fused sentence
1, 3, 6 correct

EXERCISE (7)-1, COMMA SPLICES AND FUSED SENTENCES

Revise each of the following faulty sentences in four ways to correct the spliced or fused independent clauses: (a) use a period to form two separate sentences; (b) use a semicolon between independent clauses; (c) use a coordinating conjunction and a comma to form a compound sentence; and (d) use a subordinating conjunction or relative pronoun (with any necessary commas) to form a complex sentence.

Example   Canada and the United States are both in North America they are the most ethnically diverse countries in the world.
Canada and the United States are both in North America.
a. They are the most ethnically diverse countries in the world.

b. ... America; they are ...

c. ... America, and they are ...

Though Canada and the United States are both in North
d. America, they are the most ethnically diverse countries in the world.

1. Other large nations have many ethnic groups living within their borders, China and the Soviet Union are examples.

    a. _____

    b. _____

    c. _____

    d. _____

2. North America was uniquely populated by immigrants who began arriving in the seventeenth century they are still arriving today.

    a. _____

    b. _____

    c. _____

    d. _____

3. Even the original population may have immigrated from Asia, American Indians may have crossed the Bering Strait into Alaska.

    a. _____

    b. _____

    c. _____

    d. _____

4. They were the "original population," people have since come from almost every other country in the world.

   a. _____

   b. _____

   c. _____

   d. _____

5. Immigrants often sent letters back home they were called "America letters."

   a. _____

   b. _____

   c. _____

   d. _____

6. These letters described life in the new country there were no taxes, no compulsory military service, and everyone had three meals a day.

   a. _____

   b. _____

   c. _____

   d. _____

7. By 1850, transoceanic steamships had been introduced this meant that the ocean voyage took twelve days instead of nine weeks.

   a. _____

   b. _____

   c. _____

   d. _____

8. The trip was much easier for these new pilgrims, the influx of immigrants tripled by 1850.

   a. _____

   b. _____

   c. _____

   d. _____

Name _____ Date _____ Score _____

EXERCISE (7)-2, COMMA SPLICES AND FUSED SENTENCES

The following sentences contain comma splices, fused independent clauses, or both. Revise them, correcting the errors and clarifying the logic. You may add, omit, or rearrange some words to achieve an effective revision.

Example   There are many black American military heroes, many people think otherwise.
         There are many black American military heroes, even though many people think otherwise.

1. Black Americans have served in every American military action people may be surprised to learn.

   _____

2. History books often omit the military contributions of blacks, research on this topic once was ignored.

   _____

3. In early military actions such as the Revolutionary War, the role of blacks was admittedly small, it had to be a small role, obviously.

   _____

4. The number of free blacks in America at that time was small so very few served.

   _____

5. They almost begged to be allowed to fight, blacks served with great honor.

   _____

6. Two black men crossed the Delaware with Washington, they were Oliver Cromwell and Prince Whipple.

   _____

7. General Newport, of the Royal Army, was captured by Prince Estabrook, he was a black soldier in the Continental army.

   _____

8. Peter Salem killed Major Pitcairn as he was savoring his expected victory at Bunker Hill, Salem was another black hero.

   _____

9. Black soldiers were often forced to serve in segregated units, of course, this caused morale problems.

_____

10. Blacks could not command well or use firearms accurately this was what whites had long believed.

_____

11. These bigoted views of their abilities did not keep blacks from honorable service blacks distinguished themselves in combat.

_____

12. The Medal of Honor was awarded in 1863 to William Carney, he was a later black military hero.

_____

13. Carney fought against the Plains Indians with the Massachusetts Colored Infantry, as one can conclude from name alone, they were a segregated unit.

_____

14. Isaiah Dorman was a black scout, he served and died at the Little Big Horn with Custer in 1876.

_____

15. Henry Flippes was the first black to graduate from West Point, he was a trailblazer for thousands of black West Point graduates.

_____

16. By World War I, 40,000 black combat soldiers were serving but they served with the French command.

_____

17. No U.S. commanders wished to use these men, no British commander wanted them, either.

_____

18. The Croix de Guerre is the highest decoration France offers, it had never been awarded to Americans before World War I.

_____

19. It was awarded to Henry Johnson and Needham Roberts they had distinguished themselves in fighting for France's cause.

_____

20. Both men had served in the 369th Infantry's black "Hellfighters" group, this group was "loaned" to the French.

   _____

21. During World War II, over 1.4 million black men and women served, many were drafted, but many also volunteered for service.

   _____

22. At Pearl Harbor, four enemy planes were brought down by a black mess attendant, he manned a machine gun.

   _____

23. The attendant was Dorie Miller, he was acclaimed as a hero very quickly by the Army, they needed a hero.

   _____

24. The black fighter pilots of Benjamin Davis, Jr., proved courageous and valuable, they fought during the Italian campaign.

   _____

25. American military history has been made, in large part, by black Americans, they served their country capably.

   _____

FAULTY AGREEMENT: SUBJECT AND VERB AGREEMENT (8a)

When subjects and verbs do not agree, readers are likely to misunderstand a writer's message. Suppose you have written *The first two quarters of the game was exciting.* in a letter to a friend. Reading the sentence, your friend understands that the game was exciting but doesn't quite know what the first two quarters have to do with it. Your reader has perceived the subject of the sentence to be *game*. Because *game* is a singular noun and *was* is a singular verb, the two fit together. If you had written *The first two quarters of the game were exciting.*, your friend would quickly see that *quarters* is the subject because it fits the plural verb *were*. Your reader would understand the message correctly: You found half the game exciting, but not necessarily all of it.

Subjects and verbs should agree in **person** and **number.** Agreement in per-son is achieved if the verb form corresponds to the first, second, or third person pronoun form of the subject. For example, *She buy new sneakers.* is a faulty sentence because the third person pronoun *she* does not agree with the verb *buy.* In the present tense, the *s* form of the verb is required for third person singular pronouns and all singular nouns: *She buys.* Agreement in person causes relatively few problems for writers because the *-s* form is the only exceptional verb form requiring special attention. (See "*Special Problems with Verb Tenses*," pp. 69–70.)

Agreement in number between subjects and verbs, however, can be more troublesome. Most writers are well aware that a singular subject requires a singular verb and a plural subject requires a plural verb. Agreement errors most often arise when the writer is uncertain about whether a subject is singular or plural or when intervening words obscure the real subject. The following guidelines can help you avoid subject-verb agreement errors:

1. If words or phrases come between the subject and the verb, be sure the verb agrees with the subject, not with an intervening noun or pronoun.

FAULTY   The final miles of the race was grueling.

CORRECT   The final *miles* of the race *were* grueling.

Singular subjects followed by expressions such as *with, along with, together with,* and *as well as* take singular verbs, even though they suggest a plural meaning. These expressions are not considered part of the subject.

FAULTY   Joan, together with her sisters, play in the semifinals tonight.

CORRECT   *Joan,* together with her sisters, *plays* in the semifinals tonight.

2. If the subject is an indefinite pronoun such as *everyone, somebody, another, each, either,* and *neither,* use a singular verb.

FAULTY   Everybody are here, but neither of the judges have arrived yet.

CORRECT   *Everybody is* here, but *neither* of the judges *has* arrived yet.

The indefinite pronouns *all, any, most, more, none,* and *some* take either a singular or a plural verb, depending on whether the noun to which the pronoun refers is singular or plural.

SINGULAR   *All* of the *soap is* gone.

PLURAL   *All* of my *socks are* dirty.

3. If two or more subjects are joined by *and,* use a plural verb.

FAULTY   Football and rubgy is only for the hearty.

CORRECT   *Football and rugby are* only for the hearty.

However, if the parts of a compound subject refer to the same person or thing, use a singular verb. Also use a singular verb if a compound subject is understood to be a unit.

SINGLE REFERENT   The play's *star and inspiration has stormed* off the stage.

SINGLE UNIT   *Macaroni and cheese was* his favorite lunch.

4. If two or more subjects are joined by *or* or *nor,* the verb should agree with the nearest subject.

FAULTY   My assistants or my secretary have the keys to the lockers.

CORRECT   My assistants or my *secretary has* the keys to the lockers.

FAULTY	My secretary or my assistants has the keys to the lockers.
CORRECT	My secretary or my *assistants have* the keys to the lockers.

5. If an expletive (such as *there* or *it*) precedes the verb, locate the true subject and make sure the verb agrees with it, not with the expletive.

FAULTY	There is many reasons for his success.
CORRECT	There *are* many *reasons* for his success.

6. If the subject is a singular collective noun (such as *assembly, audience, jury, flock*), use a singular verb when the group is acting as a unit. Use a plural verb when the members of the group are acting separately.

AS A UNIT	The *subcommittee addresses* the issue tomorrow.
AS INDIVIDUALS	The *staff take* turns answering the director's questions.

7. If the sentence contains a predicate noun, the verb should agree with the subject, not with the predicate noun.

FAULTY	Material things is a prime necessity with you.
CORRECT	Material *things are* a prime necessity with you.

8. If a relative pronoun (*who, which, that*) is used as the subject, the verb should agree with the pronoun's antecedent.

SINGULAR ANTECEDENT	They will release *one* of the men *who has* been injured. [Antecedent of *who* is *one*. The information *has been injured* is intended to describe only the one man.]
PLURAL ANTECEDENT	Here is one of the *shoes that were* missing. [Antecedent of *that* is *shoes*. The information *were missing* is intended to describe all the shoes.]

9. If a subject is plural in form but singular in meaning (such as *news, physics, linguistics*), use a singular verb. Similarly, titles of novels, plays, songs, and the like take singular verbs, even if their form is plural. Subjects indicating sums or quantities also usually take singular verbs.

College *athletics is* big business these days.

Wales and Nightingales was a popular record album.

Ten years is a long career in professional sports.

EXERCISE (8a)-1, SUBJECT AND VERB AGREEMENT

Select the correct verb from the choices in parentheses, and cross out the incorrect form.

Example   The oldest minority group in America (is/are) the American Indian.

1. As you probably (know/knows), Indians immigrated, too.

2. Most theories of their origin (holds/hold) that they came from Asia.

3. Many anthropologists (think/thinks) there (was/were) once a land bridge from Siberia to Alaska.

4. Anthropologists (theorize/theorizes) that the American Indians of the Stone Age crossed this land bridge and migrated southward.

5. "Indians" (is/are) a name given to these people by Christopher Columbus.

6. Columbus (was/were) on the shores of America by mistake.

7. He thought they (was/were) natives of India.

8. Most Indians (prefer/prefers) to be called "Native American" or "American Indian."

9. The single word "Indian" (is/are) a name given to them by a white man's mistake.

10. The Pima Indians, for example, (call/calls) themselves Ootham.

11. "Oima" (was/were) a derogatory name given to them by another tribe.

12. There (was/were) over 800,000 American Indians in the United States in the early 1970s.

13. The Indian population (has/have) almost doubled since 1950.

14. Long overdue improvements in health programs on reservations (has/have) been the cause.

15. Over half of the Indians in America still (live/lives) on federal reservations.

16. Most of the facts about modern life as an Indian (surprises/surprise) the average American citizen.

17. Indians who (live/lives) in cities face many problems.

18. In any given urban area, the Indian almost always (rank/ranks) at the bottom of the income scale.

19. The suicide rate among Indians at one time (was/were) 100 times that of whites.

20. Indians are the only minority that (is/are) directly, daily governed by the federal bureaucracy.

21. Two approaches, assimilation into white culture or tribal autonomy, (has/have) been argued for centuries.

22. No clear government policy (has/have) been established.

23. This (has/have) been true since the eighteenth century.

24. There (is/are) extremes of poverty and wealth among Native Americans.

25. The Aqua Caliente Indians (was/were) given land in exchange for a railroad right of way.

26. Worthless, sandy land—32,000 acres of it—(was/were) their settlement from President Grant.

27. This land, still empty for the most part, (are/is) now in downtown Palm Springs, California.

28. Palm Springs (is/are) arguably the richest town in America.

29. There (is/are) only 107 surviving Aqua Caliente Indians.

30. The members of this tribe probably (comprise/comprises) the richest minority group in America.

31. These empty lots, because they are in the center of such a wealthy city, (is/are) worth over a half million dollars per acre.

32. A treaty, signed in 1959, (allow/allows) the Aquas to sell or lease the land to white business people and homeowners.

33. The Aquas, according to the treaty, (was/were) allowed to hold their land "without encumbrance."

34. Recent court rulings (say/says) taxes and zoning laws are "encumbrances."

35. So the Aquas (pays/pay) no taxes.

36. They are the only people in Palm Springs who (is/are) free to use their land in any way they want.

37. Any other citizen (is/are) subject to very strict zoning laws.

38. One of the reasons Palm Springs is so beautiful (is/are) the city's approach to zoning.

39. There (is/are) no flashing neon signs and billboards.

40. The height and color of a building (is/are) regulated.

41. Everything (is/are) a soothing pastel color.

42. No motels (mar/mars) the landscape.

43. Each (is/are) called a "resort" instead.

44. Even a chandelier that (is/are) visible from the street must be approved by a committee.

45. The Aqua lands (are/is) leased to businesspeople and developers.

46. These long-term leases, which run well into the next century, (is/are) the source of the Aquas' wealth.

47. While the lots they (lease/leases) out (bring/brings) in money, the empty lots (increase/increases) in value.

48. The economics of their future security (cause/causes) no worries for the Aquas.

49. That's why many Rolls Royces seen in Palm Springs (belong/belongs) to the Aqua Calientes.

50. The tribe (has/have) surrounded itself with all the varied trappings of wealth.

EXERCISE (8a)-2, SUBJECT AND VERB AGREEMENT

Write sentences that contain appropriate forms of the given verbs and that use the words given as subjects and modifiers.

Example   (*Cable television*, present tense of *have*)

<u>Cable television has offbeat programming available.</u>

1. (*Foremost causes of failure*, a form of *be*)

   _____

2. (*These, disasters*, a form of *be*)

   _____

3. (*One, people, that*, a form of *be*)

   _____

4. (*Committee* [with its individuals acting separately], present tense of *arrive*)

   _____

5. (*Motivation and persistence*, present tense of *result*)

   _____

6. (*These*, a form of *be, decisions*)

   _____

7. (*Either you or one of the others*, present tense of *be*)

   _____

8. (*Algebra, trigonometry*, form of *be*)

   _____

9. (*Fifty dollars*, form of *be, high price*)

   _____

10. (*Network television*, present tense of *be*)

    _____

11. (*Most of the news*, present tense of *seem*)

    _____

12. (*None of the group*, form of *be*)

_____

13. (*Spaghetti and meatballs*, present tense of *taste*)

_____

14. (*Professors and students*, present tense of *cooperate*)

_____

15. (*Airplanes and trains*, present tense of *provide*)

_____

16. (*These*, form of *be*, *kinds*)

_____

17. (*Assembly* [acting as a unit], form of *be*)

_____

18. (*Neither the captain nor the sailors*, present tense of *believe*)

_____

19. (*Girl*, *with blue eyes*, present tense of *appear*)

_____

20. (*Justifications*, present tense of *involve*, *an essential matter*)

_____

21. (*Everybody*, present tense of *know*)

_____

22. (*Here*, *options*, form of *be*)

_____

23. (*Motivation*, present tense of *comprise*, *essential* [adjective])

_____

24. (*Nobody*, present tense of *see*)

_____

25. (*Hope* [noun], *desires* [noun], *neither*, *nor*, form of *be*)

_____

FAULTY AGREEMENT:

PRONOUN AND ANTECEDENT

AGREEMENT   (8b–d)

Pronouns should agree with their antecedents in number. If the **antecedent,** the word or words for which the pronoun stands, is singular, the pronoun should be singular; if the antecedent is plural, the pronoun should be plural.

    SINGULAR ANTECEDENT   The dog wanted its nightly run.

    PLURAL ANTECEDENT   The dogs wanted their nightly run.

    Antecedents such as *anyone, anybody, someone, somebody, each, every, everyone,* and *everybody* are singular and require singular pronouns. Collective nouns, such as *band, assembly, organization, mob, army, family, team, class,* and *brigade,* require singular pronouns when the group is being considered as a unit and plural pronouns when the individual members of the group are being considered separately.

    GROUP AS A UNIT   The crew has finished its work.

    MEMBERS OF GROUP   The crew have decided to quit their work.
    CONSIDERED SEPARATELY

    A plural pronoun is used to refer to two or more antecedents joined by *and.* A singular pronoun is used to refer to a singular antecedent joined by *or* or *nor.* If one of the antecedents is singular and the other is plural, the pronoun should agree in number with the antecedent that is nearer.

ANTECEDENTS JOINED BY *AND*	Artists and artisans know their stuff.
SINGULAR ANTECEDENTS JOINED BY *OR* OR *NOR*	Either Jack or Joe must have missed his connecting flight.
COMBINATION OF SINGULAR AND PLURAL ANTECEDENTS	Neither the coach nor the players flagged in their desire.

The demonstrative adjectives *this, that, these,* and *those* agree in number with the nouns they modify. In constructions with *kind of* and *sort of,* the demonstrative adjective modifies *kind* and *sort,* and the following noun should be singular, not plural.

INCORRECT	These kind of situation are bad.
CORRECT	This kind of situation is bad.
	These kinds of situations are bad.

Historically, masculine pronoun forms (*he, him, his*) have been used to refer to antecedents such as *one, none, everybody,* and other indefinite pronouns, as well as to antecedent nouns of indeterminate gender. In recent years, this "common gender" use of masculine pronouns has been recognized as imprecise at best and discriminatory at worst.

Unless all the members of a group are known to be male, it is inappropriate to use a masculine pronoun when referring to them. For example, to write *Every employee should fill out his time card correctly.* is inaccurate if some of the employees are women. By the same token, not all secretaries, librarians, and nurses are female. Be equally careful about the blanket use of feminine pronouns if the antecedent refers to men as well.

To avoid common gender when referring to antecedents that include both males and females, you can use one of the following methods:

INSTEAD OF	*Each job applicant must submit his resume.*
USE BOTH MASCULINE AND FEMININE PRONOUNS	*Each job applicant* must submit *his or her* resume.
USE THE PLURAL FOR BOTH ANTECEDENT AND PRONOUN	*All job applicants* must submit *their* resumes.
RECAST THE SENTENCE TO REMOVE THE PRONOUN	Each job applicant must submit a resume.

Practice: Avoiding Inappropriate Common-gender Pronouns   In which of the following sentences is the use of common-gender pronouns inappropriate? The answers are listed at the end of this section. Your instructor may ask you to revise those sentences that use pronouns inappropriately.

[1]A Hindu parent, particularly one who lives outside India, often feels that his greatest challenge is passing Hindu religion and culture on to his children. [2]Thus, many Hindu homes in America have family temples in a special room or area set aside for this purpose. [3]Both children and parents actually work hard to maintain their Hindu customs in the face of American culture. [4]The parent sometimes feels that her best solution is to ensure that each child has his or her chance to experience both cultures as fully as possible. [5]A Hindu person feels a great sense of responsibility for keeping his culture alive.

Answers to the Practice   Sentences 1, 4, and 5 should be revised to avoid common-gender pronouns.

EXERCISE (8b)-1, PRONOUN AND ANTECEDENT AGREEMENT

In each of the following sentences, select the correct form of the pronoun from the choices in parentheses and cross out the incorrect choice.

Example   My Hindu friends say that (his or her/their) most important holiday may be the Diwali festival.

1. Hindus celebrate Diwali on the last day of the year, when (his/their) entire family participates.

2. October 21 is, for the Hindu community, the end of (its/their) year.

3. Hindus feel that (this/these) kind of traditional celebration is very important.

4. Hindus think such celebrations help maintain (their/his/its) traditional values.

5. Diwali is the most important of (this/these) holidays.

6. With (their/its/his or her) lifestyle rooted in two cultures, most Hindu-Americans celebrate two sets of New Year holidays.

7. The holiday celebrates the hero Rama's return after (he/they) defeated Ravana, a mythical demon.

8. Dussera, another of Rama's days, celebrates (his/her/its) actual victory over the demon.

9. A Hindu begins (his or her/his) celebration of Dussera ten days before Diwali.

10. The whole family will set out lights to show (his/their) joy at Rama's return from victory.

11. All Hindus give thanks on Diwali because (he/they) are grateful for another year.

12. Every member of the family busies (himself or herself/themselves/itself) with cleaning the house and buying new dishes.

13. Those who can afford it light (her/their) houses with hundreds of lights.

14. One of my friends invited me to (their/her) family's festival celebration.

15. Some of my Hindu friends even let me help (them/him or her) in setting out all the tiny lamps.

16. (These kinds of/This kind of) lamps are placed in decorative rows.

17. As do many Westerners, Hindus make (themselves/itself/himself) New Year's resolutions.

18. The Hindus hope, as Westerners do, to better (himself/themselves) with (their/his or her) resolutions.

19. Lakshmi is a goddess who also receives (his/her/its) special attention on Diwali day.

20. Hindus revere Lakshmi because (she/he/they) symbolizes prosperity.

21. Doors are left ajar so Lakshmi can make (her/their) entrance.

22. On Diwali day, neither children nor any adult will forget to dress in (their/his or her) best clothes.

23. Nikhat says she and her family spend (its/their/her) day feasting and visiting.

24. After the family prays, (it eats/they eat) a huge meal of traditional curry and sweet dishes.

25. Anyone who studies Hindu culture realizes (it/they) covered a 5,000-year history.

26. Hindus have no fixed system that regulates (their/its/his) prayer, fasting, or meditation.

27. No single prophet or writer forced (his/her/their/his or her) religious beliefs into a single code.

28. Westerners find this hard to accept; (he or she/they) expect more rules.

29. Each geographical region of India has (their/its) own specific beliefs.

30. Over 82,000 Hindus have brought (his/her/its/their) culture to the United States.

EXERCISE (8a–d)-2, PRONOUN-ANTECEDENT AND SUBJECT-VERB AGREEMENT

Revise the following sentences, correcting errors of pronoun-antecedent and subject-verb agreement. Revise to avoid common-gender pronouns where their use is inappropriate.

Example   The Immigration Service says 107,000 immigrants from India is recorded since 1820.
The Immigration Service says 107,000 immigrants from India are recorded since 1820.

1. Over 60 percent of that number has arrived since 1970.

   _____

2. An anthropologist finds himself unable to account for their origins by district or province.

   _____

3. Migration to the United States were based on class rather than geography.

   _____

4. Many Indians once left his or her country to escape poverty or British rule.

   _____

5. Many of this modern immigrants are university students.

   _____

6. They come to the United States to study and ends up remaining to pursue a career or profession.

   _____

7. One exception are a growing number of Sikhs who is leaving India for political reasons.

   _____

8. The Sikhs are leaving his or her home in the Punjab region.

   _____

9. Indians have established several permanent colonies for itself in California.

   _____

10. But mainly, the Indian population live near universities in the East and Midwest.

    _____

11. They wish to remain in this sort of locations because this is where they found educational and professional opportunities.

_____

12. Many Indians, of course, returns home after completing their studies.

_____

13. But some Indians also remain to teach or to complete his or her internship at U.S. hospitals.

_____

14. Among the first Indian visitors to the United States were Swami Vive Kananda.

_____

15. He attended the 1893 Chicago Exposition to teach Americans about their Hindu philosophy.

_____

16. Many an Indian teacher has visited since to teach their philosophy here.

_____

17. Many of these teachers has become permanent citizens.

_____

18. Unfortunately, the news have focused attention on those teachers who seem most outrageous.

_____

19. More serious teachers, like J. Krishnamurti, find his contributions often ignored.

_____

20. Before making up their mind, anyone investigating Eastern philosophy should read Krishnamurti's books.

_____

21. H. G. Khorana was a biochemist who were awarded the Nobel Prize.

_____

22. The first Indian immigrants to this country were probably a group of itinerant workers that moved their base of operations from Canada to the United States.

_____

23. Large numbers of Indian immigrants began arriving after 1947, when the Immigration Act banning his entry was repealed.

   _____

24. President Kennedy, along with his advisors, were responsible for further lowering these barriers to immigration.

   _____

25. Today, the number of Indians rank third among foreign students, after Canadians and Chinese.

   _____

FAULTY REFERENCE
OF PRONOUNS   (9)

Pronouns conveniently spare us the awkwardness of having to repeat nouns monotonously in our writing. However, pronouns are more general and less precise than their antecedents, the names of people, places, and things. Consequently, writers must be careful to make pronoun references very clear. If the reader is unsure to what antecedent a pronoun refers, the pronoun becomes a source of confusion.

Pronoun reference problems usually result from vague usage. The following discussion addresses the most common usage problems.

1. A pronoun should clearly refer to only one antecedent, and that antecedent should be located as near to the pronoun as possible. Don't make the reader search for and choose among remote antecedents.

VAGUE   When Ray told his father about the accident, *he* was calm.

Who was calm, Ray or his father? Readers are used to associating a pronoun with the noun that most closely precedes it, in this case *father*. However, *Ray* and *he* are both subjects of their clauses, so the parallel positions of the two words suggest that Ray was calm. The reader cannot be sure which noun is really the intended antecedent.

CLEAR   Ray was calm when he told his father about the accident.

CLEAR   His father was calm when Ray told him about the accident.

CLEAR   When Ray told his father about the accident, his father was calm.

125

VAGUE	The neighbors decided to celebrate the Fourth of July with a block party. The morning was sunny, but by late afternoon rain began to fall. Clearing out a garage, *they* moved the picnic tables under its roof.

Neighbors is the only sensible antecedent for *they,* but because the pronoun is several sentences away from its antecedent, the reader must back-track to find the correct reference.

CLEAR	. . . Clearing out a garage, the neighbors moved the picnic tables under its roof.
CLEAR	When rain interrupted their Fourth of July block party, the neighbors cleared out a garage and moved the picnic tables under its roof.

2. The pronouns *this, that,* and *which* should not be used to refer to the general idea of a preceding clause or sentence. Always supply a specific antecedent.

VAGUE USE OF *WHICH* AND *THIS*	The dog slipped his leash but did not run away, *which* showed his training. *This* resulted from his going to obedience school.

What showed the dog's training, that he slipped his leash or that he did not run away? Was slipping the leash, not running away, or showing training the result of obedience school?

CLEAR	The dog slipped his leash, but the fact that he did not run away showed his training. This training resulted from his going to obedience school.

3. Although we commonly use *it* and *they* for general, indefinite references in informal speech, nouns should be used in writing for exactness and clarity. *You,* used in speech to mean people in general, should be replaced by nouns such as *people, person,* or the pronoun *one. You* is correct, however, when used as the subject in writing directions or when the context is clearly *you, the reader* (as in *You should sand the surface before painting it.*)

VAGUE USE OF *IT, THEY,* AND *YOU*	*It* says in the newspaper that *you* can still get tickets because *they* have added two more performances.
CLEAR	The newspaper says people can still get tickets because the theater has added two more performances.

4. A sentence containing two or more different uses of the pronoun *it* can be confusing. Especially when *it* is used as an idiom in one place in a sentence (as in *it is cold*) and as a definite pronoun referring to a specific noun in another place, the reader may have trouble keeping the uses straight.

CONFUSING	My husband and I were hiking along the mountain trail when *it* began to snow, but we decided *it* was time to turn back in case *it* drifted shut.
CLEAR	When the snow began to fall, my husband and I were hiking along the mountain trail, but we decided to turn back in case it drifted shut.

5. A pronoun should refer to a noun that is actually expressed, not to one that is merely implied. For example, a pronoun should not refer to a noun that functions as an adjective or to a word whose form does not correspond to that of the pronoun.

VAGUE	Joan's form was excellent when *she* played on the college golf team, but now she has no time for *it*.

The possessive *Joan's* implies but does not express *Joan,* the correct antecedent for *she.* Neither the adjective *golf,* nor the verb *played,* nor the nouns *form* or *team* provide an appropriate antecedent for *it.*

CLEAR	When Joan played on the college golf team, her form was excellent, but now she has no time for golf.

EXERCISE (9), FAULTY REFERENCE OF PRONOUNS

Revise the following sentences, correcting confusing, vague, remote, and implied pronoun references.

Example   It says in this book that almost all Amish are farmers.

According to this author, almost all Amish are farmers.

1. They say the Amish are a religious subculture who live in Pennsylvania.

   _____

2. They claim they have an oral rather than a written culture.

   _____

3. They use a language other than English, though most know it and can speak it.

   _____

4. When an Amish father and son speak, he speaks in German.

   _____

5. The Amish respect their elderly and care for them at home. This is why they do not accept Social Security benefits.

   _____

6. The Amish are a branch of the Mennonites; they are direct descendants of the Swiss Anabaptists.

   _____

7. The Anabaptists believed in separation of church and state, in adult baptism, and in the refusal to bear arms or take oaths of any sort, which resulted in persecution and harassment.

   _____

8. The first "Amish ships" came to America in the early 1700's, each with the families of an Amish congregation. They were soon followed by more.

   _____

9. You can't determine, however, when the first few Amish families came to America.

   _____

10. The supply of cheap land in Pennsylvania was an Amish paradise, but it soon increased so that the Amish travelled westward for more land.

   _____

11. The Old Order Amish is the largest and most conservative group of Amish in modern America, which are found in twenty states.

   _____

12. There are no Amish to be found in Europe, which is ironic, since it was their homeland.

   _____

13. It will be variations in religious practice, dress, and lifestyle among the Amish in different regions.

   _____

14. The Amish reject almost all the advances of modern civilization, including even watches, and life insurance, which creates their distinctive way of living.

   _____

15. Even their clothes haven't changed, in any way you could see, for 250 years.

   _____

16. The men wear black hats and the women wear black bonnets outdoors. It was ordered by the Bible, according to the Amish.

   _____

17. The Amish can almost be described by the things they shun. Belts, collars, lapels or pockets are all considered ornamental, and they avoid them.

   _____

18. Young men are clean-shaven, while married men must let their beards grow; they avoid mustaches.

   _____

19. You can't use makeup or ornamentation of any kind, even sun glasses or wedding rings, since they do not wish to appear "worldly."

   _____

20. The reasons for this include thrift, the desire to avoid worldliness, and conservatism, which is a religious principle with the Amish.

   _____

PRONOUN REVIEW (2, 8, 9)

Revise the following sentences, correcting errors in pronoun case, pronoun-antecedent agreement, and vague pronoun reference.

Example   What you notice most about the Amish is that they forbid automobiles.

What one notices most about the Amish is that they forbid automobiles.

1. The Amish also forbid motorcycles, bicycles, and tractors; it is a threat to their culture.

_____

2. A sick Amish farmer will find their fields tended by their concerned neighbors.

_____

3. If their barn burns down, all the neighbors will unite and build him another in a day.

_____

4. At one time, the Amish rejected doctors and hospitals, but now it is approved by most districts.

_____

5. Amish women used to have her babies at home, but now most births are in hospitals.

_____

6. Amish funerals are simple. A wooden coffin is used in a service at home, with no flowers or elaborate monuments. He is as conservative about death as he is about life.

_____

7. Amish farms are, according to experts, among the best in the world, which demonstrates their skill and training.

_____

8. You may find three to five generations of Amish living on a single farmstead.

_____

9. Some of them are so prosperous and so populated that they look like small villages.

    _____

10. Using horses presents advantages and disadvantages to the Amish farmer; they are cheap, but slow.

    _____

11. You can also fertilize the fields with a horse.

    _____

12. They allow them to use gasoline engines and other machinery, such as sprayers, cultivators, balers and haymaking equipment.

    _____

13. Often, a stationary tractor is used to power them.

    _____

14. The Amishman whom uses any rolling equipment, uses a horse to pull them, however.

    _____

15. Problems are rare; the Amish farmer is a master of his trade, and this is what his children learn as they help him.

    _____

16. Amish farm products are choice, and he sells it for top prices.

    _____

17. In addition, most of what him and his family eat is grown at home.

    _____

18. Thus, large families are no burden; on the contrary, it is a necessity.

    _____

19. Using horses rather than tractors makes them work longer, harder hours; everybody has to do their share of the work.

    _____

20. A large family is often a supply of cheap labor, they say.

    _____

SHIFTS   (10 a–d)

Point of view in a sentence is the vantage point or focus the writer provides for the reader. Unless grammar or meaning necessitates changing that focus, a sentence's subjects, verb tenses, mood, and voice, and pronoun person and number should work together to maintain a consistent point of view.

Most needless shifts occur in compound and complex sentences. The writer may begin with one focus but carelessly change to another in midsentence. The shift in point of view can distract and confuse the reader, as the following example shows:

> Terry liked to cook Chinese food, but the right ingredients were hard to find.
> [Subject changes from *Terry* to *ingredients;* voice changes from active to passive.]

The sentence focuses on Terry at the beginning, suggesting that he, his activities, or his interests are going to be emphasized. But when the sentence's subject shifts to *ingredients* in the second clause, the reader's initial assumptions are disturbed. What happened to Terry? The reader is left wondering just what the real focus of the sentence is. The following sentence illustrates a consistent point of view:

> *Terry* liked to cook Chinese food, but *he* had a hard time finding the right ingredients.

Sometimes the meaning of a sentence requires a shift in point of view. A change from one subject to another or a change in time, number, or person may be needed to keep the reader's attention in the right place and to convey the intended meaning clearly. For example, the sentence *I will wash the dishes while the cupcakes are baking.* contains shifts in subject, tense, voice, and number (first person, singular pronoun subject *I* to third person, plural noun subject *cupcakes;* active future tense verb *will wash* to passive present progressive tense verb *are baking*). These shifts are natural and necessary to convey the ideas in the sentence. *Needless* shifts in point of view, like those that follow, can make writing confusing and unfocused.

NEEDLESS SHIFT OF SUBJECT	She hated to study and, as a result, the grades she received were bad. [Subject changes from *she* to *grades*.]
REVISION	She hated to study and, as a result, she received bad grades.
NEEDLESS SHIFT OF VOICE	After a great deal of time had been spent in preparation, they started on their journey. [Voice changes from passive to active.]
REVISION	After they had spent a great deal of time in preparation, they started on their journey.
NEEDLESS SHIFT OF PERSON	When a person becomes ill, you should see a doctor. [Person changes from third, *a person,* to second, *you*.]
REVISION	When a person becomes ill, he or she should see a doctor.
NEEDLESS SHIFT OF NUMBER	If one tries hard, they will succeed. [Number changes from singular to plural.]
REVISION	If one tries hard, he or she will succeed.
NEEDLESS SHIFT OF TENSE	The mechanic first adjusts the carburetor and then set the points. [Tense changes from present to past.]
REVISION	The mechanic first adjusted the carburetor and then set the points.
NEEDLESS SHIFT OF MOOD	You must be careful; take no chances. [Mood changes from indicative to imperative.]
REVISION	Be careful; take no chances.

Another type of shift, from indirect to direct quotation (called a **shift of discourse**), is also particularly annoying to readers. Shifts from indirect to direct quotation usually involve a shift of verb tense and the omission of quotation marks.

NEEDLESS SHIFT OF DISCOURSE	The waiter asked Martha whether she wanted chopsticks or does she prefer a fork.
REVISIONS	The waiter asked Martha whether she wanted chopsticks or preferred a fork.
	The waiter asked Martha, "Do you want chopsticks, or do you prefer a fork?"

EXERCISE (10 a–d)-1, SHIFTS IN POINT OF VIEW

The sentences below contain shifts in point of view. For each, indicate the type of shift by writing the appropriate abbreviation—*s* (subject), *v* (voice), *t* (tense), *m* (mood), *p* (person), *n* (number) or *d* (discourse)—at the end of the sentence. Then revise the sentence to eliminate the shifts.

Example   For people wanting to learn about Charles Atlas, you may have a hard time learning much about him.

        People wanting to learn about Charles Atlas may have a hard time learning much about him.

1. Ask a weightlifter who started the sport and he'll have difficulty answering.

_____

2. "I'm not sure" may be his reply any time they are asked about the sport's history.

_____

3. When he was a young man, Charles Atlas takes a job as a strongman in the Coney Island circus.

_____

4. He lifted two men at a time and telephone books were torn in half in his act.

_____

5. He lay on a bed of nails and ate a banana while three men stood on his chest.

_____

6. "Women fainted at that," he said. "They can't stand watching a beautiful body being abused."

_____

7. Atlas continued working at the sideshow where eventually an artist noticed him and asked him to pose.

_____

8. He became a popular model, and public buildings all around the country were soon decorated with images of Atlas.

_____

9. His torso is part of a centaur in a theater on Broadway, and George Washington in Washington Square is also modelled after Atlas.

_____

10. He made enough money as a model so his Coney Island career was abandoned.

_____

11. In 1922, *Physical Culture* magazine held a contest to select the world's most perfectly developed man, a contest which Atlas wins easily.

_____

12. Atlas used the prize money so his own mail order business could be started.

_____

13. The early advertisements are rather clumsy; they showed Atlas in a leopard skin, his muscles flexed.

_____

14. In 1928, Charles Roman took over marketing for Atlas's course, and Atlas's ads were reworked.

_____

15. Roman coins the term *dynamic tension* and decided to concentrate on selling.

_____

16. The ads proclaimed, "Tell me where you want steel muscles and I'll add five inches to your chest."

_____

17. Roman was even responsible for the comic strip panel that the advertisements are introduced by.

_____

18. The panel shows a new Atlas graduate returning to conquer the bully who had stolen his girl and kicks sand in his face.

_____

19. Atlas returned to making personal appearances, which are his first love.

_____

20. He bent railroad spikes, he pulled six cars for a mile, and a 72-ton railroad car was towed along a track.

_____

EXERCISE (10 a–d)-2, SHIFTS IN POINT OF VIEW

The following paragraphs illustrate just how confusing and distracting shifts in point of view can be to a reader trying to follow a writer's train of thought. After reading the paragraphs, use your own paper to write revisions that eliminate the shifts.

By World War II, Charles Atlas had branch offices in London and Argentina and students all over the world were being directed by Atlas. Among his students were Max Baer, the boxer, and Fred Allen and Harry Von Zell, radio comedians. Theodore Steinway, the piano manufacturer, is a student of Atlas. Even Mahatma Gandhi wrote to Atlas, asking if Atlas can build him up. Atlas prescribed a diet and some simple exercises, remarking that "I didn't charge him a dime. The poor chap. He's nothing but a bag of bones."

A subscriber paid Atlas thirty dollars for twelve lessons. They are instructed in deep breathing, push-ups, diet and relaxation, along with isometric exercises. His students were advised to avoid alcohol, tea, plain bread, and doughnuts. Atlas also believed in moral training; young men who visit his office were told to live clean, think clean, and don't go to burlesque shows. A businessman was told by Atlas, "It's the body that counts. Burn your bonds. Tear up your stocks. Give away your property."

If you total up Atlas's reserves, you will find that over six million men bought the Atlas course. Charles Atlas, who is originally Angelo Siciliano, became a multimillionaire. He bought a home by the sea, on Long Island; he works out at the New York Athletic club; and he makes driftwood furniture. Roman directed the mail order business while Atlas posed for publicity photographs. Atlas died of a heart attack at the age of 78. The Sicilian immigrant from Brooklyn had invented a training system that is truly a revolution.

A typical day on an Amish farm begins well before dawn. Prayers are the first necessity, and then about two hours of chores are done by the family members. Cows, chickens, and hogs are fed, and then the farmer prepared the horses for the day's work. Breakfast is served around 6 A.M., and is preceded by prayer and a prayer follows the meal. An hour later, everyone was in the fields. If you are there during a particularly busy season, one will see men and women together in the fields. Otherwise, Amish women work at household duties; without modern appliances, food preparation and storage took most of the day. At 11 A.M. the bell is rung for the noon meal, and the Amish eat a large noon meal. Less than two hours later, the men and women are back at work, and the work is done usually until four in the afternoon. The farmer and his family feed their livestock again, equipment is cleaned and put away. A large supper is served, and afterward the family has about an hour and a half together, and then it is bedtime.

Since their religious beliefs rather limit their choices, the Amish do not take advantage of many recreational activities. If you believe that the "English" world is too worldly, what does that leave one to do for fun? First of all, the Amish had little time left over after all their work. Except for business trips that are absolutely necessary, you stay away from cities. Take this attitude, and what cultural activities are left open for you. The Amish do not attend operas, ballets, or concerts; movies, art shows, bars, restaurants, and sporting events are not frequented, either. At home, television, telephones, radios, popular magazines and books are all forbidden, and the Amish do not dance or play cards. The Amish do not celebrate political holidays like the Fourth of July or Washington's Birthday; Christmas and Easter are celebrated, emphasizing their religious aspects.

MISPLACED PARTS:
MODIFIERS   (11)

As a general rule, modifiers should be positioned as close as possible to the words they modify. Word order is crucial to meaning in English; readers depend on word order to follow a writer's train of thought. The following sentence illustrates what happens when a modifier is misplaced, violating the principle of word order:

> She gave the fish hook to her brother baited with a worm.

After a moment's thought, the reader can untangle the sentence, being reasonably certain it is not the brother but the hook that is baited with a worm.

However, the following sentence cannot be untangled so easily:

> The bartender handed a glass to the customer that was half full.

In this case, either the customer or the glass may be half full. Only the writer knows for sure.

Modifiers should be positioned so that the writer's intended meaning is unambiguous. The following discussion identifies some of the more common problems caused by misplaced sentence parts:

1. Adverbial modifiers such as *almost, even, hardly, just, merely, only, nearly,* and *scarcely* should be placed immediately before the words they modify.

AMBIGUOUS MODIFIER   He had only a face a mother could love. [Is his face
                          all of him a mother could love?]

| REVISION | He had a face only a mother could love. [*Only* placed thus conveys the idea the writer intends, that no one but a mother could love that face.] |

2. Modifying phrases and clauses should refer clearly to the words they modify. The **squinting modifier** is an ambiguous construction so located that it can modify what precedes it and what follows it.

UNCLEAR MODIFYING PHRASE	It is the car that won the race which has yellow wheels.
REVISION	It is the car which has yellow wheels that won the race.
UNCLEAR MODIFYING PHRASE	She had a meal in a restaurant that was low in price.
REVISION	She had a meal that was low in price in a restaurant.
SQUINTING MODIFIER	The cow he was milking irritatedly switched her tail.
REVISIONS	The cow he was irritatedly milking switched her tail.
	The cow he was milking switched her tail irritatedly.

3. As a general rule, infinitives should not be split. An infinitive is split when an adverbial modifier is positioned between the *to* and the verb: *to not go.* It is not always incorrect to split an infinitive; sometimes a sentence sounds more awkward when the writer attempts to avoid a split. But because a split infinitive usually registers in the reader's mind as unharmonious, you should avoid splitting infinitives if possible.

| AWKWARD | I want to, if I can, leave the office early. |
| REVISION | I want to leave the office early, if I can. |

4. Generally speaking, sentence parts such as subject and verb, verb and object, and parts of verb phrases should not be separated unless the result of the separation adds greatly to the effectiveness of the sentence.

AWKWARD SEPARATION	He realized, after many hours, that his course of action was wrong.
REVISION TO REMOVE AWKWARDNESS	After many hours, he realized that his course of action was wrong.
EFFECTIVE SEPARATION	The squad leader, sensing that the enemy was near, ordered the platoon to take up defensive positions.

Practice: Identifying Misplaced Parts In the following sentences, underline the misplaced words that make the sentences unclear or awkward. The answers are listed at the end of this section.

[1]Amish sermons are delivered entirely in German, which can be quite long. [2]Some of the congregation after an hour may start squirming. [3]Since they do not permit musical instruments, it is thought that they prohibit singing sometimes, but actually hymns are an important part of the Amish service. [4]Their hymnbook, the *Ausbund,* was published in 1564 first. [5]The *Ausbund* is the oldest hymnal used by any Protestant group. [6]The tunes are from one generation to the next passed down by memorization, since the *Ausbund* has no notes, the words only to 140 hymns written by Anabaptist prisoners.

Answers to the Practice [1]which can be quite long [2]after an hour [3]sometimes [4]first [6]from one generation to the next, only

EXERCISE (11a–d), MISPLACED WORDS, PHRASES, AND CLAUSES

Revise the following sentences, placing the adverbs so that the relationship to the words they modify is clear and the meaning is unambiguous.

Example   The really Amish are not dissatisfied with their lives at all.

The Amish are really not at all dissatisfied with their lives.

1. Absolutely their lifestyle denies them modern conveniences.

_____

2. But they all accept this as the will of God happily.

_____

3. They love their work and do not consider it a burden, really.

_____

4. Outsiders are amazed by the work one Amish farmer and a hired hand produce often.

_____

5. Easily the two of them can operate 200 acres almost.

_____

6. Only Amish farmers hire Amish youths when they need a hired hand.

_____

7. They say that outsiders even don't work hard enough to suit them.

_____

8. The problem actually for an Amish farmer is not running a large farm.

_____

9. The thing that is difficult is really finding a farm large enough to keep his family busy.

_____

10. Usually Amish districts are presided over by four clergymen.

_____

11. These include a bishop in most districts, two preachers, and a deacon.

_____

12. The bishop is expected to preach, but he presides at mainly ceremonies.

_____

13. His role is to prescribe and enforce constantly the rules.

_____

14. Since the rules are not written down, they are whatever the bishop says, really.

_____

15. The bishop is directed by the wishes of a certain degree the group.

_____

16. He meets with the other three clergy to discuss rules and problems before each meeting.

_____

17. The bishop must first obtain on important matters the approval of the entire group.

_____

18. Without notes of any sort, the two preachers must be able to deliver their sermons.

_____

19. Delivering the sermons is their essentially main duty.

_____

20. They assist the bishop also at ceremonies other than Sunday services.

_____

Revise the following sentences, relocating words, phrases, and clauses so their relationship to the words they modify is clear and the meaning is unambiguous.

Example   The deacon also assists at services, who is sometimes called "minister of the poor."
           The deacon, who is sometimes called "minister of the poor," also assists at services.

21. With the daily operation of the district his main duties are concerned.

_____

22. As a negotiator he serves during marriage arrangements.

_____

23. He collects about alleged violations of the rules information from witnesses.

_____

24. He arranges aid for families particularly with widows and orphans that have problems.

_____

25. The Amish have to help the needy neither a church treasury or offering plate.

_____

26. The deacon which is voluntary on the part of the members must arrange all of the details of any aid.

_____

27. The four clergymen which are not salaried hold completely voluntary positions.

_____

28. They must hold these jobs and care for their farms like any other Amishman, and their families.

_____

29. Which has no property, no treasury, no central organization, they do all this for a church.

_____

30. The bishops of different districts meet twice a year to discuss church matters in some areas.

_____

31. To a central church organization, this is as near as the Amish ever get.

_____

32. Districts agree on specific rules of dress, conduct, and so on, which are in "full fellowship."

_____

33. They may exchange preachers when districts are in full fellowship on a Sunday or two during the year.

_____

34. There is almost no contact, if the districts are not in full fellowship, between them.

_____

35. By vote and by lot, new preachers and deacons are chosen.

_____

36. Any member is entered in the lot who gets at least three votes.

_____

37. From a group of Bibles with slips of paper, each candidate chooses one.

_____

38. The candidate is new clergyman who chose the Bible with a quotation on the slip of paper.

_____

39. By man and by God, the new appointee is thus chosen.

_____

40. The bishop should be a man the Amish believe who has some prior experience.

_____

41. When a vacancy occurs, the bishop is chosen by lot from among the other three at this level.

_____

42. To have been chosen while the job may be thankless it is always an honor.

_____

43. Women altogether by tradition are excluded.

_____

44. Once usually selected, clergy hold their ranks for life.

_____

45. Some younger men never get a chance to serve who would like to be preachers.

_____

46. Others against their real wishes may be chosen.

_____

47. A system like this saves the congregation money in which there are no salaries or buildings to maintain.

_____

48. The system works to keep men in positions who are older and more conservative.

   _____

49. People, even the Amish, tend to become as they get older more conservative.

   _____

50. On conservatism the Amish people dote.

   _____

EXERCISE (11e–f), SPLIT INFINITIVES AND SEPARATED SENTENCE PARTS

Revise the following sentences, correcting awkwardly split infinitives.

Example   The bishop is expected to closely regulate the smallest details of life.

The bishop is expected to regulate closely the smallest details of life.

1. No detail of dress or behavior is too small to ever escape the bishop's eye.

    _____

2. No Amish man or woman wants to even unknowingly violate the bishop's rules.

    _____

3. The band of a hat or a reflector on a buggy might cause the bishop to someday notice a violation of the congregation's customs.

    _____

4. The bishop, in consultation with the group, is empowered to totally inflict a series of punishments or penalties.

    _____

5. Mild sanctions are those that tend to be everywhere invoked by closely knit groups.

    _____

6. Gossip, ridicule, and derision force the violators to usually correct themselves.

    _____

7. The next step is to formally be warned by one of the clergymen.

    _____

8. If the violation is serious, the bishop might want to suddenly visit the violator.

    _____

9. The violator might be asked to next Sunday appear before the whole group.

    _____

10. He or she might be asked to contritely confess the sin and ask to be forgiven.

    _____

11. The final sanction is the *Meidung*, or ban, which is to only be used as the last resort.

    _____

12. The system relies on the individual conscience to first tell him or her what is right.

    _____

13. The minor reprimands are enough to generally reform an errant member.

    _____

14. The *Meidung* is used only if a member were to openly violate a major rule.

    _____

15. Once *Meidung* has been invoked, no one is permitted to even talk to the banned member.

    _____

16. To just associate with the violator is forbidden.

    _____

17. If any persons were to even accidentally ignore the *Meidung*, the ban is extended to them.

    _____

18. All Amish districts have agreed to also honor the *Meidung*.

    _____

19. However, the *Meidung* is meant to not always be irrevocable.

    _____

20. If the violator comes to in person admit his error to the congregation, the ban will be lifted.

    _____

Revise the following sentences, eliminating awkward separation of sentence parts. If a sentence is satisfactory without revision, write *Satisfactory* in the blank below it.

Example   The Amish lifestyle bars from most of the usual meeting places young men and women.

The Amish lifestyle bars young men and women from most of the usual meeting places.

21. Amish parents forbid always their children to date "the English."

    _____

147

22. His father when an Amish boy reaches sixteen buys him his own horse and buggy.

   _____

23. This buggy is smaller than usually the family buggy.

   _____

24. The "courting buggy" has, almost always, no top.

   _____

25. The courting buggy signals that its owner has approval to start dating.

   _____

26. Young Amish at about the same age as non-Amish youth marry.

   _____

27. Courtship activities begin with on Sunday night the "singings."

   _____

28. Singings are totally run by the young Amish themselves.

   _____

29. These are very informal and allow in the course of the evening conversation and refreshments.

   _____

30. A boy may if he has a date bring her to the singing.

   _____

31. Or a boy may during the course of the singing make a date.

   _____

32. These impromptu dates allow later in the evening the boy to drive a girl home.

   _____

33. Amish youngsters possibly because of their Amish lifestyle are usually very shy.

   _____

34. A boy may ask sometimes a friend to act as a go-between.

   _____

35. Amish girls and boys do not since all dress and wear similar haircuts place much emphasis on physical attraction.

   _____

36. They look for instead those characteristics that will help make a successful farm life.

_____

37. After a couple are even "going steady," they keep their relationship secret.

_____

38. When a boy leaves in his courting buggy, he is about where he's going rather vague.

_____

39. He waits until the adults have gone to bed to "sneak over" to his girlfriend's house.

_____

40. If either about their relationship is questioned, he or she denies its existence.

_____

41. Their parents seldom ask, knowing the dating customs well themselves, any question.

_____

42. The couple themselves must appear in public disinterested.

_____

43. No display of affection is ever in public permitted.

_____

44. A young man is expected to when he has decided to marry notify the deacon.

_____

45. The deacon for him asks permission for the marriage from the bride's father.

_____

46. The wedding ceremony is held at the bride's home, which is the most festive of all Amish ceremonies.

_____

47. The ceremony, which is followed by a huge meal, itself is simple.

_____

48. The honeymoon is not a vacation but a long sequence of visits with the couple's friends and relatives.

_____

49. The newlyweds are given on this honeymoon trip many gifts for their new home.

   _____

50. The Amish believe that their children should live close enough "to see the smoke from the chimney."

   _____

DANGLING MODIFIERS (12)

A **dangling modifier** does not logically modify anything in a sentence. Sometimes it seems to modify a certain word but cannot because such a relationship does not make sense. In other instances, there is nothing it could possibly modify.

One type of dangling modifier is the **dangling participle.** Because it functions as an adjective, a participle or participial phrase must have a substantive (noun or noun substitute) to relate to. If the substantive is not present, the participle has nothing to modify. One remedy for a dangling participle is to supply a word it can logically modify. Another solution is to expand the dangling modifier into a full subordinate clause.

DANGLING PARTICIPLE	*Tied to the mast,* the storm lashed at him.
REVISION	Tied to the mast, he was lashed by the storm. [Making *he* the expressed subject supplies the appropriate word for the participial phrase to modify.]
DANGLING PARTICIPLE	*Running in a race,* the finish is hardest.
REVISION INTO SUBORDINATE CLAUSE	When you are running in a race, the finish is hardest.

Dangling gerund phrases, like dangling participles, lack a word they can logically modify. These dangling constructions are usually prepositional phrases with the gerund serving as the object of the preposition. To correct a dangling gerund phrase, you must supply a word that the phrase can modify. Another solution is to recast the sentence so that the gerund is no longer part of a modifying phrase but is instead the subject or object of the verb.

DANGLING GERUND	*After mowing the lawn,* the lemonade tasted very good.
REVISION BY SUPPLYING SUBJECT	After mowing the lawn, I found the lemonade tasted very good.
REVISION BY RECASTING SENTENCE	Mowing the lawn made the lemonade taste very good to me.

A **dangling infinitive** must also have a word to modify logically. Like a gerund, an infinitive can substitute for a noun, so an alternative method for correcting a dangling infinitive is to recast the infinitive as a noun substitute rather than a modifier.

DANGLING INFINITIVE	*To win at tennis,* practice is required.
REVISIONS	To win at tennis, one must practice.
	To win at tennis requires practice.

As with other types of modifiers, participles, gerunds, and infinitives can also be misplaced. They can be situated near nouns with which they have no connection instead of near nouns they logically modify.

MISPLACED PARTICIPLE	*Fleeing down the alley,* the police caught the thief.
REVISION	The police caught the thief fleeing down the alley.
MISPLACED GERUND	*Playing with the symphony,* she loved her job.
REVISION	She loved her job playing with the symphony.
MISPLACED INFINITIVE	*To stick to a diet,* her doctor told her she needed will power.
REVISION	Her doctor told her she needed will power to stick to a diet.

An **elliptical clause** is one that has an implied or understood, rather than a stated, subject or verb—for example, *While tying his shoes, he broke a lace.* In the preceding sentence, the subject and auxiliary verb (*he was*) of the subordinate clause are implied. An elliptical clause dangles if its implied subject is not the same as the subject of the main clause. To correct a dangling elliptical clause, be sure the objects of both clauses agree, or supply the omitted subject or verb.

DANGLING ELLIPTICAL CLAUSE	*While eating our supper,* the rain began to fall.
REVISIONS	While eating our supper, we noticed that the rain had begun to fall.
	While we were eating our supper, the rain began to fall.

Practice: Identifying Dangling and Elliptical Modifiers In the following sentences, underline the dangling or elliptical modifiers. Answers are listed at the end of this section.

[1]Having survived and prospered for hundreds of years, sociologists call the Amish culture one of the most successful folk societies in history. [2]While experiencing some problems in adapting to government regulation, separation from the majority culture has been maintained remarkably well. [3]Being occasionally lured away by the temptations of the modern world, Amish parents continue to worry about their teenage children, but very few—only about six percent—ever leave the Amish community. [4]Land scarcity has been a problem which has caused Amish families to move into more and more new districts, but even this is an advantage. [5]While coming to admire the Amish way of life, public support is more likely.

Answers to the Practice [1]Having survived and prospered for hundreds of years [2]While experiencing some problems in adapting to government regulation [3]Being occasionally lured away by the temptations of the modern world [5]While coming to admire the Amish way of life,

EXERCISE (12a–b), DANGLING PARTICIPLES AND GERUNDS

Revise the following sentences to eliminate all dangling or misplaced participles and gerunds. Write the word *Satisfactory* in the blank if the sentence requires no revision.

Example   Regulating almost every aspect of education, each state has its own laws.

Each state has its own laws regulating almost every aspect of education.

1. For not complying with these laws, some states have arrested the Amish.

   _____

2. Commonly believed, a popular idea is that the Amish are anti-education.

   _____

3. Holding fast to their beliefs, it is non-Amish education that the Amish do not like.

   _____

4. Working out compromises, laws have been passed making exceptions for Amish children.

   _____

5. Willing to attend the first eight grades, Amish parents are concerned about their children.

   _____

6. Objecting to teenage exposure to worldliness, Amish students rarely attend ninth grade.

   _____

7. Insisting that the school is an Amish school, even then the parents are careful.

   _____

8. Opening their own schools, the students are educated in the Amish community.

   _____

9. Looking encouraging, the details of certifying Amish community schools seem to be resolving themselves.

   _____

10. Looking for compromise, Amish students are allowed by most states to apply for a work permit at age fifteen.

_____

11. By attending a farm vocational school instead of high school, some states allow Amish children to avoid public school after eighth grade.

_____

12. Ruling on a 1968 court case, Amish parents were upheld in their beliefs by the U.S. Supreme Court.

_____

13. In deciding the case, religious freedom was found to outweigh the states' interest in universal education.

_____

14. Looking for the most part like any other school, modern conveniences are not present, though, in Amish schools.

_____

15. Convinced that good teaching is unrelated to college or state certification, teaching is a God-given talent and a calling, similar to preaching.

_____

16. Being Amish like the students, an eighth grade education is all that can be required of an Amish teacher.

_____

17. In choosing their teachers, most Amish teachers are female.

_____

18. Being very dedicated, their own conferences, bulletins and teacher associations are very important to Amish teachers.

_____

19. Serving only one district, the average enrollment at an Amish school is thirty students.

_____

20. Thus teaching several grades at once, even janitorial and nursing duties also are assigned to the single teacher who staffs most Amish schools.

_____

EXERCISE (12c–d), DANGLING INFINITIVES AND ELLIPTICAL CLAUSES

Revise the following sentences to eliminate dangling or misplaced infinitives and elliptical clauses. Write the word *Satisfactory* if the sentence requires no revision.

Example To visit the Amish country, trips are often arranged, for tourists.
Trips to visit the Amish country are often arranged for tourists.

1. To see the Amish customs, buses, trains, and planes bring millions of visitors each year.

———————————————————————————————————

2. To cash in on this business, motels and restaurants, even souvenir shops and museums have appeared all around the larger Amish districts.

———————————————————————————————————

3. While viewing the Amish settlements, the Amish are very annoyed by the traffic.

———————————————————————————————————

4. To bring back souvenir snapshots, the Amish taboo against cameras is constantly violated.

———————————————————————————————————

5. To challenge the Amish rules of conduct, every year brings new modern technology and conveniences.

———————————————————————————————————

6. To protest what they considered unnecessary strictness, whole congregations have seceded.

———————————————————————————————————

7. To permit the use of mechanical vehicles, a group calling itself the New Amish was formed in 1966.

———————————————————————————————————

8. While permitting the ownership of automobiles, Moses M. Beachy started a new group in 1927.

———————————————————————————————————

9. To protect themselves from the appeal of modern conveniences, the Amish may finally find themselves forced to compromise.

———————————————————————————————————

10. To judge by their past, however, such compromise is not very likely.

   _____

11. To maintain their way of life in the face of ever-increasing government regulation has been difficult.

   _____

12. To meet traffic and vehicle codes, electric lights have been installed on Amish buggies.

   _____

13. To obey health laws, inoculation and vaccination of Amish children has been approved.

   _____

14. To have their milk inspected, Amish dairy farmers have had to agree.

   _____

15. While obtaining conscientious-objector status during all major wars, the decision was not without controversy.

   _____

16. While paying income and property taxes like everyone else, some of the purposes the taxes serve are considered irreligious.

   _____

17. To maintain control of teenage Amish boys, stricter enforcement of rules has been necessary.

   _____

18. To resist the temptations of alcohol, automobiles and other violations of Amish mores, even the isolated Amish teenagers apparently sometimes find it difficult.

   _____

19. While experiencing relatively few problems of this nature, the few problems that occur are still difficult to understand and resolve.

   _____

20. To look into the future, the Amish will probably have more of these problems.

   _____

OMISSIONS; INCOMPLETE AND ILLOGICAL COMPARISONS (13)

Omissions in sentences may occur because of the writer's haste, carelessness, or lack of proofreading. A few types of omissions occur, however, because the writer is not fully aware that certain omissions common in speech can be very confusing in writing. Omissions of this sort typically fall into three categories: omitted prepositions and verbs, omissions in compound constructions, and incomplete comparisons.

1. Be sure to proofread carefully. Proofreading is difficult for almost everyone. When we have written a sentence or paragraph, we have trouble seeing our own omissions because we tend to "fill in" anything that is missing. We listen to our thoughts rather than see what is actually written on the page. Keep a list of errors you have difficulty seeing when you are proofreading. You may notice an emerging pattern that will help you to spot mistakes more easily in the future. When you proofread, do it slowly and do it some time after you have finished the final draft—when the words will be less familiar to you. Read a line at a time, using a ruler or sheet of blank paper under each line as you read it. This technique will help to isolate the line on which you are concentrating and eliminate distractions from other sentences on the page.

Careless omissions usually involve the little words our minds fill in but our pens fail to record: articles and prepositions.

CARELESS OMISSION	The car was little, green one.
REVISION	The car was *a* little, green one.
CARELESS OMISSION	I saw it parked next the gas pump.
REVISION	I saw it parked next *to* the gas pump.

2. Be sure to write out relationships that are merely implied in speech. In casual speech we may say *This type motorcycle is very powerful* or *We were roommates last semester,* but in writing we need to supply the prepositions.

OMISSION   Gasoline consumption the last few years has decreased.

REVISION   Gasoline consumption *during* the last few years has decreased.

3. Be sure compound constructions are complete. Check the verbs and prepositions in particular. When we connect two items of the same kind with a conjunction, we frequently omit words that unnecessarily duplicate each other; however, these omitted words must in fact be the same as words that do appear in the sentence: *She can [climb] and will climb the mountain.* Too often, omitted words are not duplicates of stated ones, and the result is an illogical sentence.

OMISSION   She is interested and experienced at mountain climbing.

REVISION   She is interested *in* and experienced at mountain climbing.

OMISSION   On the other hand, I never have and never will go mountain climbing.

REVISION   On the other hand, I never have *gone* and never will go mountain climbing.

Sometimes duplicate words should be repeated in a compound construction. Otherwise the expressed meaning may be illogical.

OMISSION   They lost the game because of a lack of speed and good blocking. [It is doubtful that the game was lost because of good blocking, but the reader might understand that to be the case.]

REVISION   They lost the game because of a lack of speed and *a lack of* good blocking.

4. Be sure all comparisons are clear, complete, and logical. Avoid illogical use of *than any of* or *any of.* Do not compare items that are logically not comparable. Make sure not only that comparisons are complete but also that both terms of the comparison are given and that the basis of the comparison is stated. The following sentences illustrate omissions that create illogical comparisons:

ILLOGICAL USE   She is the best player than any of them.
OF *THAN ANY OF*

REVISION   She is the best player *on the team.*

ILLOGICAL COMPARISON   The vegetables here are as high in price as any other region.

REVISION   The vegetables here are as high in price as *those in* any other region.

159

GRAMMATICALLY INCOMPLETE COMPARISON	This horse is as fast, if not faster than, the other.
REVISION	This horse is as fast *as,* if not faster than, the other horse.
TERMS OF COMPARISON INCOMPLETE	I like biology more than Jan.
REVISION	I like biology more than Jan *does.*
BASIS OF COMPARISON NOT STATED	This brand costs less.
REVISION	This brand costs less *than other popular brands.*

EXERCISE (13), OMISSIONS; INCOMPLETE AND ILLOGICAL COMPARISONS

Revise the following sentences, correcting omissions and comparisons that are illogical or incomplete. Write the word *Satisfactory* if the sentence requires no revision.

Example   The Hutterites are another type Anabaptist folk society.

The Hutterites are another type of Anabaptist folk society.

1. The Hutterites have been victims persecution of one type or another for 450 years.

   _____

2. They, like Amish, are also Anabaptists.

   _____

3. The Hutterites are mainly Swiss, German, and Austrian descent.

   _____

4. From the year 1528 to present, the Hutterites have practiced communal ownership.

   _____

5. This type belief set them apart from other Anabaptist groups.

   _____

6. It may also be the reason they have been persecuted more.

   _____

7. Even the name "Hutterites" was given to them by their enemies.

   _____

8. They prefer to call themselves "Brethren," "Hutterian Brethren."

   _____

9. Jacob Hutter was early martyr who designed the group's institutions.

   _____

10. They finally arrived United States in late nineteenth century.

   _____

11. They had slowly been driven from one European country another until they settled briefly in Russia.

_____

12. They even left the United States for Canada four years of World War One, but later returned.

_____

13. The majority of modern Hutterite communities in United States are in South Dakota.

_____

14. The lifestyle of the Hutterites is as conservative as any other Anabaptists.

_____

15. They are linked to the past just as much, if not more than, the Amish.

_____

16. The Hutterite language is obscure Tyrolean dialect of German.

_____

17. Their clothing, all homemade, is just as conservative.

_____

18. The Hutterites, however, allow use of trucks, tractors, electricity on their farms.

_____

19. The Hutterites have made the best adjustment to the modern world than any of them.

_____

20. Each Hutterite colony, Bruderhof, is governed by a five-or-six-man council.

_____

21. The council is really a combination government and business.

_____

22. The council is composed a minister, business manager, farm boss, German teacher, and two elected members of the colony.

_____

23. Their loyalty, like all colony members, is to the Bruderhof rather than to themselves or their homes.

_____

24. In fact, though each Hutterite family has its own area in a type apartment, the members do not have separate homes.

_____

25. Each "apartment" has living room and separate bedrooms, but the kitchens and dining rooms are in two large halls, one for adults and one for children.

_____

AWKWARD OR CONFUSED

SENTENCES   (14)

Sometimes sentences are clumsy, meaningless, or, in some instances, absurd. Often it is difficult to determine exactly which violation of grammar is involved. The reason may be a combination of violations or simply a heavy-handed or vague and illogical manner of saying something. However, awkwardness may be the result of faulty predication or mixed construction—sentence faults that occur when a sentence begins with one kind of construction but ends with another, incompatible one.

Faulty predication results if the verb or complement is not appropriate to the subject of a sentence.

INAPPROPRIATE VERB	The data make several errors.
REVISION	The data contain several errors.
INAPPROPRIATE COMPLEMENT	His daughter is the reason he stayed at home today.
REVISION	His daughter's illness is the reason he stayed at home today.

In the first faulty sentence, action is illogically attributed to the subject, *data.* In the second faulty sentence, the linking verb *is* joins a subject and complement that are not equal. Because the verb *to be* in its various forms equates what precedes and follows it, the two sides of such an "equation" must be logically compatible. *His daughter is the reason* makes no sense.

Another common cause of faulty predication is the construction of definitions and explanations that use *is when, is where, is what,* or *is because.* Remember that the linking verb *is* functions as an equal sign between the subject and the words that rename or define it; equivalent terms must be used on both sides.

ILLOGICAL USE OF *WHEN*	A hurricane is when the winds in a tropical storm exceed 75 miles per hour.
CORRECTED SENTENCE	A hurricane occurs when the winds in a tropical storm exceed 75 miles per hour.
ILLOGICAL USE OF *WHERE*	Skydiving is where people jump from airplanes into free-fall.
CORRECTED SENTENCE	Skydiving is jumping from an airplane into free-fall.
ILLOGICAL USE OF *WHAT*	The direct object is what receives the action of the verb.
CORRECTED SENTENCE	The direct object receives the action of the verb.
ILLOGICAL USE OF *BECAUSE*	The reason she laughed is because the joke was funny.
CORRECTED SENTENCE	The reason she laughed is the joke was funny.

To avoid a **mixed construction,** attempt to maintain throughout a sentence the type of construction you establish in the first part of the sentence. Frequently, mixed constructions are caused by unnecessary shifts between active and passive voice verbs within a sentence, as the following example illustrates:

MIXED CONSTRUCTION	Although he had the best intentions, many errors were made.
SMOOTH CONSTRUCTION	Although he had the best intentions, he made many errors.

Sometimes mixed constructions occur when the writer forgets the true subject of a sentence and constructs a predicate that fits a word in a modifying phrase or clause.

MIXED CONSTRUCTION	By packing my suitcase tonight will give me more time for breakfast tomorrow.
REVISIONS	Packing my suitcase tonight will give me more time for breakfast tomorrow.
	By packing my suitcase tonight, I will have more time for breakfast tomorrow.

The best way to avoid writing awkward, confused, or mixed sentences is to evaluate each statement critically. Is it clear? Is it precise? Is it logical? Is it sensible? Is it to the point?

EXERCISE (14), AWKWARD OR CONFUSED SENTENCES
AND MIXED CONSTRUCTIONS

Revise the following sentences, correcting awkward, confused, and mixed constructions. Write the word *Satisfactory* if the sentence requires no revision.

Example   Among the Hutterites, services are usually done in the school building.

Services among the Hutterites are usually held in the school building.

1. This is what saves them expenses, too.

   _____

2. Modern appliances such as telephones and electric ranges are admitted.

   _____

3. Movies, concerts, and sporting events are what the Brethren will not allow.

   _____

4. As a major form of entertainment, the Brethren present visiting their friends.

   _____

5. Visiting among the Brethren is always present.

   _____

6. The daily lives of the Brethren are very similar to the Amish.

   _____

7. The reason is because the goals of their societies are similar.

   _____

8. For both groups, assimilation, where they become like the English, is to be avoided.

   _____

9. One difference between the groups is when they approach the ownership of property.

   _____

10. The successful Amish society is individual initiative.

   _____

11. The Amish farming system projects independence and self-reliance.

_____

12. Everything in the Hutterite colony, though, is owned by the colony.

_____

13. Individual Hutterites cannot hold property.

_____

14. The bank account of the whole colony is what grows when crops are sold.

_____

15. Each Hutterite possesses a monthly allowance of about five dollars.

_____

16. After all, their other needs are in charge of the colony.

_____

17. The Hutterite economy is where all individual needs are less important than group needs.

_____

18. Their economy comprises, essentially, communism.

_____

19. All other attempts at communist utopias remain dismal pasts.

_____

20. One reason the Brethren's colonies are so successful is because of their birth rate.

_____

21. The Hutterites have better than ten children per family.

_____

22. The Brethren may be the highest birth rate of any ethnic group in the world.

_____

23. There appears also a low death rate among the Hutterites.

_____

24. The reason is because the Brethren are health-conscious and have excellent medical care.

_____

25. "Branching" is when a new colony must be formed because the population has increased so much at an existing colony.

_____

SENTENCE FAULTS REVIEW (6–14)

Revise the following sentences, correcting fragments, fused sentences, comma splices, faulty agreement, faulty reference of pronouns, unnecessary shifts, misplaced and dangling modifiers, and awkward constructions.

Example   Jackie Robinson was the first black player in the major leagues of the Brooklyn Dodgers.

Jackie Robinson, of the Brooklyn Dodgers, was the first black player in the major leagues.

1. As Robinson walked onto the field in 1947, journalists are examining his performance in detail.

   _____

2. Among the most popular black Americans of the time were Joe Louis, heavyweight boxing champion.

   _____

3. Dominated since its beginning in America by black champions, blacks were accepted as boxers.

   _____

4. The founding of the National Basketball Association two years away.

   _____

5. Two teams in the National Football League were integrated, pro football still had a limited number of fans.

   _____

6. Baseball was in its heyday, it had never been integrated.

   _____

7. Ending legal school segregation, it would be seven years later when the Supreme Court issued its decision.

   _____

8. Changed on opening day in 1947, with Jackie Robinson playing first base for the Dodgers against the Boston Braves.

   _____

9. Blacks had played, as many as two dozen, on major professional teams before 1887.

   _____

10. On July 14, 1887, the signing of any more black players by teams was forbidden by the International League.

_____

11. Supposedly protected from dismissal by the League, a series of ugly incidents and mysterious "releases" thinned the ranks of black players already playing in 1887.

_____

12. Baseball segregation, within five years of the league's decision, was firmly in place.

_____

13. One can easily discover this for yourself in books about baseball.

_____

14. Born into poverty as a sharecropper's son, Jackie Robinson's mother took her children to California to escape.

_____

15. All of her children excels at sports, an avenue that was open for them.

_____

16. Jackie won a football scholarship to UCLA, he played in the College All-Stars Game.

_____

17. He had always, which eventually rewarded him, developed the habit of playing in the most conservative neighborhoods.

_____

18. His pro career was postponed in World War II he served with the U.S. Army in a segregated unit.

_____

19. In limited duties because his ankles were damaged by college football.

_____

20. Robinson joined the Kansas City Monarchs, in 1945, in the Negro Leagues.

_____

21. That same year, Branch Rickey's scouts were looking for black players for the Dodgers.

_____

22. Rickey knew the plan to integrate his team were going to be unpopular.

_____

23. He felt the Negro Leagues mistreats its black players.

_____

24. Rickey had been forced to disguise his intentions to integrate their own team.

_____

25. He had announced plans for a new black league, he left the impression that desegregating the Dodgers was not an immediate plan.

_____

Revise the following sentences to make plural subjects and verbs singular and singular subjects and verbs plural. Be sure that subjects and verbs agree in number in each revision, and make sure that you change pronouns and the articles *a, an,* and *the* where necessary.

Example   A scout invited Robinson back to Brooklyn to meet with Rickey.
           Scouts invited Robinson back to Brooklyn to meet with Rickey.

26. Segregationist law forced Rickey to plan his experiment secretly.

_____

27. The meeting in Brooklyn included only three men.

_____

28. For three hours, the club president addresses Robinson in the taunting manner he thought Robinson could expect from fans and even players.

_____

29. He is so convincing that the player has to restrain himself.

_____

30. At the end of the meeting comes the famous exchange.

_____

31. "Do you want a ball player who's afraid to fight back?"

_____

32. "I want a ball player who has the guts not to fight back."

_____

33. Moments after that exchange, he signed a contract obligating Robinson to play for the Dodgers' farm club.

_____

34. The master plan was known to only five people.

_____

35. The nonviolent method Rickey wanted Robinson to use was not new.

_____

36. But in 1945, the leader of the Civil Rights Movement was a college junior in Atlanta.

_____

37. Not until 1955 would a black woman refuse to give up her seat on an Alabama bus.

_____

38. Not until the 1960s would the mass march find its leader in Martin Luther King.

_____

39. Jackie's method was compared to King's method by Hank Aaron.

_____

40. He maintained poise and dignity in the face of taunts and threats.

_____

Ten incomplete statements follow. Replace the dots with your own words, creating complete sentences from the fragments.

Example   I served ... with whipped cream ...

I served peaches with whipped cream spooned on top.

41. Neither training nor education ... necessary ...

_____

42. If a brand ... costs about the same ...

_____

43. Stuck in the mud ...

_____

44.   ... used more ...

_____

45. Someone will plead . . . your version of the facts.

_____

46. The jury . . . secret ballot.

_____

47. . . . flying through the air . . .

_____

48. Overtime . . . because the orders aren't filled.

_____

49. Jodie likes . . . better . . .

_____

50. . . . nearly . . .

_____

NUMBERS; ABBREVIATIONS; ACRONYMS, INITIALISMS, AND CLIPPED FORMS; SYLLABICATION (15–18)

NUMBERS (15)

In writing for general readers, **numbers** are usually spelled out if they can be expressed in one or two words and are less than 100: *four, ninety-nine, fifteen.* Journalistic, scientific, business, and technical writing, however, tend to favor using figures over spelled-out numbers, especially if numbers are used extensively, because figures are clearer and less time consuming to read. Often, business, scientific, and technical writers, as well as journalists, use the "rule of ten": isolated numbers of ten or less are spelled out, whereas numbers greater than ten are written as figures. For example, *The machine took two years to design and 12 years to be accepted by the industry.*

A good rule of thumb for writing numbers is to follow the conventions of the field to which your readers belong. (You can find these conventions in the style manual for that field.) The most important thing is to be consistent in your use of numbers. The following guidelines explain the prevalent conventions for general, nontechnical writing:

1. Spell out numbers or amounts less than 100; use figures for larger numbers or amounts.

> My son is *twelve.*
> We saw *thirty-five* horses.
> The mountain is *15,000* feet high.

2. Use figures for dates and addresses.

July 4, 1776   1426 Homer Avenue
1914–1918   Route 2
908 B.C.   P.O. Box 606

3. The suffixes *-st, -nd, -rd,* and *-th* should not be used after dates if the year is given.

May 1, 1985   May 1st of last year

4. Figures are ordinarily used in the following situations:

DECIMALS   2.67
                                      3.14159

PERCENTAGES   45% *or* 45 percent

MIXED NUMBERS AND FRACTIONS   10 ½ (but *one-fourth* of the class)

SCORES AND STATISTICS   The vote was 67–24 against the plan.

IDENTIFICATION NUMBERS   Flight 457
                                      Channel 6

VOLUME AND CHAPTER NUMBERS   Volume 2
                                      Chapter 3
                                      page 17

ACT, SCENE, AND LINE NUMBERS   Act IV, Scene 1, lines 10–11

NUMBERS FOLLOWED BY SYMBOLS   8″ × 10″
                                      55 mph
                                      89°

EXACT AMOUNTS OF MONEY $35.79
                                      25¢

TIMES   2:45 P.M.
                                      11:00 A.M.

BUT   quarter to three, eleven o'clock

5. Except in legal or commercial writing, a number that has been spelled out should not be repeated as a figure in parentheses.

LEGAL   The easement is twenty (20) feet wide.

STANDARD   The ladder is twenty feet long.

6. Numbers that begin sentences should always be spelled out. If such a number is long or falls into a category of numbers usually expressed in figures (e.g., 40,000; 33 1/3), recast the sentence to eliminate its beginning with a number.

> One thousand five hundred refugees stepped off the boat.
> Off the boat stepped 1,500 refugees.

ABBREVIATIONS (16)

Abbreviations should generally be avoided in writing, with a few standard exceptions. These exceptions and other conventions governing the use of abbreviations include the following:

1. The abbreviations *Mr., Mrs., Ms.,* and *Dr.* are appropriate only before surnames, as in *Mr. Brown, Mrs. Sanchez, Ms. Trent, Dr. Jacobson.*

2. Abbreviations such as *Hon., Rev., Prof., Sen.,* and *Gen.* are appropriate only when both the surnames and given names or initials are given, as the *Rev. Oscar Smith.*

3. The abbreviations *Jr., Sr., Esq., M.D., D.D., J.D., LL.D.,* and *Ph.D.* are used when a name is given, as in *John Roberts, Jr. is the new district manager.* However, academic degrees are also used alone in abbreviated form, as in *Gloria Jones received her M.A. last year and is now working toward her Ph.D. in economics.,* in all but the most formal writing situations. Do not use equivalent titles and/or abbreviations both before and after a name—for example, *Dr. Jan Russ, M.D.*

4. The abbreviations *B.C.* (before Christ), *A.D.* (*anno Domini,* after Christ), *A.M.* or *a.m.* (*ante meridiem,* before noon), *P.M.* or *p.m.* (*post meridiem,* after noon), *Vol.* or *vol.* (volume), *No.* or *no.* (number), and *$* are used only when specific dates, times, and figures are given, as in *12 B.C., No. 4, $50.00.* The twentieth century's two world wars are abbreviated—*World War I* and *World War II; WW I* and *WW II* should not be used.

5. Latin abbreviations such as *i.e.* (that is), *e.g.* (for example), and *etc.* (and so forth) are appropriate in most contexts. However, avoid using *etc.* in formal writing and do not use it as a catch-all in any type of writing. Instead of saying, for example, *I like seafood such as shrimp, clams, etc.,* say *I like such seafood as shrimp and clams.*

6. Personal names and names of countries, states, months, days of the week, and courses of instruction should be spelled out. For example, *On September 17 we studied Germany and France in our history class.* instead of *On Sept. 17 we studied Ger. and Fr. in our hist. class.* Three exceptions are the District of Columbia, abbreviated *D.C.* when it follows the city name, Washington; the United States, abbreviated *U.S.A.* (or *USA* or *U.S.*); and the Soviet Union, abbreviated *U.S.S.R.* (or *USSR*). The names of states may, of course, be abbreviated when they are parts of addresses.

7. Names of agencies, organizations, corporations, and persons commonly referred to by initials do not need to be spelled out unless you believe your reader will not be familiar with them. In that case, spell out the name the first time you use it and place the abbreviation in parentheses. Thereafter you may

use the abbreviation by itself: *The president of the United Auto Works (UAW) refused to comment on the UAW's negotiations with Ford.*

Use abbreviations such as *Inc., Co., Bros.,* or *&* (for *and*) only if they are part of a firm's official title, as in *MacLauren Power & Paper Co.*

8. Place names and the words *street, avenue,* and *boulevard* should be spelled out. References to a subject, volume, chapter, or page should also be spelled out. The only exceptions are special contexts such as addresses and footnotes.

9. In writing for general audiences, spell out most scientific and technical terms unless the abbreviations are well known to the majority of readers or the terms themselves are too cumbersome. After you have spelled out the term and presented it with the abbreviation, you may use the abbreviation alone: *The number of rems (for roentgen equivalent man—a unit of measure for radiation) sufficient for a 50 percent chance of death ranges between 200 and 600.*

ACRONYMS, INITIALISMS, AND CLIPPED FORMS (17)

Like abbreviations, acronyms, initialisms, and clipped forms are shortened forms of words. An **acronym** is an abbreviation formed from the initial letters of words and is pronounced as a single word: *NATO (North Atlantic Treaty Organization; SADD (Students Against Drunk Driving).* Some acronyms are so well known that they have become words in their own right and are no longer capitalized: *scuba (Self-Contained Underwater Breathing Apparatus); laser (Light Amplification by Stimulated Emission of Radiation); radar (RAdio Detecting And Ranging).* An **initialism** is also an abbreviation formed from the first letters of words, but the initials are pronounced letter by letter rather than as a single word: *CRT (cathode ray tube); DOD (Department of Defense); CEO (chief executive officer).*

Clipped forms are not abbreviations and are not followed by periods. Notice that the following sentence contains both an abbreviation for a title and a clipped form of the word not used as a title: *The prof giving the lecture is Prof. Scaletta.* Other familiar clipped forms include words such as *lab, phone, prep (preparation), stew (stewardess), doc (doctor), exam (examination), grad (graduate).*

The conventions that apply to acronyms, initialisms, and clipped forms are as follows:

1. Spell out or define acronyms and initialisms at the first reference if your reader is likely to be unfamiliar with them: *During the past twenty-five years, most TB (tuberculosis) sanitariums have closed for lack of patients. The World Health Organization (WHO) now has statistics that show TB is far from cured, however; WHO notes a startling increase in the last decade.*

2. Although clipped forms may be appropriate for some types of informal writing, such as where a casual, conversational tone is desired, avoid them in formal writing.

CONVERSATIONAL	The vet called the lab tech on the phone.
FORMAL	The veterinarian called the laboratory technician on the telephone.

Syllabication, or word division, at the end of a line properly occurs only between syllables. If you are in doubt about where a word's syllable breaks occur, consult your dictionary. When you must divide a word between one line and the next, place the hyphen, which indicates the break, after the first part of the divided word, not before the remainder of the word at the beginning of the next line: *inter- esting,* not *inter -esting.*

Dictionaries indicate syllabication by means of dots: in•ter•est•ing. However, not every syllable division is an appropriate place to break a word at the end of a line. Three general rules govern word division at ends of lines:

1. Do not divide one-syllable words or words pronounced as one syllable (*thrust, blanched, stream*).

2. Do not divide a word so that a single letter stands alone on a line. If necessary, leave the line short and carry the whole word over to the next line.

INCORRECT	The neighbors moved a- way.
CORRECT	The neighbors moved away.

3. Divide hyphenated compound words at the hyphen only, to avoid awkwardness.

AWKWARD	The committee re-ex- amined the issue.
IMPROVED	The committee re- examined the issue.

EXERCISE (15), NUMBERS

Assume an audience of general readers. Cross out incorrectly expressed numbers in the following sentences, then write the correct forms in the blanks at the right.

Example   I was born in ~~nineteen forty~~-eight, and I weighed nine pounds.   *1948*

1. The first Indian-English dictionary was published in sixteen forty-three. _____

2. Louis W. Ballard wrote the 1st American Indian ballet. _____

3. Ballard, a Cherokee-Sioux from Oklahoma, was born in nineteen thirty-one. _____

4. His ballet, *Koshare,* was 1st performed in nineteen sixty. _____

5. Thus, Ballard was twenty nine when he first saw his work. _____

6. It was not performed in a major American city for 7 more years, however. _____

7. Ballard's ancestry combines 2 of the most numerous ethnic groups among American Indians. _____

8. The Cherokees number over 66 thousand, making them the 2nd largest tribe. _____

9. There are forty seven thousand, eight hundred and twenty-five Indians of Sioux descent. _____

10. The Sioux were the 3rd largest tribe in 1970. _____

11. 25 candidates reported for the ceremony. _____

12. She will arrive in thirty (30) days. _____

13. On January twenty-third, we observe Martin Luther King's birthday. _____

14. I am 6 feet tall and weigh two hundred pounds. _____

15. Their address is forty-three One Hundred Twenty-third Street. _____

16. They saved $2,500 and spent one hundred fifty nine dollars and seventy cents of it on airfare.

_____

17. Reduce your weight by fifteen percent.

_____

18. I ran the one-hundred-yard dash in nine and two-fifths seconds.

_____

19. The assignment is on page two hundred forty-nine of Chapter 11.

_____

20. We arrived at eleven twenty A.M. and left at ten P.M.

_____

21. Buy 10 jalapenos, 1 pound of masa, and 2 pimientos.

_____

22. The radius was twenty six-hundredths of an inch.

_____

23. Phone me at five seven two 3 one nine one at 7 o'clock.

_____

24. 25 times 25 equals 625.

_____

25. His grade point average for the term was two point nine.

_____

26. Physics three hundred thirty-two is the last of the twelve physics courses offered.

_____

27. They will arrive at three fifteen A.M. on track seven.

_____

28. I was driving fifty mph when the hose burst.

_____

29. We drive 2 miles Monday through Friday and 5 miles on Saturday.

_____

30. At half-time the score was tied at fourteen to fourteen.

_____

EXERCISE (16), ABBREVIATIONS

Cross out inappropriate abbreviations in the following sentences, and then write the corrections in the blanks at the right.

Example   He became a citizen on J̶u̶e̶ 20, 1982.   *June*

1. Senator Charles Curtis of Kansas was the first VP with an Indian ancestry.

   _____

2. In 1946, the Indian Claims Comm. was established to set-tle treaty disputes.

   _____

3. The first Am. Indian to be declared venerable by the RC church was K. Tekakwitha.

   _____

4. This is the first step toward becoming a St.

   _____

5. Curtis served under Pres. Hoover.

   _____

6. The first Indian Day was held on May 13, 1916, by the Soc. of American Indians.

   _____

7. In 1940, Indians registered for the mil. draft for the first time.

   _____

8. There are Fed. Indian reservations in twenty-three states.   _____

9. The Indian Civ. Rights Act was passed in 1968.   _____

10. Indian consent must be given before states can assume power over reserv. land.

    _____

11. Lemons, oranges, etc. are grown in FL.   _____

12. Her office is on Westview St.   _____

13. She was the Sr. member of the firm.   _____

14. She made the firm many $, I believe.   _____

15. He has previously lived in Ger. and Eng.   _____

16. John Werdt, Sr., and John Werdt, Junior are certainly highly dissimilar persons.

    _____

17. Walter Cronkite retired from the CBS eve. news in 1981. _____

18. I don't know whether the Dr. will approve. _____

19. The Lamson Co. manufactures hardware specialties. _____

20. I like the month of Aug. better than I do the month of Feb. _____

21. Rev. McIntoch preached an inspiring sermon on tolerance. _____

22. The No. is either four dollars or five $. _____

23. He drove his new Cad. to the Co. meeting. _____

24. They settled in the Blue Ridge Mtns. of Va. _____

25. Span. is an easier language than Fren. or Ger. for English speakers to learn. _____

26. Ms. Jare could not find the answer in vol. 9 of the encyclopedia. _____

27. Hon. George Dorain will address the meeting of the Hibernian Society at 121 Birch Ave. _____

28. The Jr. looked a great deal like his father, Matt Brown, Sr. _____

29. The boss told Sandy to bring his wife with him to the office New Yrs. Eve party. _____

30. Way back in B.C., Gen. Julius Caesar won some important Roman victories. _____

EXERCISE (17), ACRONYMS, INITIALISMS, AND CLIPPED FORMS

In the following sentences, revise by spelling out (or by substituting a longer form) any acronym, initialism, or clipped form that would be inappropriate for use in writing for a general audience. Your dictionary may be helpful in identifying some terms. Write your revision in the blank beneath each sentence; if a form seems appropriate, write the word *correct* in the blank.

Example   The UMW is a union with a long history.

   The United Mine Workers is a union with a long history.

1. Jacques Cousteau developed the scuba apparatus into its current form.

   _____

2. The prez has often been of ethnic stock.

   _____

3. Who was the sales rep for the new computer?

   _____

4. Every ambulance must have a crew of three EMTs.

   _____

5. How old is the AFL-CIO?

   _____

6. Muhammad Ali was world champ three times.

   _____

7. Our soc prof says that is a rare achievement.

   _____

8. The new DOE directives are not in the least ambiguous.

   _____

9. For years, the BIA was responsible for administering the feds' programs for American Indians.

   _____

10. Indians refer to people "on the res" when those people live on a reservation.

   _____

11. There aren't many HUD programs to provide reservation housing.

_____

12. The NIH has taken an interest in community health programs on the reservation since the agency was established.

_____

13. SIDS is one health concern among many the NIH studies.

_____

14. The MOS of many Navajos in the military is cryptographer.

_____

15. A cryptographer often works in a computer lab these days.

_____

16. They transmit coded messages for military organizations like NATO.

_____

17. Even laser transmission of messages can be intercepted.

_____

18. Not many spies can comprehend the Navajo language.

_____

19. However, cryptography isn't a very marketable skill for a vet.

_____

20. A sarge with a few years of experience with digital instrumentation will find his or her military background useful.

_____

21. I'm considering a career in med tech.

_____

22. My advisor met me at the dorm this morning.

_____

23. I had left her a phone message.

_____

24. She says econ and bio are required subjects.

_____

25. I imagine my chem courses would be useful, too.

_____

EXERCISE (18), SYLLABICATION

Some of the following word groups contain errors in word division or hyphenation. In the blank to the right, show by means of a slash where the word should be divided. If the word cannot be divided, write *ND* (no division) and then write out the whole word. If the word division is acceptable, copy the word as it is given. For each word in question, indicate each of its syllable points with a dot. Indicate any hyphens with a dash.

Example	workb-ook	work/book	must-ache	must-ache
	longwind-ed	long/wind·ed	raz-zle-dazzle	raz-zle-daz·zle

1. pyr-amid _____

2. tel-evision _____

3. Mas-ter's _____

4. ca-ble _____

5. sunn-y _____

6. can-tilever _____

7. pre-mium _____

8. jutt-ing _____

9. qual-ity _____

10. prohib-ited _____

11. pack-ed _____

12. ans-wering _____

13. cus-hion _____

14. cond-ition _____

15. hind-rance _____

16. non-support _____

17. in-flation _____

18. high-strung _____

19. malig-nant _____

20. barb-aric _____

21. pre-medical _____

22. pre-judice _____

23. court-
martial _____

24. ver-
y _____

25. post-
office _____

26. re-en-
actment _____

27. coll-
ective _____

28. e-
qual _____

29. pre-his-
toric _____

30. inacc-
essible _____

31. exh-
ibition _____

32. learn-
ed [adjective] _____

33. defi-
nite _____

34. re-
al _____

35. pre-
sent
[adjective] _____

36. int-
elligent _____

37. guil-
ty _____

38. undou-
btedly _____

39. pre-
sented [verb] _____

40. o-
pen _____

41. flatt-
er _____

42. gi-
ant _____

43. gyro-
stabilizer _____

44. aff-
inity _____

45. utopia-
nism _____

46. a-
cute _____

47. trimm-
ing _____

48. gho-
ul _____

49. ghos-
tly _____

50. merchan-
dise _____

51. e-
rupt _____

52. twe-
lve _____

53. re-en-
list _____

54. leth-
al _____

55. yearn-
ed _____

56. tourn-
ament _____

57. ca-
mel _____

58. barb-
ecue _____

59. eight-
een _____

60. le-
vel _____

MECHANICS REVIEW (15–18)

The following sentences contain errors involving numbers, abbreviations, and word division. Assume a general audience and rewrite the sentences, correcting the errors.

Example   The PO lists millions of inventions the feds have registered.

The Patent Office lists millions of inventions the federal authorities have registered.

1. The number of inventions listed there is well over 4 mill.

_____

2. The Patent Office first opened in seventeen ninety.

_____

3. A pat. gives its owner 17 years of exclusive rights to the invention.

_____

4. Many famous inventions are the results of mods to earlier inventions.

_____

5. Akiba Horowitz landed in New York in eighteen-nineteen.

_____

6. Horowitz, a Russ., quickly changed his name to Conrad Hubert.

_____

7. Horowitz opened a small restaurant, where he met Joshua Lionel Cowen.

_____

8. Cowen was the owner of the Lionel Train Co.

_____

9. Hubert closed his restaurant and became a salesman for Cowen's toys.

_____

10. Cowen had invented an artificial plant w/ flowers that lit up.

_____

11. He called this invention the elec. flowerpot.

_____

12. Cowen had no real int. in the future of the elec. flowerpot.

_____

13. He was glad to sell his lice-
nses for the invention to his sales rep, Hubert.

_____

14. Hubert 1st threw away the plant and the pot.

_____

15. He designed better batteries & bulbs.

_____

16. Then he sealed the 2 inside a long cylindrical tube.

_____

17. He obtained patent number seven hundred thousand four hundred ninety seven.

_____

18. He later received patent # seven hundred thousand six hundred fifty.

_____

19. He called his invention "a port. elec. light."

_____

20. We refer to his device today as a fla-
shlight.

_____

21. Hubert called his company the Ever Ready Co.

_____

22. He sold his business in nineteen fourteen.

_____

23. Within only 12 years, Hubert had made his fortune.

_____

24. At his death, his estate was worth $ eight million.

_____

25. Almost all his money was made w/his modification of the electric flowerpot.

_____

END PUNCTUATION   (19)

Three punctuation marks signal the end of a sentence: the period, the question mark, and the exclamation point. The **period** signals the end of an assertion or a mild command. It is also used at the end of an indirect question.

ASSERTION	She mailed the letter.
MILD COMMAND	Please mail the letter.
INDIRECT QUESTION	He asked if she had mailed the letter.

A period is also used for abbreviations—for example, *Jr., Ms., Mr., Mrs., Ph.D., C.P.A.* Omit the period in abbreviations that serve as names of organizations or government agencies: *NAACP, UNESCO, NCTE, NSF, AMA, USAF, IBM.*

The **question mark** signals the end of a direct question. It is also used to indicate doubt or uncertainty about the correctness of a statement. When used to express uncertainty, the question mark is placed in parentheses. A good substitute for (?) is simply to say *about.*

DIRECT QUESTION	Have you paid the bills?
EXPRESSIONS OF UNCERTAINTY	This house is 150 (?) years old.
	This house is about 150 years old.

A polite request phrased as a direct question is usually followed by a period rather than a question mark. Phrasing a request as a question rather than as a command is considered to be courteous and tactful, but the underlying intention of such a statement is not interrogative.

POLITE REQUEST   Will you please mail your payment as soon as possible.

A period rather than a question mark is used for an indirect question because such a statement implies a question but does not actually ask one. Although the idea expressed is interrogative, the actual phrasing is not.

DIRECT QUESTION   Had he turned off the water?

INDIRECT QUESTION   He wondered whether he had turned off the water.

The **exclamation point** signals the end of an emphatic or exclamatory statement. It is also used for emphatic commands and for interjections. Interjections are exclamatory words and phrases capable of standing alone: *Oh!, Ouch!, My goodness!,* and so forth.

EXCLAMATORY STATEMENT   Help! I'm drowning!

INTERJECTION WITH   Ouch! Stop pinching me!
EMPHATIC COMMAND

Be careful not to overuse exclamation points in your writing. Inexperienced writers tend to use exclamation points for indicating everything from mild excitement to full-scale disaster. Whereas exclamation points used sparingly can provide genuine emphasis, too many of them will make the tone of your writing seem hysterical. Furthermore, your reader may begin to distrust you; like the boy in the fable who falsely cried "Wolf!" too often, you will not be able to attract your reader's attention with an exclamation point if you have previously misused it.

Practice: Using End Punctuation   Supply the missing end punctuation.

[1]Who is the most successful entertainer in America [2]The answer, of course, depends on the way one defines success [3]What are the easiest aspects of success to measure [4]In the 1980s, one might argue that Lionel Richie is America's most successful entertainer [5]Richie has been nominated for thirty-three awards. [6]Isn't it a record that he has actually won five Grammys [7]Consider the fact that he has also won thirteen American Music Awards, a Golden Globe, and shelves full of People's Choice statues [8]One of his albums, *Can't Slow Down,* sold more than any other album produced by Motown Records [9]That album sold a phenomenal 15,000,000 copies [10]And that's only part of the story of Lionel Richie's appeal

Answers to the practice   [1]America? [2]success. [3]measure? [4]entertainer. [5]awards. [6]Grammys. [7]statues. [8]Records. [9]copies! *or* copies. [10]appeal! *or* appeal.

EXERCISE (19), END PUNCTUATION

Circle any errors involving the use of periods, question marks, or exclamation points in the following sentences; then write the correct forms in the blanks at the right. If the punctuation is correct, write *Correct* in the blank.

Example   She asked me if I knew how Lionel
            Richie got his start as a singer⟨?⟩   _____singer._____

1. Isn't it true that Richie didn't start out to be
    an entertainer.   _____

2. I don't know whether he really dreamed of
    being a singer or not?   _____

3. He was raised across the street from Tuskegee Institute!   _____

4. Tuskegee is the school founded by Booker T.
    Washington.   _____

5. I wonder if Washington's philosophy of hard work
    and self-improvement played a role in Richie's life?   _____

6. No one can really be sure if that is true?   _____

7. Lionel's father was a systems analyst.   _____

8. Wasn't his mother an elementary school principal.   _____

9. I do know that music was not Lionel's major interest.   _____

10. He even went to Tuskegee on a tennis scholarship!   _____

Punctuate each of the following sentences as indicated, changing the wording if necessary so the sentence will be appropriate to the end punctuation requested.

Example   Lionel joined the Commodores after a freshman talent show.
            (question) _Did Lionel join the Commodores after a freshman_
                        talent show?
            (exclamation) _Lionel joined the Commodores after a freshman_
                           talent show!

11. The Commodores wanted to become "the Black Beatles."

    (question) _____

    (exclamation) _____

12. Until then, Richie carried a saxophone case mainly to meet girls.

   (question) _____

   (exclamation) _____

13. What a surprising fact!

   (period) _____

   (question) _____

14. Wasn't their first tour with the Jackson Five?

   (exclamation) _____

   (period) _____

15. I question whether or not that was really their big break.

   (question) _____

   (exclamation) _____

Write sentences with end punctuation appropriate to the instructions below.

Example   (expression of uncertainty) __*Turn the page ?*_____

16. (indirect question) _____

17. (polite request phrased as a question) _____

18. (mild command) _____

19. (direct question) _____

20. (assertion) _____

21. (interjection with assertion) _____

22. (expression of uncertainty) _____

23. (emphatic command) _____

24. (indirect question) _____

25. (polite request phrased as a question) _____

THE COMMA: MAIN CLAUSES AND SUBORDINATE CLAUSES (20a–b)

The **comma** is the most frequently used (and misused) punctuation mark. It is an internal punctuation mark that indicates relationships between sentence elements. One of its principal functions is to signal relationships between clauses. (See also Sections 1d(1–3) and 7.)

1. A comma separates main clauses (independent clauses) joined by the coordinating conjunctions *and, but, or, nor, for, so,* and *yet.* The comma always precedes the coordinating conjunction.

> She was a good student, and she was also a good athlete.

When you use a comma with a coordinating conjunction, be sure that the conjunction introduces an independent clause and not just a compound sentence part. For example, no comma is necessary before the conjunction linking compound predicate nouns (see Section 1a).

INCORRECT	She was a good student, and also a good athlete.
CORRECT	She was a good student and also a good athlete.

If two main clauses are not joined by a coordinating conjunction, use a semicolon between them (see also Section 21).

> She was a good student; she was also a good athlete.

A semicolon may also be used before the coordinating conjunction when one or both of the main clauses are very long or are internally punctuated with commas.

> She was a good student, getting nearly all *A*'s in even the most difficult courses; and she was also a good athlete with many conference records to her credit.

2. A comma separates introductory words, phrases, or subordinate clauses from the main clause. Such introductory elements function as modifiers—either adverbial modifiers qualifying the verb or the whole main clause or adjectival modifiers qualifying the subject of the main clause. A comma following a modifying word, phrase, or clause signals the reader that the main clause is about to begin.

INTRODUCTORY PARTICIPLE	Depressed, George thought about all his unpaid bills.
INTRODUCTORY PREPOSITIONAL PHRASE	Without enough money for his tuition, he looked for a part-time job.
INTRODUCTORY SUBORDINATE CLAUSE	Because he could type well, he found work as a temporary secretary.

Be sure not to confuse modifying verbal phrases with verbals used as subjects. An introductory verbal modifier needs a comma; a verbal used as a subject does not.

INTRODUCTORY VERBAL MODIFIER	Having learned to type in high school, he now put his skill to use.
VERBAL AS SUBJECT	Having learned to type in high school was a blessing now that he needed to earn money for tuition.

3. The comma may be omitted after a very short introductory clause or phrase if there is no chance the reader will misunderstand your meaning. Remember that your use of a comma may be your reader's only clue to the exact meaning you intend. Note, for example, the following sentence: *Watching my sister Barbara was no fun.* The sentence might mean that Barbara is my sister. On the other hand, it might mean that Barbara was watching my sister.

CLEAR	Watching my sister, Barbara was no fun.
CONFUSING	After rolling the ball fell into the hole.
CLEAR	After rolling, the ball fell into the hole.
CONFUSING	In case of fire escape down the stairs instead of using the elevator.

CLEAR	In case of fire, escape down the stairs instead of using the elevator.
CLEAR	Before breakfast we went for a walk.
CLEAR	Next Tuesday my vacation begins.

The decision to use a comma after short introductory elements is sometimes a matter of emphasis. If, when you say a sentence aloud, you find yourself pausing for emphasis, a comma is probably desirable to ensure that the reader will distinguish the same emphasis.

CLEAR	Unfortunately my car needs new tires.
COMMA USED FOR EMPHASIS	Unfortunately, my car needs new tires.

EXERCISE (20a–b)-1, PUNCTUATION BETWEEN CLAUSES

Insert a caret (∧) to show where punctuation should be placed between main clauses or between an introductory element and the main clause in each of the following sentences. Then indicate whether the sentence requires a comma (,) or a semicolon (;) by writing the correct punctuation mark in the blank at the right. If the sentence requires no additional punctuation, write *NP* in the blank.

Example   In October 1945 the Montreal team
           announced that Jackie Robinson would
           play for them.   __1945,__

           A nationwide uproar began immediately.   __NP__

1. After a few difficult games Canadian fans began to support Robinson.

   ———— ————

2. Two Florida minor league teams cancelled their games
   with Montreal.

   ——————

3. Even though he faced taunting fans and segregated facilities Robinson turned down an offer to play in the
   Mexican League.

   ——————

4. If he had played in Mexico Robinson would not have
   been faced with the problems of discrimination.

   ——————

5. Despite opposition from other team owners Branch
   Rickey announced in January 1947 that Robinson would
   play for the Dodgers.

   ——————

6. Rickey moved spring training to Havana so the segregation laws of the South would not pose further problems.

   ——————

7. More than half of all major league players were Southerners and the most popular Dodger in 1947 was Dixie
   Walker of Alabama.

   ——————

8. Walker immediately asked to be traded when he learned Robinson was a Dodger.

9. There was a small players' rebellion on the team but the manager and coaches were firm in their support of Robinson.

10. Of course many players supported Robinson from the beginning Pee Wee Reese was one of Robinson's earliest friends on the team.

11. After about a month of practice and play Robinson had the support of most of his teammates.

12. Reese was sensitive to both Robinson and the Southerners on the team the shortstop from Kentucky was important in bringing the team together.

13. His teammates may have supported him but Robinson still faced enormous odds.

14. Baseball teams travelled by train in those days and hotels were often inhospitable to blacks.

15. Robinson had always been a fiery competitor in college and in the Army he had not concealed his outrage when he encountered racism.

16. As badly as Jackie might have wanted to reply to abusive fans he had made a pact with Rickey.

17. He agreed to ignore the abuse and show his talents on the field.

18. Jackie knew how important his mission was and black leaders had told him that it was important that he succeed.

19. During his first two seasons with the Dodgers, Jackie was very subdued.

20. He and Rickey knew that the cause of integration might be set back if Jackie had reacted to the abuse.

21. Hank Aaron says that Robinson made it possible for black children to dream of playing in the major leagues.

   _____

22. Jackie was the right person for the job he was articulate and educated.

   _____

23. By his third season with the Dodgers Robinson could speak his mind more openly.

   _____

24. Though his outbursts were mostly about baseball and were without racial overtones the public was shocked by the change in the quiet black player.

   _____

25. They were simply seeing and hearing the real Jackie Robinson for a change.

   _____

26. From 1949 until his retirement in 1956 Robinson was a controversial player because he was outspoken.

   _____

27. Robinson was aware of his roles as a black athlete and as a spokesman he fought for equal rights until his death in 1972.

   _____

28. Having "broken the color line" in baseball was Robinson's great achievement.

   _____

29. Concerned about the view black historians may take of his contribution many of Robinson's fellow athletes speak out in his behalf.

   _____

30. With financial help from major league teams the Jackie Robinson Foundation keeps his memory alive with books, exhibits, and educational materials.

   _____

EXERCISE (20a–b)-2, PUNCTUATION BETWEEN CLAUSES

Expand each of the core sentences in the following ways: first, by adding another main clause; second, by adding an introductory subordinate clause; third, by adding an introductory phrase. Use appropriate internal punctuation.

Example   I visit my dentist three times a year.

(main clause) _I visit my dentist three times a year, but never do I enjoy it._

(subordinate clause) _Because I enjoy talking to him, I visit my dentist three times a year._

(phrase) _In order to prevent problems, I visit my dentist three times a year._

1. The dog barked all night.

   (main clause) _____

   (subordinate clause) _____

   (phrase) _____

2. I cleaned the porch.

   (main clause) _____

   (subordinate clause) _____

   (phrase) _____

3. There was no mail for you.

   (main clause) _____

   (subordinate clause) _____

   (phrase) _____

4. Three catalogs arrived for me.

   (main clause) _____

   (subordinate clause) _____

   (phrase) _____

5. Hooking up a video recorder is simple.

   (main clause) _____

   (subordinate clause) _____

   (phrase) _____

6. Reading instructions requires patience.

(main clause) _____

(subordinate clause) _____

(phrase) _____

7. We went to a Braves game.

(main clause) _____

(subordinate clause) _____

(phrase) _____

8. It's too hot to attend day games.

(main clause) _____

(subordinate clause) _____

(phrase) _____

9. The traffic is too heavy.

(main clause) _____

(subordinate clause) _____

(phrase) _____

10. We bought our tickets in February.

(main clause) _____

(subordinate clause) _____

(phrase) _____

THE COMMA: NONRESTRICTIVE AND RESTRICTIVE SENTENCE ELEMENTS (20c–f)

Nonrestrictive elements are nonessential modifying words, phrases, or clauses that add useful but incidental information to a sentence. **Restrictive elements** are essential modifying words, phrases, or clauses that affect a sentence's basic meaning. Nonrestrictive sentence elements are set off with commas; restrictive elements are not.

We noted previously, in Section 20a–b, that commas can be crucial to the reader's understanding of the writer's meaning. In the case of nonrestrictive and restrictive elements, the presence or absence of commas is particularly important because the meaning can be quite different, depending upon their use. A simple example illustrates the difference:

NONRESTRICTIVE	Children, *who hate vegetables,* should take vitamins.
RESTRICTIVE	Children *who hate vegetables* should take vitamins.

In the first sentence, the subordinate clause *who hate vegetables* can be removed without changing the sentence's basic message: *All* children ought to take vitamins. The subordinate clause adds the incidental information that all children also dislike vegetables.

The second sentence says something very different. Its meaning is that the *only* children who ought to take vitamins are those who hate vegetables. In this sentence, the subordinate clause *restricts* the category, children, to those hating vegetables.

This is the crucial point: Readers have no way of knowing whether the writer intends the category to be all-inclusive (nonrestrictive) or limited (restrictive) unless the commas are used (or omitted) correctly. The words are identical in both sentences.

A reader can occasionally distinguish whether a sentence element is restrictive or nonrestrictive even though the writer has misused commas.

RESTRICTIVE
BUT INCORRECTLY
PUNCTUATED

A waiter, *who gives good service,* gets generous tips.

NONRESTRICTIVE
BUT INCORRECTLY
PUNCTUATED

Max *who gives good service* gets generous tips.

If the reader follows the signals provided by the faulty punctuation in the first sentence and interprets the basic message to be *a waiter gets generous tips,* he or she will recognize this as a false statement. Generally, waiters do not get generous tips unless they give good service. The subordinate clause is essential to the meaning because it *restricts* the category of waiters to those who give good service. The clause *should not* be set off with commas.

Conversely, the subject of the second sentence designates a particular waiter who gets generous tips. The proper noun *Max* restricts the category to one individual. The subordinate clause merely supplies additional but nonessential information. Consequently, the clause *should be* set off with commas.

CORRECT
(RESTRICTIVE)

A waiter *who gives good service* gets generous tips.

CORRECT
(NONRESTRICTIVE)

Max, *who gives good service,* gets generous tips.

As you can see, a reader may eventually be able to figure out the meaning in spite of faulty comma usage. Nevertheless, writers who fail to follow the punctuation conventions that signal whether a sentence element is restrictive or nonrestrictive run the risk of confusing their readers—or, at the very least, of annoying them and thus detracting from the contents of the message.

Now analyze the preceding sentence, containing the subordinate clause *who fail to follow . . . ,* and decide why that clause is restrictive (not set off by commas). If you determined that without the clause (i.e., *writers run the risk of confusing their readers*) we won't know *which* writers—and surely *not all* writers confuse their readers—then you are well on your way toward understanding the difference between nonrestrictive and restrictive elements.

Be sure to use *two* commas to set off a nonrestrictive element unless it begins or ends a sentence.

NOT   That restaurant, specializing in Cuban cooking is one of my favorites.

BUT   That restaurant, specializing in Cuban cooking, is one of my favorites.

OR   Specializing in Cuban cooking, that restaurant is one of my favorites.

Typical nonrestrictive sentence elements are clauses, prepositional, verbal, and absolute phrases, appositives, and elements that slightly interrupt the structure of a sentence. Of these, clauses, prepositional and verbal phrases, and appositives may also be restrictive.

NONRESTRICTIVE CLAUSE	Key West, *where my brother lives,* is semitropical.
RESTRICTIVE CLAUSE	The city *where my brother lives* is semitropical.
NONRESTRICTIVE PREPOSITIONAL PHRASE	His boat, *on its side,* needs repairs.
RESTRICTIVE PREPOSITIONAL PHRASE	The boat *with a hole* is sure to sink.
NONRESTRICTIVE VERBAL PHRASE	The tourists, *tired and sunburned,* crowded the dock.
RESTRICTIVE VERBAL PHRASE	A woman *wearing sunglasses* dipped her feet in the water.
NONRESTRICTIVE APPOSITIVE	The tour guide, *a perspiring matron,* herded her charges.
RESTRICTIVE APPOSITIVE	"The novelist Ernest Hemingway once lived in Key West," she said.

An **appositive,** shown in the last two examples, is a noun or group of words functioning as a noun substitute. An appositive renames another noun and usually follows immediately after the noun. Most appositives of more than a word or two are nonrestrictive. Restrictive appositives, like other restrictive sentence elements, limit, define, or designate the noun they follow in such a way that their absence would change the basic meaning of the sentence.

Absolute phrases are always nonrestrictive; they provide explanatory detail rather than essential information. An absolute phrase is a noun or pronoun followed by a present participle or past participle verb form. The phrase modifies the entire main clause rather than specific words in the clause. Because they are nonessential and therefore nonrestrictive, absolute phrases are always set off by commas.

Thousands of refugees came ashore at Key West in 1980, *Fidel Castro having allowed them to leave Cuba.*

Interrupting expressions—words, phrases, or clauses that slightly disrupt the flow of a sentence—are sometimes called **parenthetical elements.** These elements should be set off by commas because they are not integral to the grammatical structure of the sentence. Words of direct address, mild interjections, transitional words and expressions, phrases expressing contrast, and words such as *yes* and *no* are usually considered interrupting expressions.

Other sentence elements also fall into the category of interrupting expressions if they are inserted out of their normal grammatical order. When they disrupt a sentence's grammatical flow (see Section 1a), they require commas.

DIRECT ADDRESS	Please let us know, *Dad,* when you will arrive.
MILD INTERJECTION	*Well,* I had better get some sleep.
TRANSITIONAL WORDS	*Despite the storm, however,* the plane landed on time.
CONTRASTED ELEMENTS	Dogs, *unlike cats,* usually love to play in the water.
DISRUPTED SENTENCES	Promptness, *my mother always said,* is a virtue.
	The package, *battered and dented,* had been labeled "fragile."

One final category of sentence elements needs to be discussed: **clauses and phrases that follow the main clause.** In Section 20a–b, we examined punctuation for introductory subordinate clauses and phrases that precede the main clause. These usually require a comma to prevent misreading and to signal the start of the main clause. But what about a subordinate clause or lengthy phrase that follows the main clause? Here, again, you must decide whether the information provided by the clause or phrase is restrictive or nonrestrictive.

If the information is essential to the meaning of the main clause, then the sentence element is restrictive and does not need a comma. If the information is nonessential and does not restrict the main clause's meaning, then the sentence element is nonrestrictive and should be separated from the main clause by a comma. Such phrases and clauses usually explain, amplify, or offer a contrast to the main clause, but the main clause does not depend on them for its meaning. Consider the following examples:

RESTRICTIVE	We cannot leave on vacation *unless the airline strike ends.*
NONRESTRICTIVE	I should pick up our tickets, *before I get busy and forget to do it.*

In the first example, the subordinate clause presents a condition for leaving on vacation. The meaning of the main clause depends on the qualification presented in the dependent clause. In the second example, the subordinate adverbial clause adds a kind of afterthought—an explanation, but not a condition that is essential to the meaning of the main clause. Consequently, a comma is necessary in the second sentence, but not in the first.

Usually subordinate clauses and phrases that follow the main clause are so closely tied to its meaning that they are considered restrictive. Using a comma after the main clause is generally the exception rather than the norm.

A good guide to whether or not a clause, phrase, or other sentence element is restrictive is the pitch and pause of your voice when you read the sentence. If your voice dips and hesitates before and after reading an expression, the element is likely to be nonrestrictive and require commas. If you read the sentence fairly even-toned and even-paced, the element is probably restrictive and does not need commas.

Remember that your readers will pause where you insert commas. Readers depend on you to provide the appropriate signals for meaning and emphasis.

Practice: Punctuating Restrictive and Nonrestrictive Sentence Elements   Some of the following sentences use commas correctly; some do not. Examine the sentences and determine whether they are correct or incorrect as punctuated. The answers are listed at the end of this section.

[1]Lionel Richie's first hit record, "Machine Gun," appeared in 1974. [2]This first hit record, like his next five, was performed with the Commodores. [3]The group which earned four gold and three platinum albums stayed together, until 1980. [4]Richie angered the Commodores that year when "Lady," a song the Commodores had rejected for being "corny," was sold to Kenny Rogers. [5]Lionel's song became Rogers' biggest hit selling more than 15,000,000 copies. [6]"Endless Love" a duet with Diana Ross became the biggest single of Ross's career. [7]Richie, finally, left the Commodores in 1982. [8]His career which has continued to excel has made Lionel Richie one of the most successful black entertainers of the last two decades.

Answers to the Practice   [1]correct [2]correct [3]incorrect [4]correct [5]incorrect [6]incorrect [7]incorrect [8]incorrect

EXERCISE (20c–f)-1, THE COMMA: NONRESTRICTIVE AND RESTRICTIVE SENTENCE ELEMENTS

Although the following sentences are not punctuated to indicate the presence of nonrestrictive elements, many of them should be. In the blanks following the sentences, indicate whether the expressions set off or preceded by asterisks are restrictive or nonrestrictive.

Example   Most ethnic groups do not name themselves*
           which surprises most people.   nonrestrictive

1. The Pima Indians* who live in the Southwest* call themselves the Ootham.   _____

2. "Pima" is a name* that the tribe considers derogatory.*   _____

3. It is a name* that was given to them by another tribe.*   _____

4. It is quite rare to find an ethnic name* created by the group it describes.*   _____

5. Disagreement is almost inevitable* especially when a group consciously attempts to create a name for itself.   _____

6. Having* decided on a name* the group may find itself more unified.   _____

7. This is a result* that justifies the process.*   _____

8. There are many names* that have been used to name Americans of Mexican descent.*   _____

9. Hispano, Latino, Chicano, Hispanic-American, or Mexican-American are some* of these names.*   _____

10. All* of these names* have been found objectionable by one group or another.   _____

11. All Chicanos* for example* are Mexican-Americans.   _____

12. But not all Mexican-Americans consider* themselves* Chicanos.   _____

13. A single name would create an impression* of unity.*   _____

14. So the issue of a single name* one that has been agreed upon by all Mexican-Americans* is a very serious issue.   _____

15. Recently, the name "Hispanic" has been promoted* as a way to solve this problem.*   _____

16. This name currently seems acceptable to Americans*
    who are of Mexican descent.*   _____

17. Many Chicanos resent the term "Mexican-American"*
    which they think was forced on them by Anglo-Saxons.*   _____

18. Many Hispanics resent the term "Chicano"* a word they
    feel was created by militants demanding political rights.*   _____

19. "Chicano" is a word* that is used by younger Hispanics.*   _____

20. "Latino"* a more recent creation* is beginning to be-
    come popular.   _____

Expand each of the following core sentences with nonrestrictive and restrictive
clauses or phrases, using commas correctly.

Example   All employees are urged to make suggestions.
                      All employees, who are our best critics, are
           (nonrestrictive) _urged to make suggestions._____
                      All employees who work in the shipping area
           (restrictive) are urged to make suggestions._____

21. The suggestions poured in.

    (nonrestrictive) _____

    (restrictive) _____

22. The solution was found.

    (nonrestrictive) _____

    (restrictive) _____

23. The insurance business is good nowadays.

    (nonrestrictive) _____

    (restrictive) _____

24. An unpopular decision was made by the manager.

    (nonrestrictive) _____

    (restrictive) _____

25. I've just gone on a diet.

    (nonrestrictive) _____

    (restrictive) _____

EXERCISE (20c–f)-2, THE COMMA: NONRESTRICTIVE AND RESTRICTIVE SENTENCE ELEMENTS

In the following sentences, insert commas when they are needed for nonrestrictive elements or interrupting expressions. If a sentence contains a restrictive element and needs no additional punctuation, write *NP* at the end of the sentence.

Example   For years after the first colonists landed in America, indentured servants arrived by the thousands.

1. Surprisingly many early colonists were indentured servants.

2. Germany for example was a country that sent many peasants to America.

3. German peasants who had heard stories of the freedom in America were willing to "enslave" themselves for passage.

4. Many English peasants however also found the system attractive.

5. Having no money to pay for passage to the colonies a peasant found the indenture system often the only choice.

6. Indentured servants who sold their labor to a wealthier colonist had the price of their passage to America paid by their new "owner."

7. Ship captains as a matter of fact relied on indentured servants as a major source of income.

8. Many captains as part of their contract with ship owners were allowed to provide passage for a number of servants.

9. Upon arrival in the colonies the captain offered these servants for sale to the highest bidder.

10. In Georgia for example the period of service lasted from four to fourteen years.

11. The governing body of Georgia the Trustees of the Georgia Colony gave land to an indentured servant who had served the full period.

12. The former master of the servant who was now technically fully freed was required to give tools.

13. There was always a supply of people who were willing to pay their passage in such a way.

14. Wealthier colonists who found indentured servants a source of very cheap labor at first were enthusiastic too.

15. However the system was a failure.

16. Anxious to get started on their own indentured servants were often discontented.

17. There were several minor uprisings all of which frightened colonists who kept indentured servants.

18. Eventually the system of indentureship faded away.

19. Tom Carter one of President Jimmy Carter's ancestors sold himself as a servant to get to Virginia in 1635.

20. In 1678 one hundred Irish families all of whom were fleeing Oliver Cromwell's armies sold themselves as servants for passage to the Carolinas.

As you have seen from the text and exercises in Section 20c–f, nonrestrictive and restrictive sentence elements are modifiers used to expand core sentences with additional information. At each number below, write a core sentence. Then expand that core sentence by adding modifying words—subordinate clauses, phrases, and interrupting elements. Make sure that at least two of your expanded sentences contain nonrestrictive modifying elements and at least two contain restrictive modifying elements. Set off nonrestrictive or interrupting elements appropriately with commas. Be ready to explain why you consider the modifying elements you have added to be restrictive or nonrestrictive.

Example (core sentence) _Limburger cheese smells terrible._

If you ask me, limburger cheese, a very soft white cheese, smells terrible.

21. (core sentence) _____

_____

22. (core sentence) _____

_____

23. (core sentence) _____

_____

24. (core sentence) _____

_____

25. (core sentence) _____

_____

THE COMMA:

ITEMS IN A SERIES (20g–i)

Commas are used to separate **three or more coordinate words, phrases, or clauses in a series.** Items in a series are coordinate if they are of approximately equal grammatical rank or importance.

> Artesians are an ethnic group of *unknown origin, undetermined ancestry, and mysterious habits.* [Three nouns modified by adjectives]

> No one knows for sure *who they are, where they came from, or how they got here.* [Three dependent clauses]

You have probably seen sentences in newspapers and magazines that omit the comma before the final element in a series: *The candidate offered a platform that Democrats, Republicans and Independents could support.* Although omitting the final comma is not incorrect, doing so can lead to confusion for the reader. Consider the following sentence, for example:

> It is known that Artesians like bowling, beer, pickles and ice cream with fudge sauce.

A reader may be unsure as to whether Artesians like pickles *and* also like ice cream with fudge sauce or whether they like a weird concoction of pickles and ice cream, both ingredients covered with fudge sauce. To prevent such confusion, establish the habit of always using a comma to signal the final element in a series.

> It is known that Artesians like bowling, beer, pickles, and ice cream with fudge sauce.

Commas are used to separate coordinate adjectives in a series, but they are **not used between adjectives that are not coordinate.** Adjectives are coordinate if each one separately modifies the noun—that is, (1) if *and* can be placed between each of the adjectives without distorting the meaning; and (2) if the order of the adjectives can be changed without distorting the meaning.

> Artesians are said to be quiet, peaceful, law-abiding folks. (Artesians are said to be quiet and peaceful and law-abiding folks. Artesians are said to be peaceful, law-abiding, quiet folks.)

Adjectives in a series are not always coordinate; sometimes they are **cumulative,** as the following sentence shows:

> Some people claim Artesians dislike congested suburban shopping centers.

Clearly, the adjectives cannot be moved around without reducing the sentence to nonsense. *Shopping* modifies the noun *center,* but we ordinarily use the two words together in such a way that they really constitute a single concept and function together as a compound noun—like *baseball* or *timekeeper. Suburban,* in fact, modifies the whole concept formed by the two words taken together. Of the three adjectives, *congested* is the most independent and loosely attached. We could say *congested and suburban shopping centers* without destroying the sentence's meaning.

Coordinate adjectives are rather like the spokes of a wheel, each one focused on the noun at the hub, each one separated from the others by a spacing comma. Cumulative adjectives, adjectives in series that are not coordinate, are more like funnels tightly stacked one inside the other, each one often modifying a word or words ahead of it and the last one modifying the noun itself.

The same principles governing punctuation for adjectives in a series apply when only two modifiers precede the word being modified. If the two modifiers are coordinate but not joined by a conjunction, use a comma between them. If they are cumulative rather than coordinate, do not use a comma.

> Apparently Artesians are shy, retiring types, but they are rumored to be fantastic poker players.

Commas are also used to set off **items in dates** following the series order month, day, and year. Commas are not used if just the month and year are given or if the series order is day, month, and year.

> An Artesian was seen publicly on July 4, 1986, but at no time since then.

> Before May 1903 only four Artesian sightings were recorded, two of them occurring on 21 June 1902 at a local pub.

Commas are used to set off **items in addresses and geographical names.** A comma should be placed after the last item if the geographical name or address appears within a sentence. No comma is used before a zip code.

ADDRESS
The pub was located at 212 Happy Hollow Road, Short Order, Oregon, and still stands at that address today.

GEOGRAPHICAL NAME
Other Artesians have been seen in Moffat, Scotland, and Cromwell, New Zealand, during the last decade.

Commas are also used to set off **titles that follow names.** In addition, commas are used in **numbers** to indicate thousands, but not in social security numbers, telephone numbers, zip codes, and so forth.

According to Professor George Arcane, Ph.D., who is an authority on the subject, Artesians have a terrific sense of humor. He claims to have interviewed 11,405½ of them and says they all share the same telephone: Olympia 555-7426.

EXERCISE (20g–i), THE COMMA: ITEMS IN A SERIES

After each of the following sentences, write *C* if the sentence is punctuated correctly and *NC* if it is punctuated incorrectly.

Example   Martin Steinway and Wurlitzer are three German names famous for making musical instruments. NC

1. Christian Frederick Martin's company makes guitars banjos, and mandolins.

2. It is the nation's oldest and finest guitar company.

3. Martin emigrated to America, settled in New York City and finally moved to Nazareth Pennsylvania.

4. Martin guitars are popular with folk artists, country artists, and even rock artists.

5. Bob Dylan, Judy Collins, and Willie Nelson, all own Martin guitars.

6. H. E. Steinway founded what became the single most famous piano factory in the world.

7. He built his first piano as a hobby then won a prize for his work and finally decided to open a factory in New York in 1854.

8. H. E. Steinway T. E. Steinway and Henry Z. Steinway are just three of the four generations of Steinway piano builders.

9. Concert halls, individual artists and even the armed forces are some of the Steinway Company's best customers.

10. During World War II, the Steinways supplied over 3,000 upright, olive-drab "GI pianos."

11. Rudolph Wurlitzer emigrated to America, saved his money and became a dealer in fine quality handcrafted musical instruments.

12. He saved his money earned at his job as a porter in a dry goods store, then as a bank clerk, and finally as a salesman.

13. His thrift his strategy of selling directly to customers and his hard work made Wurlitzer's business a great success.

14. Wurlitzer manufactured his own Wurlitzer piano for the first time in 1880.

15. The first coin-operated music box was sold in 1896, the first 10-tune jukebox in 1934, the first electronic organ in 1947.

Insert commas at all points where they are required in the following sentences. (Use an ink or lead color other than black.) Write *NC* at the end of the sentence if it needs no commas.

Example   John Philip Sousa was one of the Marine Corps' most famous band-leaders. **NC**

16. He led the Marine Band wrote songs for them and designed new instruments for the band members.

17. His father emigrated from Portugal to the United States.

18. John Philip threatened to run away join the circus and become a circus musician.

19. His father enlisted John Philip as a boy musician with the Marine Band.

20. Sousa wrote over 100 marches for the Marines, including *Semper Fidelis* "The Washington Post March" and "Stars and Stripes Forever."

21. The Sousaphone was patterned after Sousa's suggestions then built for his Marine musicians and finally named for Sousa.

22. The Sousaphone is simply a modified tuba.

23. Sousa also served as bandmaster for the Navy wrote an operetta in 1896 and wrote the theme song for Harry Houdini.

24. Arthur Fiedler was the son of Austrian-Jewish immigrant violinists.

25. Radio television and concert audiences knew him as the conductor of the Boston Pops Orchestra.

26. In 1911 he was accepted into the Berlin Royal Academy in 1926 he conducted his first performance with the Pops Orchestra and in 1930 he became the orchestra's permanent conductor.

27. Fiedler was one of America's most popular best-known beloved conductors of his time.

28. Leopold Stokowski was born in London, England in 1882 came to the United States in 1905 and became a citizen in 1915.

29. In his seventy-year career Stokowski conducted the Philadelphia the NBC and the America Symphony Orchestra.

30. Stokowski brought great classical music to the masses when he conducted the sound track for Disney's *Fantasia*.

COMMA REVIEW (20)

Insert commas where they are required in the following sentences. (Use a pen or pencil that writes in a color other than black). Write *NC* after any sentence that requires no commas.

Example   As a matter of fact, many of America's artists, sculptors, and designers are proof of its multiethnic origins.

1.   Born in Bottrop Germany Josef Albers came to the United States in 1933.

2.   O. H. Ammann an American of Swiss origin designed the Verrazano-Narrows Bridge.

3.   It is the longest single-span suspension bridge in the world.

4.   Amman also designed the George Washington Bridge and the Lincoln Tunnel both of which allow traffic across the barrier of the Hudson River.

5.   John Borglum began carving the Mount Rushmore memorial but it was eventually finished by his son Lincoln.

6.   Mount Rushmore's carvings include the heads of Washington Lincoln Jefferson and Theodore Roosevelt.

7.   The son of Danish immigrants to Idaho Borglum did not live to see his masterpiece finished.

8.   Willem de Kooning was born in the Netherlands and came to America not as an immigrant but as an illegal alien.

9.   He settled in Hoboken New Jersey and later moved to New York.

10. For 35 years he never left the United States fearing that he would not be readmitted.

11. He finally flew to Canada obtained a visa and returned to apply for citizenship.

12. Only two years later de Kooning was awarded the Medal of Freedom.

13. President Johnson presented the medal our nation's highest civilian award to de Kooning.

14. Gustav Lindenthal designed the Manhattan Bridge and the Queensboro Bridge major connectors between Manhattan and Long Island.

15. He also designed the Hell Gate Bridge one of the world's largest steel-arch bridges.

16. Peter Max with his bold graphic designs became a famous artist in the 1960s.

17. Max was born in Berlin and raised in Shanghai.

18. His surrealistic psychedelic patterns were influenced by Eastern religion.

19. When the Nazis came to power in 1933 Walter Gropius fled to England.

20. He eventually came to America where his ideas about design were welcomed.

21. Gropius had founded the Bauhaus school whose members believed that "form should follow function."

22. He made great advances in industrial design city planning and the design of everyday household objects.

23. His aim was to design objects that would be functional as well as attractive.

24. Born in China in a well-to-do family I. M. Pei studied at MIT and Harvard.

25. He studied under Gropius the founder of Bauhaus design.

26. In 1954 Pei became a naturalized citizen.

27. Pei designed the Syracuse Museum terminals at JFK Airport and the John Hancock Building.

28. When he designed the National Gallery's East Wing he used a unique standard of judgment.

29. The gallery was designed to allow visitors to see the exhibits in less than forty-five minutes.

30. Pei believes that in forty-five minutes one doesn't get bored one's feet don't hurt and one comes away with a sense of accomplishment.

THE SEMICOLON   (21)

A **semicolon** is used to separate main clauses not joined by a coordinating conjunction. (See also Sections 7 and 20a–b.)

> One thinks of cathedrals as creations of medieval Europe; one does not associate them with twentieth-century New York City.

Like a period, a semicolon marks the end of a complete, grammatically independent statement. Although it can be substituted for a period, a semicolon is most effectively used between two independent clauses that are closely related in thought. Whereas a period is a "full stop," marking a complete break between sentences, the semicolon separates and stops but does not fully break the flow of thought between grammatically independent statements.

> Work on Manhattan's Cathedral Church of St. John the Divine stopped in 1941; construction began again in 1979.

This close relationship of thoughts is underscored by another of the semicolon's uses: to separate main clauses joined by a conjunctive adverb. Conjunctive adverbs, words such as *however, moreover, therefore,* and *consequently,* carry a thought from one main clause to the next. (See Section 1d(1–3) for additional discussion of conjunctive adverbs and a more extensive list of them.)

> Much of the cathedral had been completed by 1941; *however,* the church's two towers had not been built.

Conjunctive adverbs are easy to distinguish from coordinating and subordinating conjunctions if you remember that, unlike the other connectives, they can be moved from the beginning of their main clauses without destroying the sense.

> Work was suspended because of the Japanese attack on Pearl Harbor; *consequently,* the church stood without towers for twenty years.

> Work was suspended because of the Japanese attack on Pearl Harbor; the church stood, *consequently,* without towers for twenty years.

Coordinating and subordinating conjunctions cannot be moved around in this way. *Work was suspended, and the church stood without towers* makes sense, but *Work was suspended, the church and stood without towers* does not.

Note that when a conjunctive adverb comes within the second main clause instead of at the beginning, the clauses still must be separated by a semicolon and the conjunctive adverb set off by a pair of commas.

A semicolon is also used to separate main clauses joined by a coordinating conjunction if the clauses are exceptionally long or contain internal commas. This uses of the semicolon helps the reader to see clearly where one main clause stops and another starts. When you compare the following sentences, you will appreciate a reader's relief at finding a semicolon among the welter of commas:

> Building a cathedral is like putting together an enormous, multiton, three-dimensional jigsaw puzzle, and it requires not an afternoon, but decades, even centuries, to finish.

> Building a cathedral is like putting together an enormous, multiton, three-imensional jigsaw puzzle; and it requires not an afternoon, but decades, even centuries, to finish.

Similarly, semicolons are used in place of commas to separate items in a series if the items themselves contain internal commas.

> At the Cathedral of St. John the Divine, the stonecutters have included Poni Baptiste, a sculptor from Harlem; James Jamieson, an ex-butcher from the Bronx; and D'Ellis Kincanon, who is part Chickasaw Indian.

Practice: Using Semicolons   In the following passage, underline those punctuation marks—either commas or periods—that you think could be replaced by semicolons. The answers are listed at the end of this section.

> [1]Fannie M. Farmer was forced to leave high school at the age of sixteen. [2]A paralytic stroke made sitting in class impossible. [3]She developed an interest in cooking during her struggle to regain her health. [4]Eventually, she established her own school of cookery. [5]Her *Boston Cooking School Cookbook* was first published in 1896. [6]It sold over four million copies. [7]It was this cookbook and her column in *Woman's Home Companion* that revolutionized home cooking in America. [8]Fannie Farmer took the "guesswork" out of American recipes.

Answers to the Practice   [3-4]health; eventually   [5-6]1896; it

EXERCISE (21), THE SEMICOLON

Insert semicolons where they are needed in the following sentences. (Use a pen or pencil that writes in a color other than black.)

Example   Fannie Farmer was a Boston cooking instructor of English descent; she popularized the use of level measurements in the kitchen.

1. Before Farmer's cookbook, no one knew exactly how big a "pinch" or "dash" should be thus a recipe might easily go wrong.

2. Spoons were even of varying size a "spoonful" could vary depending on the spoon used.

3. Farmer's cookbook provided clear instructions more importantly it used exact measurements.

4. She gave recipes that could be duplicated all over the country an inexperienced cook could prepare perfect Hollandaise the first time.

5. All ingredients were carefully measured amounts down to one-eighth of a teaspoon were included in Farmer's recipes.

6. Farmer continued to manage her cooking school even after a second stroke confined her to a wheelchair, she taught a class ten days before her death in 1915.

7. Mary Harris Jones was born in Cork, Ireland she emigrated to America at the age of ten.

8. She lost her family to a yellow fever epidemic in Memphis four years later her business was destroyed by the Chicago Fire.

9. The fire was a turning point in her life for the next fifty years she fought for labor reforms.

10. She attended only a few meetings of the Knights of Labor obviously she was ready to hear their message.

Combine or repunctuate the sentences below, substituting semicolons for periods and commas where appropriate and changing capitalization if necessary.

Example   Mother Jones was jailed three times for organizing strikes, and she was once sentenced to twenty years in prison.

Mother Jones was jailed three times for organizing strikes; she was once sentenced to twenty years in prison.

11. Mother Jones did not look like a labor leader. She was, in fact, described as "a little old woman in a black bonnet."

_____

_____

12. She had a very high falsetto voice, and she had curly white hair.

_____

_____

13. Some of her tactics were unheard of for a woman. She always said, "No matter what your fight, don't be ladylike."

_____

_____

14. She followed her own advice for fifty years. Once, she even armed workers' wives with brooms and mops.

_____

_____

15. Railroad workers and miners were two of her causes, but she also spent time and energy fighting child labor and unsafe working conditions.

_____

_____

16. She was a real revolutionary about some things, yet she opposed prohibition and women's suffrage.

_____

_____

17. She died at the age of one hundred and she was still making public appearances when she was ninety-nine.

_____

_____

18. Another speaker once introduced Mother Jones as a "great humanitarian." She denied his remarks, saying, "No, I'm a hell raiser."

_____

_____   _____

19. Henrietta Szold was nicknamed "the Jewish Florence Nightingale" for her work with the poor in Palestine. She is also called "Mother of Hadassah."

_____

_____

20. Henrietta was born in Baltimore. She was the eldest daughter of a Hungarian rabbi.

_____

_____

21. She went to Palestine to recover from a failed love affair. It was there she took up the Zionist cause.

_____

_____

22. Disease and poverty were rampant in the Holy Land in 1910. Szold was determined to eliminate these problems.

_____

_____

23. She returned to Baltimore in 1912, and it was there that she founded Hadassah, the Women's Zionist Organization of America.

_____

_____

24. She and her colleagues worked quickly, because the first medical dispatch unit arrived in Jerusalem in 1913.

_____

_____

25. Today, Hadassah has over 350,000 members raising funds for medical and education centers in Israel. It is the world's largest Zionist group.

_____

_____

THE COLON   (22)

THE DASH

AND PARENTHESES   (23)

The **colon** has some characteristics similar to the semicolon and some similar to the dash. In fact, from time to time you may be unsure about whether to use a colon or one of the other two punctuation marks. In this section, we examine the distinctions that will help you determine the appropriate punctuation to use.

Like a semicolon, a colon can be used between main clauses that lack a coordinating conjunction. However, whereas the semicolon indicates a stop, the colon indicates an addition or expectation. The colon separates main clauses, the second of which explains, illustrates, or amplifies the first.

> Stonecutting is not something you can learn in a day: it requires a four-year apprenticeship.

A colon can also be used to set off a long final appositive (words that rename a nearby noun or noun substitute) or to set off a long summary. A dash is used to set off a short final appositive or short summary.

LONG APPOSITIVE USING COLON	Medieval cathedrals were built by apprentices: young workers learning their trade under a master craftsman.
SHORT APPOSITIVE USING DASH	Medieval masters paid their apprentices not with money but with subsistence—food and lodging.
LONG SUMMARY USING COLON	The apprentices working on the Cathedral of St. John the Divine today are an unusual bunch: They have come from New York's ghetto to learn a medieval European craft.

SHORT SUMMARY USING DASH	They receive not only wages but also a place in history for their work—a kind of immortality.

A colon can be used to introduce examples, a series, or a list. When it introduces a list, the colon may be preceded by the phrases *as follows* or *the following,* or these phrases may be only implied.

COLON PRECEDED BY *THE FOLLOWING*	Some of the world's great cathedrals are in the following cities: Chartres, Amiens, Canterbury, Cologne, Barcelona, and Milan.
COLON USED WHERE *AS FOLLOWS* IS IMPLIED	Two architectural styles dominate European cathedrals: the Romanesque and the Gothic.

Do not use a colon after the linking verb *are* or after the participle *including.*

Several features distinguish Gothic cathedrals, including pointed arches, ribbed vaults, and buttresses.

A colon is used to introduce a formal quotation. Also, established convention requires a colon to separate items in biblical citations, titles with subtitles, and divisions of time.

FORMAL QUOTATION	In 1170 four knights murdered Archbishop Thomas à Becket in Canterbury Cathedral, acting upon the words of King Henry II: "Will no one rid me of this priest?"
BIBLICAL CITATION	Ecclesiastes 3:1–8
TITLE WITH SUBTITLE	*Poets and Pilgrims: Chaucer's Canterbury Tales*
DIVISION OF TIME	11:55 P.M.

The **dash** is best used for emphasis and clarity to indicate shifts in sentence structure or thought or to set off parenthetical elements that might be confusing if punctuated with commas.

SHIFT IN SENTENCE STRUCTURE	A cathedral in New York City—its presence seems almost an anachronism—sets a bit of the Old World down in the New World.
SHIFT IN THOUGHT	The stonecutters at St. John the Divine—the best go to Bath, England, for special training—work from scale drawings of the structure.
EMPHASIS ON PARENTHETICAL ELEMENT	James Robert Bambridge—a master builder from England—is directing the construction of the cathedral's gallery and two towers.

INTRODUCTORY LIST OR SUMMARY	Measuring, marking, and chiseling—these are the steps in "tapping stone."
INTERRUPTION OR HESITATION IN SPEECH	"The feeling I get from working here is like—like soaring. It makes me want to—"
	"To sing," says another stonecutter, finishing the sentence for his friend.

The dash is also used for clarity to set off internally punctuated appositives. Remember that a semicolon can be used between items in a series containing internal commas (see Section 21). Using dashes to set off an appositive made up of an internally punctuated series serves a similar clarifying purpose.

A cathedral's architectural elements, gables, turrets, pinnacles, and spires, reach heavenward, designed as a celebration of glory to God.

A cathedral's architectural elements—gables, turrets, pinnacles, and spires—reach heavenward, designed as a celebration of glory to God.

The dashes quickly signal to the reader that the words following *elements* are a series of appositives and that *elements* is not part of the series.

When typing a dash, use two hyphens with no space beside or between them.

Parentheses are used to set off nonrestrictive parenthetical information, explanation, or comment that is incidental to the main thought of a sentence. Parentheses used instead of dashes downplay the importance of the information, whereas dashes emphasize it. Parentheses are also used to enclose numerals or letters that label items listed within a sentence.

PARENTHETICAL INFORMATION	The Cathedral Church of St. John the Divine will take a great deal of money ($21 million) and thirty years to finish.
NUMBERED OR LETTERED ITEMS	Other modern cathedrals built according to medieval architectural styles are (1) St. Patrick's Cathedral in New York City; (2) the National Cathedral in Washington, D.C.; and (3) the Anglican Cathedral in Liverpool, England.

EXERCISE (22–23), THE COLON, THE DASH, AND PARENTHESES

Insert carets at the points in the following sentences where dashes or colons are required. Then write the dashes or colons above the line.

Example   The kindergarten˄literally, a garden for children˄was the idea of a German educator.

1. Two women Martha Meyer and Susan Blow popularized the kindergarten.

2. Its founder Friedrich Froebel was by many standards at least a failure.

3. Froebel was considered a fool for romping he was in his seventies at the time with children in the fields.

4. He was disgraced the Prussian government had banned kindergartens in his final years of life.

5. His experience told him that much educational opportunity was lost if a child did not begin attending school until the age of six the custom in almost all countries.

6. He devised songs, games and activities all designed to teach basic concepts to four-year-olds.

7. Froebel believed that knowledge must come from within that parents and teachers are merely guides.

8. One of his students who spread the idea of the kindergarten was Margaretha Meyer, a German-Jewish refugee she later married the great German-American statesman, Carl Schurz.

9. Meyer established the first kindergarten in the United States but it is not she who is called the mother of the kindergarten.

10. That honor falls to Susan Blow a Missouri woman of English ancestry who helped make kindergartens available in the U.S.

11. Blow focused her efforts on making kindergartens part of public education making this revolutionary schooling available to millions of children.

12. Susan Blow learned of Froebel's work she was interested in reform while traveling through Germany in 1870.

13. She begged the superintendent of schools she began before she was back home in St. Louis to introduce a kindergarten in the school system there.

14. Because of her efforts, the first public kindergarten at the DesPeres School in St. Louis was established in 1873.

15. Blow later spread the concept she established a training school for kindergarten teachers throughout America.

16. Not many Americans remember the name of the woman who organized the Sabbath School movement in America Joanna Bethune.

17. Joanna who was born in Scotland was merely following in the footsteps of another reformer her mother.

18. Both were involved in educating immigrant children on the sabbath many of these children worked the rest of the week.

19. Joanna's mother began a Sunday School in New York in 1792 but it was unsuccessful the movement languished.

20. Joanna organized the Female Sabbath School Union the name "Sunday School" had already come to mean religious training in New York in 1816.

Insert carets at the points in the following sentences where dashes, colons, or parentheses are required. Then write the dashes, colons, or parentheses above the line.

Example   Clarissa Barton (1821–1912) was born on Christmas day.

21. Clarissa better known to the world as Clara earned the name Angel of the Battlefield for her work in the Civil War.

22. She helped care for the wounded and brought them food meat pies, mostly.

23. She was in Europe she was recovering from a nervous breakdown in 1869 when she first heard about the International Red Cross.

24. She began lobbying American legislators the United States had not signed the Red Cross treaty in 1864 to ratify the Geneva Convention.

25. Barton organized the American Association of the Red Cross better known simply as Red Cross in 1881.

26. Under her leadership she served as its president until 1904 she amended the Red Cross purpose to include peacetime relief for victims of natural disasters.

27. Edward Barton Clara's first ancestor in America had come to Salem, Massachusetts, from England.

28. But in 1692, the family's life there was disrupted by one of America's oddest historical events the Salem witch trials.

29. One of the witches hanged there was a distant relative the aunt of Edward's grandson's wife, to be precise.

30. That was enough, though, to convince the Barton family to settle in Oxford, Massachusetts where Clara was born on that Christmas Day in 1821.

SUPERFLUOUS INTERNAL PUNCTUATION (24)

If you have not provided enough internal punctuation to guide your readers, they may have to go over your sentences several times to understand the meaning. But using too many internal punctuation marks can be just as confusing. If punctuation is inserted where it is not necessary, or if it separates words that belong together, readers will have to struggle to untangle your message. Punctuation should aid meaning, not detract from it. The following guidelines discuss some common instances of superfluous (unnecessary) internal punctuation:

1. Do not separate a single or final adjective from a noun.

INCORRECT   The magnificent, unchanging, ceaseless, restless, surge of the sea.

CORRECT   The magnificent, unchanging, ceaseless, restless surge of the sea.

2. Do not separate a subject from a verb unless there are intervening words that require punctuation.

INCORRECT   My car, is at the service station.

CORRECT   My car is at the service station.

              My car, which is at the service station, requires repair.

3. Do not separate a verb from a complement or an object unless there are intervening words that require punctuation.

INCORRECT   My car is, a beautiful automobile.

CORRECT   My car is a beautiful automobile.

              My car is, unlike many cars of its type, a beautiful automobile.

4. Do not separate two words or phrases that are joined by a coordinating conjunction. A comma is used to separate independent clauses joined by a coordinating conjunction; however, if constructions other than independent clauses are involved, a comma does not precede the coordinating conjunction.

INCORRECT	She was captain of the swim team, and president of the class.
CORRECT	She was captain of the swim team and president of the class.

5. It is not necessary to separate an introductory word, brief phrase, or short clause unless such a separation is necessary for clarity or emphasis.

CORRECT	In my opinion, he will not win.
OR	In my opinion he will not win.
CORRECT	In brief, bathing suits can help or hinder competitive swimmers. [The comma is necessary after *In brief* to prevent a momentary misreading.]

6. Do not separate a restrictive modifier from the main part of a sentence. (See Section 20 c–f).

INCORRECT	All men, who want to volunteer, report to the adjutant.
CORRECT	All men who want to volunteer report to the adjutant.

7. Do not separate indirect quotations, or single words or short phrases in quotation marks, from the rest of the sentence.

INCORRECT	She said, she could go no further.
CORRECT	She said she could go no further.
INCORRECT	He was voted, "most popular teacher" by the senior class.
CORRECT	He was voted "most popular teacher" by the senior class.

8. Do not separate a preposition from its object with a comma.

INCORRECT	I went to, the grocery store, the dry cleaners, and the shoe repair shop.
CORRECT	I went to the grocery store, the dry cleaners, and the shoe repair shop.

9. Do not use a semicolon to separate a main clause from a subordinate clause, a phrase from a clause, or other parts of unequal grammatical rank.

INCORRECT	I rode my bicycle; although it was raining.
CORRECT	I rode my bicycle although it was raining.

INCORRECT	My glasses got raindrops on them; making it very hard to see clearly.
CORRECT	My glasses got raindrops on them, making it very hard to see clearly.
	My glasses got raindrops on them; I found it very hard to see clearly. [Equal rank: two main clauses]

10. Do not use a semicolon before a direct quotation or before a list.

INCORRECT	She asked; "What's for dinner?"
CORRECT	She asked, "What's for dinner?"
INCORRECT	The back yard was full of junk; an old washing machine, a pile of inner tubes, and four overflowing garbage cans.
CORRECT	The back yard was full of junk: an old washing machine, a pile of inner tubes, and four overflowing garbage cans.

11. Do not use a colon between a verb and its object or complement or between a preposition and its object—even if the objects or complements are in series (see also Section 22–23).

INCORRECT	The back yard also contained: three dog houses, a beat-up car, and a lot of rats.
CORRECT	The back yard also contained three dog houses, a beat-up car, and a lot of rats.
INCORRECT	Rats are: unsightly, unclean, and unhealthy.
CORRECT	Rats are unsightly, unclean, and unhealthy.
INCORRECT	The Health Department ordered the owners to: clean up the trash and spray for: rodents, mosquitoes, and roaches.
CORRECT	The Health Department ordered the owners to clean up the trash and spray for rodents, mosquitoes, and roaches.

EXERCISE (24), SUPERFLUOUS INTERNAL PUNCTUATION

Write out each of the following sentences, correcting any superfluous internal punctuation. If the sentence is correctly punctuated, write *Correct* in the blank.

Example   William Procter, was an English candlemaker who arrived in the United States in 1832.

<u>William Procter was an English candlemaker who arrived in the United States in 1832.</u>

1. James Gamble, a Scots-Irish soapmaker, arrived, in this country, in 1819.

_____

_____

2. Procter and Gamble, each, invested almost $3,600 in the company, that is today named after both men.

_____

_____

3. Today the company has net sales, well in excess of eight billion dollars.

_____

_____

4. Procter, and Gamble, were also brothers-in-law.

_____

5. They had each married, one of the Norris sisters, Olivia and Ann.

_____

_____

QUOTATION MARKS AND SLASH MARKS (25)

BRACKETS AND THE ELLIPSIS MARK (26)

Quotation marks signal to the reader that you are writing someone else's words rather than your own. If you decide to insert your own words within a quotation, those words are set off with brackets to let the reader know they are not part of the original, quoted material. If you omit any of the quoted words, ellipsis marks are used to indicate the omission. These three types of punctuation marks enable the reader to distinguish between your words and those of another source.

Double quotation marks are used to enclose a direct quotation from either a written or a spoken source. Commas or periods that occur at the end of the quoted matter are always placed within the quotation marks. Colons and semicolons are always placed outside, after the quotation marks.

> She answered very shortly, "I don't want to."

> The boys' leader replied, "The driver of the yellow car was driving recklessly," and the others in the group agreed with him.

> He answered very shortly, "I don't want to"; this was not the answer we had expected.

> She said, "There are several reasons for my actions": One was that she was tired, a second was that she was bored, and a third was that she didn't know the guest of honor.

A dash, question mark, or exclamation point belongs inside the quotation marks when it applies only to the quotation; it belongs outside the quotation marks when it applies to the entire statement.

> She asked, "When may I see you again?"

> Did she say, "I'll probably see you again"?

A comma is used to separate an opening quotation from the rest of the sentence unless the quotation ends in an exclamation point or a question mark.

"This is the book I'm looking for," he said.

"Drat it!" he roared.

"When do we leave?" she asked.

When a quotation is broken to designate the speaker, a comma should be used after the first part of the quotation. The quotation following the interrupting construction should be punctuated as would any phrase or clause.

"I don't believe," said Ms. Wicket, "that I understand you."

"I don't believe it," said Ms. Wicket. "There are just too many reasons why it can't be true."

"I don't believe it," said Ms. Wicket; "you really can't mean it."

Although a comma ordinarily follows the designation of the speaker, as the foregoing examples show, the comma may be omitted if the quotation is grammatically closely related. When the quotation is fairly long or formally introduced, a colon may precede it.

CLOSELY RELATED: NO PUNCTUATION	He growled "Now you just wait a minute" and barred the door.
	I remember the words "Four score and seven years ago," but I can't remember the rest of the speech.
FORMAL INTRODUCTION: COLON	My mother's disciplinary lectures always began: "When I was your age, I had funny notions, too. But I outgrew them."

Quotation marks are used to set off poems and song titles and also to indicate titles of articles, short stories, and parts of longer works.

"The Death of the Hired Man" is one of Robert Frost's best poems.

Glenn Miller's theme song was "Moonlight Serenade."

You can use quotation marks to set off words in a special sense, but do not use them around common nicknames, slang, colloquialisms, trite expressions, or for emphasis or apology. If a word is appropriate, it will stand on its own.

	This is what I call a "foppish" metpahor.
BUT NOT	"Silly" means "stupid" or "foolish," according to the dictionary.
	In these supposedly "modern" times, I feel "out of it."

When words ordinarily placed within quotation marks appear within another quotation, use single quotation marks to set them off. Single quotation marks should never be used for anything but a quotation within a quotation.

> She told the class, "Please read 'The Tell-Tale Heart' for Monday."

BUT NOT   I said, 'Where did you put my notebook?'

A prose quotation more than four lines long should be displayed—that is, set off from your own words with each line indented from the left margin. A displayed quotation does not take quotation marks at its opening and close; setting it off serves to signal the reader that it is a quotation. If quotation marks occur within material you intend to use as a displayed quotation, include them as they appear in the original material.

As Hayes says in *The Crane Papers:*
> Part of the distinctly American tradition is a belief in the New World. America was the land fondly dreamed of as the New Eden, a second chance for men and women to begin again on virgin shores. They could build a new civilization—and this time do it right. It is this tradition that the poet Hart Crane inherits and expounds in his poem "The Bridge" (254).

Quoted poetry and song lyrics should be enclosed in quotation marks and run into the text if three or fewer lines are being quoted. Indicate the end of a run-in line of poetry with a **slash mark** (/).

> Crane is sure unity is possible. He writes, "The stars have grooved our eyes with old persuasions / O, upward from the dead."

If you are quoting more than three lines of poetry, display them. Like displayed quotations of prose, displayed quotations of poetry do not take quotation marks at opening and close unless they occur in the original. Displayed lines of poetry are not run on and consequently do not need slash marks.

Use **brackets** to set off editorial remarks in quoted material and to enclose *sic* ("thus it is") to indicate that a mistake in a quotation is that of the original writer and not that of the quoter.

> "He [Tennyson] was poet laureate of England for several years."

> The dispatch continued: "It was a climatic [*sic*] battle. Everyone knows the end is near."

Ellipsis marks (three spaced periods) show you have deliberately omitted a word or words from the material you are quoting. If you omit words at the end of a quotation, use four periods: the first is the usual sentence period, and the last three are the ellipses. The closing quotation mark encloses all the periods.

> "Part of the distinctly American tradition is a belief in the New World. America was ... the New Eden ... a second chance to begin again.... "

Name _____ Date _____ Score _____

EXERCISE (25), QUOTATION MARKS

Rewrite the following indirect quotations as direct quotations.

Example   Janice said that she was happy about the meeting.
           Janice said, "I am happy about the meeting."

1. She told us that today's speaker was from the Board for Certification of Genealogists.

   _____

2. The speaker indicated that professional genealogists will research your family's background for a fee.

   _____

3. Did he ask how we can find out about these people?

   _____

4. [Make a split quotation out of the following.] Yes, the board, according to the speaker, will mail a list to anyone who's interested.

   _____

5. One of the students remarked that the board provides a valuable service.

   _____

6. She said that she had heard of many people who had been victimized by companies claiming to do genealogical research.

   _____

7. The speaker answered that the Certification Board existed to help people avoid unscrupulous researchers like those.

   _____

8. Many people, according to the lecture, still perform their own research.

   _____

9. He asked the lecturer what was the best way to get started.

   _____

10. [Make a split quotation out of the following.] There are, he was told by the speaker, many books, libraries, and other sources of information that should help you.

    _____

Rewrite the following sentences to punctuate each correctly. In addition to other changes, be sure to capitalize where necessary.

Example   Do you know what I think, she asked I think I'll start my research at home.

"Do you know what I think?" she asked. "I think I'll start my research at home."

11. That way Marge said all I'll need are a pen and some paper.

_____

12. There was an article entitled Tracing Your Ancestry in this morning's paper Marge said.

_____

13. The first thing you should do said Professor House is talk to your relatives.

_____

14. You may be surprised she said sometimes tracing your ancestry is easier than you thought.

_____

15. Most families keep wills diaries birth and marriage certificates she said.

_____

16. Since 1820 Professor House added records of passengers traveling by ship have been kept in every major port.

_____

17. It has long been customary in many families Marge said to keep an informal genealogy in the family Bible.

_____

18. Yes the speaker said those can be invaluable.

_____

19. It is relatively easy said Marge to track down church and government records in the United States.

_____

20. Parish records in other countries also record births deaths and marriages Ernest said but very few people really have to travel abroad to consult them.

_____

EXERCISE (25–26), QUOTATION MARKS AND SLASH MARKS; BRACKETS AND THE ELLIPSIS MARK

Punctuate the following sentences by inserting punctuation marks where they are necessary. Circle any letters that should be capitalized.

Example "Here we are," the librarian said, "this is the records section."

1. We are taking a course we explained that requires us to use these records.

2. This week were studying the chapter Getting Started in *A Basic Course in Genealogy* by D. E. Gardner.

3. Our instructor claims that over a million people actively pursue genealogical research.

4. Mr. Bole stated categorically no specific education is required to perform this kind of research.

5. Are you sure asked Liza.

6. The text I had read as follows correspondent sic courses are helpful.

7. I know I said but no courses or licenses are required just to use the material.

8. Surely Liza said training will make you a better researcher.

9. Who wrote the chapter Public Records in *Tracing Your Civil War Ancestor?*

10. Our instructor said authoritatively all researchers hope to find a royal ancestor.

11. I know everyone might enjoy that but I think he may be overstating his case Alex maintained.

12. The dictionary says that the word genealogy doesn't mean the same as ancestry.

13. I'm not interested in finding a noble ancestor aren't there other things to be discovered asked Judy.

14. One saying that turns out to be good advice for a genealogist is he who hesitates is lost.

15. Many sources of information Judy informed us are really quite permanent.

16. She also said board-certified genealogists are in demand at many institutions.

17. A professional genealogist Mr. Bole said also maintains record collections.

18. But he continued professional genealogists rarely started as amateurs.

19. Many people in this field Bole said are trained first as librarians or archivists.

20. However he said there are literally thousands of publications designed to aid the amateur.

Using the verse printed below, write two paragraphs. In the first paragraph show (1) how to quote three lines or less of poetry and (2) how to use ellipsis marks to show the omission of word(s) from a quotation. In the second paragraph, show (1) how to quote more than three lines of poetry and (2) how to insert editorial remarks into quoted material. For your editorial remarks, you might want to indicate that the author, Emma Lazarus, was a Jewish poet who donated her sonnet, from which these lines are taken, at a fund-raising auction for the Statue of Liberty in 1883. These words are, of course, engraved on a plaque inside the statue's pedestal.

> Give me your tired, your poor
> Your huddled masses yearning to breathe free
> The wretched refuse of your teeming shore,
> Send these, the homeless, tempest-tossed, to me;
> I lift my lamp beside the golden door.

(Paragraph 1) _____

_____

_____

_____

_____

_____

_____

(Paragraph 2) _____

_____

_____

_____

_____

_____

ITALICS (27)

Word punctuation signals that a word has a special use or particular grammatical function. Italics, capitals, apostrophes, and hyphens are the punctuation marks used to signal special word uses and functions. For example, when you write a word with an apostrophe, you are signaling that the word is either a possessive form or a contraction because convention has led readers to recognize possessives and contractions by means of the apostrophe.

Italics are letters sloped to the right in print. In handwritten or typewritten manuscripts, italics are indicated by underlining. This word punctuation is used for titles of books, newspapers, magazines and journals, computer programs, and all works that are published separately—that is, not published as part of another work.

An item such as a short story, article, chapter, or poem that is published as part of a larger work is set off by quotation marks (see Section 25–26). For example, John Milton's lengthy poem about creation and the fall of Adam and Eve is punctuated *Paradise Lost* when it appears as a separate publication; it is punctuated "Paradise Lost" when it appears in the collection *John Milton: Complete Poems and Major Prose.*

Be sure to italicize the word *The* only if it is actually part of a specific title:

The New York Times

BUT

the *Reader's Digest*

The names of plays, movies, record albums and tapes, television or radio programs, computer software works of art, and the like, as well as the names of ships and aircraft, are italicized.

Hamlet	*Casablanca*	the *Mona Lisa*
Sesame Street	the *U.S.S. Nimitz*	*MacNeil/Lehrer News Hour*
Hard Day's Night	the *Concorde*	*Swan Lake*

Italics are used to set off foreign words and expressions that have not yet been adopted into English. They are also used to indicate letters, words, and numbers used as words. Quotation marks are also used to set off words used in a special sense (Section 25–26), but if your subject requires you to refer to words as words frequently, italics are the more scholarly convention. Finally, italics can be used to give special stress to a word. However, don't overuse italics for stress or emphasis. Otherwise, your writing will seem shrill and immature sounding.

He graduated *magna cum laude.*

I cannot distinguish your *n*'s from your *u*'s.

The word *empathy* does not mean the same as *sympathy.*

That was *her* suggestion, not mine.

EXERCISE (27), ITALICS

In the following sentences, indicate by underlining the words or expressions that should be italicized.

Example   Was <u>Santa Maria</u> the first ship to visit American shores?

1. Anyone doing historical research should watch her p's and q's.

2. The miniseries George Washington was very well researched.

3. In the word ancient does the i go before or after the e?

4. The word yogurt is borrowed from Turkish.

5. So are the words tulip and meander.

6. Caviar and shish kebab are also words English borrowed from Turkish.

7. Sometimes the a in shish kebab is replaced by an o.

8. The word robot comes from the Czech word for work.

9. Robot was first used in Karel Capek's play, R.U.R., in 1923.

10. The Oxford English Dictionary says the word jazz is of black origin.

11. Webster's New International says the word is a Creole word from West Africa.

12. Up until the 1880s black was considered a slave term; blacks used the word colored to refer to their race.

13. By 1919, The Negro Year Book stated that the word Negro was acquiring a dignity it had previously lacked.

14. On June 7, 1930, The New York Times announced that in the future the n in Negro would be capitalized.

15. In 1933 the U.S. Government Printing Office began to capitalize Negro.

16. Many people, including leaders such as W. E. B. DuBois and Adam Clayton Powell, continued to use the word black.

17. DuBois wrote The Souls of Black Folk and Black Folk Then and Now.

18. In 1967, the Amsterdam News, the leading black newspaper, announced that its writers would no longer use the word Negro.

19. Today the publishing industry uses black almost exclusively.

20. Most book indexes use the word black as a heading rather than Negro or Afro-American.

Write sentences including the information called for in parentheses. Be sure to use correct word punctuation.

Example   (word used as word; letter used as word)

It's difficult to remember the second r in occurred.

21.   (title of magazine and title of magazine article)

_____

22.   (title of work of art and word punctuated for emphasis)

_____

23.   (title of book and title of short story or poem)

_____

24.   (title of movie, television program, or play)

_____

25.   (foreign expression or word used as word)

_____

26.   (title of record album, audio tape, or computer program)

_____

27.   (title of a newspaper)

_____

CAPITALS   (28)

A century or more ago, writers commonly capitalized almost all nouns. Today conventions governing capitalization have changed so that we capitalize only proper nouns, their derivatives and abbreviations, and common nouns used as part of proper nouns. A proper noun is one that names a particular person, place, or thing rather than a general category: *Chrysler* versus *car*.

We also always capitalize the first word of a sentence or a line of poetry as well as the pronoun *I* and the interjection *O*.

The following guidelines illustrate uses of capitals for categories of proper nouns:

1. Specific persons, races, nationalities, languages, ethnic or religious groups.

Robert	African	Chicanos	Gypsies
Liz	Cuban	Quakers	Eskimos
Thomas G. Brown	Chinese	Moslems	French

2. Specific places.

Miami	Iceland	Rockefeller Center	Saturn
Delaware	Lake Michigan	Nile River	U.S.S.R.

3. Specific organizations (including widely used abbreviations), historical events, and documents.

Knights of Columbus	NAACP
World War II	Declaration of Independence
Gray Panthers	New York Philharmonic Orchestra

4. Days of the week, months, holidays.

Monday	Christmas	Ramadan
May	Passover	Memorial Day

5. Sacred religious terms.

the Virgin Mary	Allah	the Torah
the Savior	the Creation	Mass

6. Titles of books, plays, magazines, newspapers, articles, poems and the like. Capitalize the first word and all other words except articles, conjunctions, and prepositions of fewer than five letters.

Mutiny on the Bounty	*Newsweek*	*The Wall Street Journal*
Fiddler on the Roof	*King Lear*	*Ms.*

7. Titles when they precede a proper noun.

President Truman	Mr. John Doe	the Reverend Paul Mills
General Bradley	Dr. Hilda Vail	Treasurer Jean Ritchie

8. Common nouns used as part of a proper name.

Fifth Street	Yale University	First National Bank
Atlantic Ocean	Shedd Aquarium	Exxon Corporation

Avoid unnecessary capitalization. The following items are usually *not* capitalized:

1. Directions. *North, east, south,* and *west* are capitalized only when they occur at the beginning of a sentence or when they refer to specific geographical locations.

He drove south for ten miles.	the Middle East
He liked the Deep South.	the northern states

2. Seasons. *Fall, autumn, winter, spring,* and *summer* are not capitalized.

3. Family Relationships. Capitalize nouns indicating family relationships only when they are used as names or titles or in combination with proper names.

I hoped to hear from Mother soon.	My sister Harriett is a lawyer.
I have great regard for my mother.	I received a letter from Uncle Carl.

4. Common nouns and adjectives used in place of proper nouns and adjectives.

	He graduated from high school.
BUT	He graduated from Cedar Falls High School.
	He traveled by car.
BUT	He traveled by Delta Airlines.
	She enjoyed sociology and statistics.
BUT	She registered for Sociology 235 and Mathematics 201, Statistical Analysis.

Sometimes it is difficult to decide whether a word is a proper noun or a common noun. For example, if you write *The wedding was held at a Lutheran church.,* should *church* be capitalized or not? In this case, no, it should not be capitalized. However, if you write *The wedding was held at the Lutheran Church.,* you need to capitalize *Church.* In the first instance, the word *church* is a general term (common noun) rather than a reference to a specific church (proper noun), as is the case in the second instance. It may help you to think of proper nouns as being like formal titles or given names.

One indicator to help you decide whether or not to capitalize is the article used with a word. If the article is *a* or *an,* the word is probably a common noun: *a board of directors.* Sometimes, but by no means always, the article *the* will indicate that a word is a proper noun: *the Board of Directors of General Motors.* Your best bet is to determine if a word belongs to a collective category or if it refers to a "titled" person, place, or thing.

A second issue is whether or not to capitalize nouns that refer to and are the same as proper nouns—for example, *The Mulberry City Council met Tuesday, and the council voted to deny the rezoning request.* When the complete title of a person, place, or thing is not used, ordinarily the repeated words are treated as common nouns (as in category 4 under "Unnecessary Capitalization"). Sometimes, however, the shortened form of a proper noun will be capitalized to signify respect, as in *The Reverend Joseph West will deliver Sunday's sermon; the Reverend is a well-known member of the clergy.* Of course titles shortened to just proper names are always capitalized: *Visit Custom Upholstery Company for your upholstery needs because Custom guarantees satisfaction,* not ... *because custom guarantees satisfaction.* The following sentences provide further illustrations of capitalization:

He traveled by Delta Airlines because, he said, the airline's staff was courteous and Delta flights are usually on time.

My favorite lake is Lake Louise.

The school board president attended a meeting of the National Association of Public School Boards.

Columbiana County is a county in eastern Ohio.

EXERCISE (28), CAPITALS

Rewrite the following sentences, correcting all errors in capitalization.

Example   Lena himmelstein arrived in new york from lithuania in 1895.

Lena Himmelstein arrived in New York from Lithuania in 1895.

1. Lena moved her dress shop to fifth avenue in 1904.

———————————————————————————————————————

2. Her company found its name, lane bryant, when lena reversed the vowels in her first name on a bank deposit slip.

———————————————————————————————————————

3. Lena's first husband, david bryant, had urged her to go into business.

———————————————————————————————————————

4. It was her second husband, albert maislin, who took a great interest in lane bryant, incorporated.

———————————————————————————————————————

5. Ebenezer butterick was descended from an english immigrant who came to the united states in 1635.

———————————————————————————————————————

6. Ebenezer was apprenticed to a tailor in worcester, massachusetts.

———————————————————————————————————————

7. In 1867, butterick began designing paper patterns for women's clothing.

———————————————————————————————————————

8. His most popular pattern was a suit patterned after the suit worn by the italian revolutionary garibaldi and his men.

———————————————————————————————————————

9. Maroun hajjar, a lebanese immigrant, founded the haggar clothing company in dallas, texas.

———————————————————————————————————————

10. Many people in the east didn't think a texas clothing company would succeed.

———————————————————————————————————————

11. In one month of 1978, paul guez sold over two million dollars worth of sasson jeans.

_____

12. Guez, who immigrated from tunisia, named the jeans after his partner, maurice sasson.

_____

13. Sasson's name means "happiness" in hebrew.

_____

14. Thus, the jeans have no connection with australian-born hairstylist vidal sassoon.

_____

15. Frederick mellinger is descended from a long line of orthodox jewish rabbis.

_____

16. Mellinger is the founder of frederick's of hollywood.

_____

17. Ida rosenthal, according to the text *ethnic fashion almanac,* was a russian jewish immigrant from minsk.

_____

18. She started making dresses in hoboken, new jersey, in april 1920.

_____

19. Her company, maidenform, is one of america's largest clothing companies.

_____

20. Jonathan schwartz says he wanted a wasp-sounding, ethnically neutral name for his line of jonathan logan clothing.

_____

THE APOSTROPHE   (29);
THE HYPHEN   (30)

THE APOSTROPHE

An **apostrophe** signals the possessive case of nouns and indefinite pronouns. The following guidelines illustrate its use in forming the possessive case:

1. Words not ending in *s* add an apostrophe and *s* to form the possessive.

the man's suitcase   the women's suitcases

2. Singular words ending in *s* add an apostrophe and *s* unless the second *s* makes pronunciation difficult.

James's bike   Euripides' plays

3. Plural words ending in *s* add only the apostrophe.

the dogs' food   the babies' shoes   the Browns' mailbox

4. With compounds, only the last word is made possessive.

my father-in-law's chair   someone else's locker

5. With nouns of joint possession, only the last noun is made possessive.

George and John's bedroom

6. With nouns of individual possession, both nouns are made possessives.

Beth's and Bart's swimsuits.

Do not use an apostrophe with the possessive form of personal pronouns *his, hers, its, ours, yours, theirs,* and *whose.*

An apostrophe indicates the omission of a letter or number.

you are	you're
cannot	can't
it is	it's
would not	wouldn't
of the clock	o'clock
class of 1978	class of '78

An apostrophe is also used to form the plurals of letters, numbers, and words used as words. Note that these are the *only* instances in which apostrophes are used in forming plurals. Apostrophes are *never* used to form the plurals of proper names or other nouns.

Mind your *p's* and *q's.*

The *'30's* were called the Jazz Age.

Don't put too many *and's* in one sentence.

THE HYPHEN

The **hyphen** has two different uses. It is used to indicate that a word is continued from one line to the next (see "Syllabication," Section 15–18), and it is used to punctuate compound words. The following guidelines give the conventions for using hyphens in compound words:

1. To form compound words that are not accepted as single words. Since there is no general rule that can be applied to such compounds, the best way to determine whether a compound word is hyphenated is to consult the dictionary.

2. To join two or more words serving as a single adjective before a noun.

a well-liked person   an ill-fitting suit   a five-year-old child

Omit the hyphen when the first word is an adverb ending in *-ly.*

a rapidly fired pistol   a slowly sinking ship

Do not hyphenate adjectives that follow the verb as predicate adjectives.

> They were well-known actors.

BUT   The actors were well known.

3. To avoid an awkward union of letters such as *bell-like*.
4. To form compound cardinal and ordinal numbers from twenty-one through ninety-nine and to designate spelled-out fractions.

twenty-two   twenty-second   three-fourths

5. In conjunction with prefixes *self-, all-,* and *ex-,* and the suffix *-elect*.

self-confidence   all-important   ex-President Carter

vice president-elect   Governor-elect Orr   ex-champion

EXERCISE (29), APOSTROPHES

In the blanks, write the singular possessive for the following nouns.

Example   *baronet*   <u>baronet's</u>

1.	*Sue* _____	2.	*Kansas* _____
3.	*Toyota* _____	4.	*Jim* _____
5.	*everyone* _____	6.	*anybody* _____
7.	*industry* _____	8.	*Janis* _____
9.	*Moses* _____	10.	*Pericles* _____

In the appropriate blanks, write the singular possessives and the plural possessives for the following nouns.

		SINGULAR	PLURAL
Example	*class*	<u>class's</u>	<u>classes'</u>
1.	*deer*	_____	_____
2.	*dog*	_____	_____
3.	*check*	_____	_____
4.	*brother-in-law*	_____	_____
5.	*thief*	_____	_____
6.	*cook*	_____	_____
7.	*juggler*	_____	_____
8.	*night*	_____	_____
9.	*bus*	_____	_____
10.	*company*	_____	_____
11.	*treasurer*	_____	_____
12.	*acrobat*	_____	_____
13.	*man*	_____	_____
14.	*life*	_____	_____
15.	*city*	_____	_____

		SINGULAR	PLURAL
16.	*swatch*	_____	_____
17.	*mask*	_____	_____
18.	*file*	_____	_____
19.	*Jones*	_____	_____
20.	*camera*	_____	_____
21.	*watch*	_____	_____
22.	*desk*	_____	_____
23.	*task*	_____	_____
24.	*hero*	_____	_____
25.	*tusk*	_____	_____
26.	*woman*	_____	_____
27.	*secretary*	_____	_____
28.	*day*	_____	_____
29.	*month*	_____	_____
30.	*week*	_____	_____

Form the correct contractions for the following words.

Example   *we have* ___we've___

1. *I will*   _____
2. *they are*   _____
3. *do not*   _____
4. *I am*   _____
5. *were not*   _____
6. *you are*   _____
7. *it is*   _____
8. *they will*   _____
9. *was not*   _____
10. *who is*   _____

EXERCISE (29–30), HYPHENS AND APOSTROPHES

Insert apostrophes, *'s*, and hyphens where they are needed in the following sentences.

Example Some of America's most famous music was written by immigrants or their descendants.

1. Some of the best loved songs have been written by or for ethnic Americans.

2. *Aloha Oe,* Hawaiis traditional farewell song, was written by a Hawaiian queen.

3. Queen Liliuokalanis reign lasted only two years.

4. The queens name became Mrs. Lydia Dominis after she married a native Bostonian.

5. She formed her new name from her old names first two syllables.

6. Kate Smiths trademark song, "God Bless America," was also a best seller in sheet music.

7. She performed the song for GIs and for the home front during World War II.

8. "God Bless America" was written by a Russian Jewish immigrant named Israel Baline.

9. Balines stage name was Irving Berlin.

10. He wrote the record breaking song twenty two years before the 1940s, when Ms. Smith made it famous.

11. All Berlins royalties were donated to the Girl Scouts and Boy Scouts.

12. "Home Sweet Home," with its humble, all American words, was written in 1823.

13. Some say John Paynes music was borrowed from a Sicilian opera.

14. James A. Bland, sometimes called "the prince of Negro songwriters," was born to well to do free parents in New York in 1854.

15. Blands education included stints at Howard University.

16. He worked as a representatives page in the House of Representatives.

17. He joined Callenders Original Georgia Minstrels when he was twenty one.

18. In the 1870s, Bland wrote "Carry Me Back to Ol Virginny."

19. "Carry Me Back" became Virginias official state song in 1940.

20. Almost unknown in America, Bland was the idol of Englands music halls in the 1880s and 1890s.

21. The never ending refrains of "La Cucaracha" were written by a Spanish composer.

22. The song concerns a marijuana smoking cockroach who dries out in the sun.

23. One line, "now hes just another raisin," may be the least appetizing line ever written in such a popular song.

24. "The Anacreontic Song" got its name from a British gentlemens club.

25. The complicated tune was written by a London born composer, John Stafford Smith.

26. Different words were added to the songs music by Francis Scott Key.

27. "The Anacreontic Song," of course, became Americas national anthem.

28. A sixty year old soprano, Adelina Patti, was the inspiration for "Sweet Adeline."

29. "Yes We Have No Bananas" was inspired by a reply heard at a Greek immigrants fruit stand in New York.

30. The tune was borrowed from Handels *Messiah.*

Provide two examples for each use of the hyphen listed below.

31. (compound words) _____

32. (two words serving as a single adjective before a noun) _____

_____

33. (an awkward union of letters) _____

34. (compound numbers) _____

35. (spelled-out fractions) _____

36. (words using the prefix *self-*) _____

37. (words using the prefix *all-*) _____

38. (words using the prefix *ex-*) _____

39. (words using the suffix *-elect*) _____

40. (two words serving as a single adjective before a noun) _____

_____

PUNCTUATION REVIEW (19–30)

Revise the following sentences, providing necessary end, internal, and word punctuation.

Example   In fact many foods that sound as through they are foreign actually were invented in America

In fact, many foods that sound as though they are foreign actually were invented in America.

1. Vichyssoise for example was invented in 1910 by a French chef.

   _____

2. But that French chef who was named Louis Diat lived and worked in America

   _____

3. Vichyssoise is made from leeks and potatoes it is best served cold

   _____

4. Diat who used a recipe from his mothers kitchen worked at the Ritz Carlton Hotel in New York

   _____

5. Lebanon bologna which sounds as if its origins are in the Middle East is a smoked beef sausage made in Lebanon Pennsylvania.

   _____

6. Spaghetti and meatballs was in point of fact first served in Brooklyn

   _____

7. Cioppino which is a fish stew may have an Italian name but it was first cooked in Montereys restaurants.

   _____

8. It was however made popular in San Francisco

   _____

9. For years people have wondered whether the United States had its own distinct foods

   _____

10. Baked Alaska sounds as though it should have some connection with the north with Alaska or with Eskimos in fact it was invented in the 1860s by a new york chef.

_____

11. Chop suey in point of fact was invented by a chinese diplomat

_____

12. However the inventor of chop suey li hung chang was in new york when he invented it

_____

13. The dish an attempt to recreate authentic chinese food with modern utensils and available ingredients caught on quickly

_____

14. The name combines chop sticks and soya sauce into chop soya which eventually became chop suey

_____

15. Chow mein is another staple of chinese restaurants it was also first made by chinese railroad workers in san francisco

_____

16. Only two cheeses out of the hundreds of varieties that exist can actually be called american cheeses

_____

17. One is brick cheese developed by a swiss American John Jossi

_____

18. The other is liederkrantz a pungent smelling cheese in the same group as Limburger.

_____

19. The inventor Emil Frey tested his cheese on members of a choral society

_____

20. Did they like the cheese

_____

21. Isnt it true they gave the cheese the name of their group Liederkranz

_____

22. George Crum an american indian working as a chef in saratoga springs invented the potato chip

---

23. One guest complained about the french fried potatoes he asked if Crum would slice a new batch just for him

---

24. The old batch apparently were too thick for the guests gourmet tastes

---

25. Dutifully Crum sliced the new batch

---

26. Once again the guest sent them back to the kitchen

---

27. Crum by this time really exasperated sliced up a paper thin batch and fried them to a crisp

---

28. To Crums total amazement the guest loved this third batch

---

29. Every year thereafter the new way of cooking potatoes became more popular

---

30. Crum himself called them saratoga chips and served them every night at the posh resort

---

Insert punctuation where it is needed in the following sentences. (Use a pen or pencil that writes in a color other than black.)

31. Popcorn is a native American food apparently it was brought to the first Thanksgiving by the Indians

32. F. W. Rueckheim a German American inventor experimented with popcorn trying to make it even more popular

33. By adding sugar syrup and peanuts Rueckheim created a new candy which he called Cracker Jack

34. It was first offered for sale in the late 1800s

35. Cracker Jack is made even today according to Rueckheims original recipe

36. Rueckheim developed the idea of putting a prize in each box and he coined the Cracker Jack advertising slogan "The more you eat the more you want"

37. Doesnt everybody paw through the box to find the prize first

38. The sailor boy on the box Jack was modeled after Rueckheims grandson Jack who died at the age of eight

39. Another German American horticulturist Orville Redenbacher experimented for years with hybrid popcorn seeds

40. He turned popcorn growing into a science but he was able to grow a superior popcorn

41. Redenbacher's hybrid makes a larger lighter fluffier kernel when it is popped

42. His "gourmet" popping corn as he calls it has made him rich

43. Americans eat almost 400 million pounds of popcorn every year that figure works out to about two pounds per person

44. Almost half the total consumed 200 million pounds is cooked at home

45. Popcorn in all its forms eaten plain strung on a string coated with syrup or pressed into syrup-covered balls has become a part of most of America's festive occasions

EFFECTIVE SENTENCES: COORDINATION AND SUBORDINATION (31)

Sections 1c through 1d(4) on phrases, clauses, and sentence types introduced some ideas we now need to review. As you discovered in those earlier sections, phrases enable a writer to elaborate, amplify, and qualify the information provided in the core of the sentence—in the simple subject and simple predicate. Clauses enable a writer to combine several related ideas into one sentence. Using coordination and subordination, a writer can express related thoughts in one sentence, instead of having to write a separate sentence for each thought. By using different types of sentence patterns, a writer can achieve greater sentence variety and emphasis.

In the next four sections, we explore these techniques in detail, techniques that can give you more control over your writing and thus improve your ability to express your meaning in interesting and effective ways.

COORDINATION (31a)

The simplest kind of coordination involves joining words, phrases, or clauses with the coordinating conjunctions *and, but, or, nor, for, so,* and *yet.* Coordination establishes relationships of approximately equal rank or importance between ideas. Coordination also allows you to condense and compress information. Notice how the information in the following series of sentences is compressed and smoothed when it is combined into one sentence using coordinating conjunctions:

Peas are harvested in the spring. They cannot tolerate hot weather. Pumpkins need hot weather to mature. They are harvested in the fall.

Peas cannot tolerate hot weather *and* are harvested in the spring, *but* pumpkins need hot weather to mature *and* are harvested in the fall. [Two independent clauses coordinated by the conjunction *but*, showing contrast; verbs within clauses coordinated by the conjunction *and*.]

You have probably also noticed that the coordinated sentence makes more sense than the four separate sentences—because the relationships among ideas have been clearly expressed by the conjunctions, rather than left for the reader to figure out.

In addition to the coordinating conjunctions previously mentioned, parts of sentences can be joined by correlative conjunctions—coordinating conjunctions that work in pairs—such as *both ... and, either ... or, neither ... nor, not ... but, not only ... but also*. For example: *I **not only** planted peas **but also** spread mulch around the strawberries.*

Conjunctive adverbs such as *however, nevertheless, therefore,* and *furthermore* do not connect words, phrases, and clauses but, when used with a semicolon, link whole sentences: *A late frost killed the tender seedlings; **therefore,** we will have to replant the peas this weekend.*

SUBORDINATION (31b)

Another effective method of combining and relating ideas is subordination. Coordination will not provide the focus you need if, for example, two ideas are not of equal importance or one depends on the other for its meaning. Consider the following pair of sentences:

IDEAS COORDINATED	The rain ended, *and* the sun came out.
IDEAS SUBORDINATED	*When* the rain ended, the sun came out.

In the first sentence the two events are given equal importance and rank by the coordinating conjunction *and*. The second sentence, however, expresses a more specific relationship, a time relationship, which establishes the dependence of one event upon the other: first the rain ended; then the sun came out.

If you combine too many ideas—or illogically combine ideas—with coordinating conjunctions, your writing will reflect what is known as "primer style," parts of sentences monotonously and unemphatically connected by *and* or *but: The rain ended, and the sun came out, and we went back to the garden, but it was too muddy to work.*

Another form of primer style is successive, short, choppy sentences: *The ground was soaked. Everything had turned to mud. The water ran down the gutters. Children played in the puddles.*

Subordinating details, qualifications, and ideas of lesser importance indicates your focus to the reader. Subordinating conjunctions include *although, because, if, when, since, before, unless,* and *after,* as well as the relative pronouns *who, which,* and *that* (see Section 1d(1–3) for a more complete list).

Remember that because a subordinate clause is of lesser importance, the information in it should not contain your main idea. The main idea belongs in the main clause. You do not want to mislead your reader by illogically burying the most important idea in a dependent clause.

| ILLOGICAL SUBORDINATION OF MAIN IDEA | When the sun came out, the storm ended. |
| LOGICAL SUBORDINATION OF QUALIFYING IDEA | When the storm ended, the sun came out. |

In many cases, of course, only you know for sure which idea is your primary focus and which is a modifier. The following examples show how subordination can affect meaning by changing the focus in the same collection of information:

Because they raise gardens, many people save money on food bills.
[Stresses saving money in main clause]

Many people raise gardens because doing so saves money on food bills.
[Stresses raising a garden in main clause]

APPOSITIVES, PARTICIPIAL PHRASES, AND ABSOLUTE PHRASES (31c)

Besides subordinate clauses, three other types of constructions can be used to subordinate ideas and economically add details to core sentences.

An **appositive** is a word or phrase that renames or further identifies another word, usually a noun or pronoun. In the sentence *The potato, a tuber, is characterized by its swollen underground stem,* the words *a tuber* are the appositive renaming *potato.* An appositive can often be substituted for a subordinate clause or even several subordinate clauses or sentences, thus providing a more streamlined way of supplying details. Notice how the following examples proceed from separate ideas in separate primer-style sentences, to sentences combined using clauses, to sentences combined using an appositive:

PRIMER-STYLE SEPARATE SENTENCES	The potato is a tuber. A tuber is characterized by a swollen underground stem.
SENTENCES COMBINED WITH CLAUSE	The potato is a tuber *that is characterized by a swollen underground stem.*
SENTENCES COMBINED WITH AN APPOSITIVE	The potato, *a tuber,* is characterized by a swollen underground stem.

A **participle** is a verb form ending in *-ing* (present participle: *moving, eating, sleeping*), ending in *-ed* or *-en*, or having another irregular form (past participle: *moved, eaten, slept*). Participles, together with their objects and modifiers forming participial phrases, can function as adjectives. They offer another alternative to subordinate clauses for combining ideas in sentences, as the following examples show:

SEPARATE SENTENCES	The potato was probably first grown in the Andes region of South America. It was transported to Europe by the Spanish. It became a staple of the northern European diet.
SENTENCES COMBINED WITH CLAUSES	The potato, *which was probably first grown in the Andes region of South America,* was transported to Europe by the Spanish *where it became a staple of the northern European diet.*
SENTENCES COMBINED WITH PARTICIPIAL PHRASES	The potato, *probably first grown in the Andes region of South America and transported to Europe by the Spanish,* became a staple of the northern European diet.
	Probably first grown in the Andes region of South America and transported to Europe by the Spanish, the potato became a staple of the northern European diet.

Participles are fairly flexible in their placement, as the previous examples show. However, be careful not to create misplaced or dangling modifiers when you use participles to combine ideas. (See Sections 11 to 12.)

An **absolute phrase** is an especially compressed modifier that, because it modifies the whole sentence rather than any single word, can be placed effectively at many locations in a sentence. An absolute phrase consists of a subject (usually a noun or pronoun), a participle, and any modifiers of the participle. Almost any sentence containing a form of the verb *be* followed by a present or past participle can be transformed into an absolute phrase by omitting the *be* form of the verb. Absolute phrases can also be formed by changing a main verb into its *-ing* form.

SENTENCE	The potatoes were mashed, so I put them into a bowl.
ABSOLUTE	*The potatoes mashed,* I put them into a bowl.
SENTENCE	The food was tasty, and the guests asked for second helpings.
ABSOLUTE	*The food being tasty,* the guests asked for second helpings.

These different ways of subordinating information and combining ideas allow you to construct denser, more compact and streamlined sentences. You can also vary the structure of your sentences and achieve a tighter focus on ideas you want to emphasize.

Practice: Identifying Subordinated Modifiers   Underline the appositives, participial phrases, and absolute phrases in the following sentences. The answers are listed at the end of this section.

[1]Settling on frontier lands as they found them, the Scotch-Irish found these lands occupied by Indians or by other white settlers. [2]"Squatting" on these lands, the pugnacious Scotch-Irish became superb frontiersmen and Indian fighters. [3]Experienced in the secrets of whiskey distilling, they established stills almost everywhere they went. [4]In fact a very religious people, the Scotch-Irish were careful to also establish churches. [5]Their detractors said the Scotch-Irish kept the Sabbath, along with anything else they touched. [6]Holding no love for the British, who had uprooted them twice, the Scotch-Irish eagerly joined in the American Revolution. [7]About a dozen U.S. presidents were of Scotch-Irish descent.

Answers to the Practice   [1]Settling . . . them [participial phrase] [2]"Squatting" on these lands [participial phrase] [3]Experienced . . . distilling [participial phrase] [4]In fact a very religious people [absolute phrase] [6]Holding . . . British [participial phrase] who had uprooted them twice [appositive]

EXERCISE (31a–b), COORDINATION AND SUBORDINATION

Revise the following sentences using coordinating conjunctions, subordinating conjunctions, and relative pronouns to combine ideas and eliminate primer style.

Example   Dozens of black newspapers have been started. Many famous black Americans have worked on these papers.

Dozens of black newspapers have been started, and many famous black Americans have worked on these papers.

1. *Freedom Journal* was first published in New York in 1827. It was the nation's first newspaper published by blacks.

   _____

2. The editors were Samuel Cornish and J. B. Russwum. Russwum was one of the first American blacks to earn a college degree.

   _____

3. Cornish was a freeborn black. He started the first Presbyterian church in America, too.

   _____

4. All the other New York papers were owned by whites. They were very critical of freed slaves.

   _____

5. White papers were critical of allowing ex-slaves to vote. *Freedom Journal* was a response.

   _____

6. *Freedom Journal* closed in two years. There were disagreements over editorial policy.

   _____

7. Its editors urged blacks to educate themselves. The editors could not agree. They dissolved their partnership.

   _____

8. They were undecided. Should blacks stay in America? Should they return to help colonize Africa?

   _____

9. Many black Americans were, by this time, freed. Many of them went to settle in Liberia.

_____

10. Many other black papers were printed before the Civil War. They had equally short lives.

_____

11. Forty black-owned newspapers were first printed between 1829 and 1860. None lasted long at all.

_____

12. But they were founded and printed for a while. A black audience for newspapers existed at the time.

_____

13. *Freedom Journal* was the first to demand equal rights. Many of these papers have shared that message.

_____

14. Frederick Douglas was a famous early black writer. He published the *North Star* in New York.

_____

15. W. E. B. DuBois became editor of *The Crisis*. He also helped found the NAACP.

_____

16. Marcus Garvey was an editor of *Negro World*. There he advocated emigration back to Africa for American blacks.

_____

17. These publishers helped change minds in America. They sometimes suffered for their beliefs.

_____

18. The messages of black papers were heard. A paper like *The Living Way* might have its offices burned.

_____

19. Thousands of blacks moved north. The *Chicago Defender* told blacks of the jobs available in northern industry.

_____

20. Black publishers asked President Truman to integrate the armed services. He ordered their complete integration immediately after World War II.

_____

EXERCISE (31c–d), PARTICIPLES, ABSOLUTES, AND APPOSITIVES

Combine the following sentences, expressing what you believe to be the most important idea in the main clause, using participial phrases, appositives, or absolute phrases to subordinate other ideas. Be sure to avoid dangling or misplaced modifiers in your revisions.

Example   Black newspapers and magazines are widely distributed. They have the largest ethnic reading audience.

Black newspapers and magazines, which are widely distributed, have the largest ethnic reading audience.

1. The National Newspaper Publishers Association (NNPA) was formed in 1940. It represents black-owned newspapers.

_____

2. This group represents 125 newspapers. Its offices are in New York and Washington.

_____

3. It functions as a trade association. The NNPA helps black newspapers with all sorts of business problems.

_____

4. NNPA officers serve as business consultants. They serve as lobbyists on occasion.

_____

5. Some problems of black papers are the same as problems faced by white-owned newspapers. These problems include circulation, advertising revenues, and delivery schedules.

_____

6. The black press is now thriving in America. The NNPA has been a major factor.

_____

7. The black press has overcome its problems. It now reaches well over 25 million readers every week.

_____

8. The black press is the most visible ethnic press in America. There are many other newspapers and magazines aimed at specific ethnic groups.

_____

9. *The Echo of Poland* was the first Polish language newspaper in America. It was published in 1863–1864.

_____

10. *The Pacific Citizen* contains news of interest to Americans of Japanese descent. *The Pacific Citizen* is published by the Japanese American Citizens League.

_____

11. The oldest Lebanese newspaper in the United States is *The Guidance*. It is published in New York City.

_____

12. *France-Amérique* recently celebrated its 160th anniversary. It is the oldest French language newspaper in the United States.

_____

13. It is a weekly paper with a circulation of 20,000. *France-Amérique* was established in 1827.

_____

14. *France-Amérique* is a 16-page weekly. It was originally titled *Le Courrier*.

_____

15. *Italian-American Progress* is the only Italian daily in the United States. It stresses news about events in Italy.

_____

16. In contrast, the *Tribune-News* concentrates on the Italian culture in the United States. It even publishes Italian language lessons.

_____

17. (Write your own sentence using a participial phrase to combine ideas.)

_____

18. (Write your own sentence using an appositive to combine ideas.)

_____

19. (Write your own sentence using an absolute phrase to combine ideas.)

_____

20. (Write your own sentence using coordinating and subordinating conjunctions to combine ideas.)

_____

PARALLELISM (32)

If successive parts of a sentence, or successive sentences, use the same grammatical construction, they are parallel. Parallel constructions emphasize coordinate relationships, stressing equal importance or rank by means of the repeated grammatical patterns.

You can create parallel structures in just about any part of a sentence by using coordination.

SUBJECTS	*Art, music, and dance* are virtually international languages.
VERBS	These forms of expression *attract and captivate* audiences everywhere.
DIRECT OBJECTS	Audiences understand *art, music, and dance* without translation.
INFINITIVE PHRASES	They only need *to see and hear* to understand and appreciate the message.
PARTICIPLES MODIFYING NOUNS	*Dancing feet or singing voices* communicate across political barriers.
ADJECTIVE COMPLEMENTS	Art forms are both *universal and personal* at the same time.
NOUN COMPLEMENTS/ PREPOSITIONAL PHRASES	They are *importers of cultural exchange and exporters of human understanding.*

The equal emphasis stressed by parallel form provides you with yet another tool for indicating and reinforcing meaning in your sentences. Rather than having to say "this is ranked the same as that," you can indicate the ranking through sentence structure. Consequently, parallel structures are particularly useful for combining sentences, as the following examples show.

SUCCESSIVE SENTENCES	Music is a good cultural ambassador. Dance is another effective international communicator.
SENTENCES COMBINED USING PARALLELISM	Music and dance are good cultural ambassadors as well as effective international communicators.

Because parallel structures are formed with coordinators—either coordinating conjunctions (*and, but, or, nor,* etc.) or correlative conjunctions (*either, or; neither, nor; not only, but also; both, and; whether, or*), you must be careful to avoid faulty parallelism which would destroy the sameness of structure and thus the equality of emphasis on each side of the coordinator. If you use a noun phrase on one side of the conjunction, for example, be sure to use a noun phrase on the other side as well. If you use *and who, and which,* or *and that* in the second half of a parallel structure, you must be sure to introduce the same type of structure in the first half, too.

CORRECT	That is Wolfgang Steinmetz, who is a great pianist and who is also an excellent mathematician.
FAULTY	That is Wolfgang Steinmetz, a great pianist and who is also an excellent mathematician.
CORRECT	That is Wolfgang Steinmetz, a great pianist and an excellent mathematician.
	That is Wolfgang Steinmetz, who is a great pianist and an excellent mathematician.
FAULTY	You are either wrong or I am wrong. [Adjective *wrong* is not really parallel with clause *I am wrong.*]
CORRECT	Either you are wrong or I am. [Two parallel clauses.]
FAULTY	They not only have insulted me but everyone. [Verb *have insulted* is not properly parallel with pronoun *everyone.*]
CORRECT	They have insulted not only me but everyone. [Pronouns *me* and *everyone* are parallel.]

EXERCISE (32), PARALLELISM

Revise the following sentences to express coordinate ideas in correct parallel form.

Example   Early records of the lives of black women are incomplete and not able to be trusted.

Early records of the lives of black women are incomplete and untrustworthy.

1. Sojourner Truth became a preacher and for women's rights she was an advocate.

   _____

2. She was born into slavery in 1797 in Hurley, New York, and slavery was the topic she spoke out against in later life.

   _____

3. She was the first black woman to lecture against slavery, and she was first to speak out for women's rights.

   _____

4. In 1851, Francis Gage organized a woman's convention in Ohio, and Sojourner was invited by her to speak.

   _____

5. In 1851, it was not simple for whites and for people who were black to cooperate in public activity.

   _____

6. When Sojourner asked to speak, many women wanted to refuse her the right of speaking.

   _____

7. She rose slowly to her full height of almost six feet; for the audience to be quiet her arms were raised.

   _____

8. As she spoke of her life of hard work on a farm, her muscular arms were bared for the audience to see.

   _____

9. She returned to her seat amid roars of applause, and many women had tears in their eyes.

_____

10. C. J. Walker started selling her hair conditioner door to door, and her own manufacturing plant in Indianapolis was the result.

_____

11. She developed a line of hair care products and was discovered to be America's first black female millionaire in 1915.

_____

12. Maggie Walker founded the St. Luke Bank and Trust Company in 1903; the first female bank president was Maggie Walker, who was also black.

_____

13. The first black Congresswoman was Shirley Chisholm, who was elected in 1968, and the 12th District in Brooklyn was represented by her.

_____

14. Rebecca Lee, the first black woman to receive a medical degree, was also the New England Female Medical College's first black graduate.

_____

15. Charlotte Ray was the first female law student at Howard University and was among black women lawyers also the first.

_____

16. Judge Jane M. Bolin was the first black woman to graduate from Yale Law School and when she was admitted to the Bar in New York.

_____

17. She graduated from Wellesley with honors in 1928 and, despite her father's objections, Yale Law School was where she enrolled next.

_____

18. He assumed she would teach school, since women shouldn't have to hear unpleasant, criminal topics, he thought.

_____

19. When she was appointed to the New York Family Court in 1939, the first black woman judge in the United States was what she discovered herself to be.

_____

20. Her most serious problem, she said, was not discrimination, but attempting to balance a high-pressure career with being a mother.

_____

EMPHASIS (33)

As you learned in Section 31 on coordination and subordination, the structure of a sentence plays a key role in focusing a reader's attention on the ideas you want to emphasize. If the most important idea appears in the main clause and information of lesser importance is subordinated, the reader has received valuable signals about the emphasis you intend. Parallel arrangements of information also provide emphasis, as Section 32 explained. Emphatic positioning, use of loose, periodic, and balanced sentences, and appropriate use of active and passive voice verbs also help you achieve emphasis in your writing.

One of the hazards of combining sentences, as you did for the exercises in Section 31, for example, is that emphasis can disappear as you join phrases and clauses together. Even though sentence combining helps to establish relationships between ideas and reduces unnecessary repetition, if you put too many ideas in a sentence that is not constructed with a clear emphasis, readers won't know where to focus their attention. First, don't be tempted to pile too much information into a single sentence. Second, be sure to structure your sentences for emphasis.

UNFOCUSED SENTENCE CONTAINING TOO MUCH DETAIL	The car with the broken axle and the smashed front end had turned over in the ditch after being hit by the train, but the tow truck began to right the wrecked vehicle because miraculously no one was injured.
SENTENCE REVISED FOR EMPHASIS	After being hit by the train, the car turned over in the ditch, its axle broken and its front end smashed. Miraculously, no one was injured, so the tow truck began to right the wrecked vehicle.

Generally, the most emphatic place in a sentence is the ending. The next most emphatic place is the beginning. The middle of the sentence receives the least amount of emphasis. A good writer achieves forcefulness by inserting the strongest points either at the ends or at the beginnings of sentences.

WEAK	Most politicians can be trusted, in my opinion.
STRONGER	In my opinion, most politicians can be trusted.
	Most politicians, in my opinion, can be trusted.
WEAK	We will have a picnic if it does not rain.
STRONGER	If it does not rain, we will have a picnic.

Naturally, you are the one who must decide which information merits emphasis. In the first example, the writer has decided in one case that *In my opinion* should be stressed. In the second case, *in my opinion* becomes the least important information in the sentence and so is inserted parenthetically in the middle. The point is that you should not inadvertently structure a sentence to destroy the emphasis you intend.

LOOSE, PERIODIC, MIDBRANCHING, AND BALANCED SENTENCES (33b)

A **loose** or **right-branching sentence,** sometimes called a **cumulative sentence,** is a sentence that concerns itself with its main idea first and its subordinate details later. The **periodic** or **left-branching sentence** has an exactly opposite arrangement: its subordinate details come first and its main idea comes last. Thus, the periodic sentence often achieves an effect of drama and suspense. Although it provides forcefulness and a sense of climax, the periodic sentence must be used judiciously since its overuse may result in a loss of the very effect you want to achieve. A **midbranching sentence** places modifying details between the subject and the verb. Like the periodic sentence, it must be used carefully because it varies from readers' expectations—from ordinary, cumulative thought patterns and sentence patterns. A midbranching sentence can either emphasize or deemphasize subordinate details, depending on whether it is punctuated with dashes or commas.

A **balanced sentence** is a compound sentence in which the independent clauses are exactly, or very nearly, parallel in all elements. Balanced sentences are useful for showing contrasts.

LOOSE, RIGHT-BRANCHING	The dog came home with its collar gone, its fur full of burrs, and its tail between its legs.

PERIODIC, LEFT-BRANCHING	Its collar gone, its fur full of burrs, and its tail between its legs, the dog came home.
MIDBRANCHING EMPHASIZED	The dog—its tail between its legs—came home.
MIDBRANCHING DEEMPHASIZED	The dog, its tail between its legs, came home.
BALANCED	The dog came home with burrs in its fur, but it came home without its collar.
	An undisciplined puppy is "disobedient"; an undisciplined dog is a menace.

EXPLETIVE CONSTRUCTIONS (33c)

Expletive constructions such as *there are, there was,* and *it is* (*there* or *it* together with forms of the verb *to be*) can be used for emphasis in sentences. These constructions are often considered to be wordy time-wasters, especially if they occur too frequently in writing; but the very properties that make them wordy can also occasionally have beneficial effects in sentences. The expletives slow down the sentence, delaying the arrival of the true subject or the delivery of other information and creating anticipation or suspense. Notice how in the following example the expletive signals the reader to pay attention.

| EXPLETIVE "IT WAS" | It was cold as the grave, it was dark as pitch, it was quiet as death in the passageway. Somewhere a door creaked. |

ITEMS IN PARALLEL SERIES (33d)

As you learned in Section 32, parallel constructions can add to a sentence's effectiveness. Items in parallel series are especially good for creating cumulative emphasis. Parallel series indicate an order or importance to readers, whether it be greater to lesser, earlier to later, small to large, or whatever. Be sure that the order you select for a series will reinforce the meaning you intend. In the example that follows, the writer uses the natural emphasis that falls on the last item in a parallel series to create a sense of climax.

| CUMULATIVE EMPHASIS PARALLEL PARTICIPIAL PHRASES | First looking for his mother amid the forest of unfamiliar knees, calves, and thighs in the aisle, then searching for her among the alien overcoats and jackets in the lobby, finally the child crumpled into tearful sobs by the theater door. |

REPEATED KEY WORDS (33e)

Like parallelism, repeated key words can be effective means for achieving emphasis, if not overdone to the point of monotony. Examine the following two examples, noticing the difference between effective and ineffective repetition.

EFFECTIVE REPETITION   The poverty of the family expressed itself in the absence of color: the children were pasty white, the mongrel dog by the step was pasty yellow, the clothes on the line were pasty grey.

INEFFECTIVE REPETITION   When I was in high school, all my high school friends and I could think about was dating older high school boys. A date with a senior for the high school dance made a girl the envy of her friends at school.

Not surprisingly, repeated key words often occur in combination with parallel constructions. The word and construction repetitions can reinforce and emphasize one another, often with effective results.

ACTIVE AND PASSIVE VOICE VERBS (33f)

The **active voice** places emphasis upon the performer of the action, whereas the **passive voice** places emphasis upon that which receives the action. For the most part, you should utilize the active voice since the effect is more forceful. The passive voice results in a slower movement of context and in impersonal and colorless writing. Use it only if you wish to place emphasis upon the recipient of an action rather than to emphasize the action itself. In some instances, the performer of the action may not be known. In this case the passive voice is often used. (See Section 5 for more discussion of active and passive voice.)

ACTIVE   John broke the news to her at midnight.

PASSIVE   The news was broken to her by John at midnight.

PASSIVE   He was murdered between ten and eleven o'clock last night.

ACTIVE   Someone murdered him between ten and eleven o'clock last night.

In the second example here, the passive voice is probably preferable since the important aspect is the murder. With active voice and the emphasis that "someone did it," self-evident information gets the emphasis.

EXERCISE (33a–e), EMPHASIS

Revise the following sentences to achieve greater emphasis. Decide which elements are more important and position sentence elements to reflect your choice. Use expletive constructions, parallel series, and repetition where appropriate.

Example   The first patent registered by a black inventor was granted to Thomas L. Jennings, a tailor, in 1821.

The first patent registered by a black inventor was granted in 1821 to a tailor, Thomas L. Jennings.

1. More than a thousand patents have been granted to more than 400 black inventors since that day in 1821.

2. Some black inventors never bothered to patent the inventions they created, which was unfortunate for them.

3. Lewis Temple never patented his whale harpoon, which doubled the whaling catch in New England once it began to be used.

4. Almost every black was self-taught who registered a patent before the 1870s.

5. Andrew Beard invented the Jenny Coupler, the device that holds together railroad cars.

6. Mechanisms that oil machinery automatically were invented by Elijah McCoy, and they reduced machine wear and manpower requirements.

7. His name became so synonymous with successful inventions that "the real McCoy" was the name used for a useful invention in many places.

8. The third rail for electric railways was invented by Granville T. Woods and patented by him in 1901.

9. Woods patented more than fifty inventions, though he never finished elementary school and could not benefit from a high school education or experience the training of a college engineering program.

_____

10. The automatic traffic light was invented by Garret Morgan, another black inventor, in 1923.

_____

Revise the following sentences, making them periodic.

Example   A breathing device that is now used on the safety helmets of firefighters was also developed by Morgan.

A breathing device that is now used on the safety helmets of firefighters was also developed by Morgan.

11. He proved the worth of his device by using it himself in a rescue in the Lake Erie tunnel.

_____

12. The patents of early black inventors were a triumph because of the difficulties of patent registration.

_____

13. Generations of Black inventors were denied patent protection for their creations, held back by early laws regarding slavery.

_____

14. Their successes became more conventional as education became more readily available to blacks.

_____

15. Black inventors' triumphs began to occur in laboratories and in classrooms.

_____

16. A black man, Frederick Jones, invented the automatic refrigeration system for trucks, opening a new era in produce transportation.

_____

17. This system changed the way we eat because foods could be shipped farther without spoilage.

_____

18. Lewis Latimer showed skill with electricity that drew the attention of the famous white inventors of his day.

_____

19. Latimer got to know the inventor of the telephone when he worked with Alexander Graham Bell.

_____

20. He worked even more closely with Thomas Edison, as a member of the "Edison pioneers."

_____

Using your own paper, write a paragraph containing at least two loose sentences, two periodic sentences, one midbranching sentence, and one balanced sentence. Give each sentence a label in parentheses after the sentence.

EXERCISE (33f), ACTIVE AND PASSIVE VOICE

Where appropriate, revise the following sentences using the active voice. If you believe that the passive voice is preferable in a sentence, write *correct* in that blank.

Example   Great things have been achieved by black explorers and inventors.

<u>Black explorers and inventors have achieved great things.</u>

1. The first American flag at the North Pole was planted by Matthew Hensen.

   _____

2. The pole was reached by Hensen 45 minutes before the rest of the party.

   _____

3. Hensen, a black scientist, was invited to accompany the expedition by Commander Peary himself.

   _____

4. Hensen was born into poverty.

   _____

5. During his teen years, school was not found particularly attractive by Hensen.

   _____

6. He was hired as an aide to Peary.

   _____

7. While serving as Peary's aide, surveying and navigation were learned by Hensen.

   _____

8. He even taught himself anthropology and the customs of Eskimos were found fascinating.

   _____

9. Benjamin Banneker was a self-taught mathematical genius who was discovered by Thomas Jefferson.

   _____

10. Banneker's manuscripts were forwarded to the Academy of Science by Jefferson himself.

_____

11. A treatise on entomology was being written by Banneker.

_____

12. A record of all tides was being kept by him, as well.

_____

13. Banneker's interests were wide-ranging; a solar eclipse was even predicted by his writings on astronomy.

_____

14. Errors in his textbooks were soon being corrected by Banneker.

_____

15. Eventually, the position of assistant to the Geographer of the United States was offered to Banneker.

_____

16. In this office, the plan for the city of Washington was created, at least in part, by Banneker.

_____

17. Before the Civil War, patents could not be registered in the names of black men or women.

_____

18. This was due to the fact that the status of a slave was not recognized by the patent and copyright laws.

_____

19. Nevertheless, some patents were registered by blacks who had been freed.

_____

20. This fact can be discovered easily if records at the patent office are checked.

_____

VARIETY   (34)

Throughout the preceding three sections of this text, we have been considering various ways to achieve effective expression in sentences. Coordination and subordination, parallelism, emphatic positioning of sentence elements, a mixture of loose, periodic, midbranching, and balanced sentences, proper use of active and passive voice are all means for adding variety to your writing.

Even though you may feel satisfied if you can simply put your ideas into grammatically correct sentences, your ideas will lose much of their impact if they are always presented in the same types of sentence constructions. If you rely too heavily on short, simple sentences, always use subject-verb-object sentence patterns, or begin every complex sentence with a subordinate clause, your writing may become monotonous and predictable. Consequently, the reader can be lulled, almost hypnotized, by the unvarying sentence style and may pay less attention to the meaning. Learn to vary the length, type, and pattern of your sentences to fit your meaning, to establish emphasis, and to keep your reader's attention engaged.

SENTENCE LENGTHS AND PATTERNS

Section 33 discussed the advantages and disadvantages of combining a series of short sentences into a larger sentence that relates ideas. The best writing uses a mixture of short sentences and long ones. Readers appreciate having related ideas combined into compound and complex sentences, because then they do not have to work at and guess about connections between thoughts. On the other hand, if you wish to establish a point dramatically, a short sentence will emphatically break the rhythm of a paragraph and draw the reader's attention. Compare the following two paragraphs, and notice how sentence variety helps to achieve emphasis in the second one.

> We could hear the wind howling above us. We huddled in the storm shelter. The tornado roared through the neighborhood like a freight train. It was quiet suddenly, so we climbed the stairs carefully. Our knees were shaking. Father opened the door, and our house was gone.

> We could hear the wind howling above us as we huddled in the storm shelter. Sounding like a freight train, the tornado roared through the neighborhood. Suddenly it was quiet. Our knees shaking, carefully we climbed the stairs, and Father opened the door. Our house was gone.

The second paragraph gains much of its dramatic effect from careful sentence construction. The writer has combined sentences in the first part of the paragraph, piling details together to reinforce the sense of chaos associated with the storm. The use of the participial phrase *Sounding like a freight train* and the absolute phrase *Our knees shaking* vary the subject-verb-object arrangement established in the first sentence. The free adverbial modifiers (ones that can be moved to several positions in the sentence) *suddenly* and *carefully* have been located near the front of their sentences for contrast and emphasis. A short sentence has been used to draw the attention to the contrast between the storm's noise and the ominous silence after it had passed. Finally, to emphasize the shock, the writer has used a short, blunt statement to say the house had been destroyed. As a result, the reader can participate in the feelings the writer experienced during the incident—from fear to shock—partially because of the varied sentence lengths and patterns.

Varying the beginnings of sentences often achieves effective expression. Note the revisions of the following sentence:

Little trouble developed in the beginning, and the manager looked forward to a harmonious future.

BEGINNING WITH A PREPOSITIONAL PHRASE	In the beginning, little trouble developed, and the manager looked forward to a harmonious future.
BEGINNING WITH AN ABSOLUTE PHRASE	Little trouble having developed in the beginning, the manager looked forward to a harmonious future.
BEGINNING WITH A PARTICIPIAL PHRASE	Having little trouble in the beginning, the manager looked forward to a harmonious future.
BEGINNING WITH AN EXPLETIVE	There was little trouble in the beginning, and the manager looked forward to a harmonious future.

BEGINNING WITH A SUBORDINATE CLAUSE	Because little trouble developed in the beginning, the manager looked forward to a harmonious future.
BEGINNING WITH A COORDINATING CONJUNCTION	But little trouble developed in the beginning, and the manager looked forward to a harmonious future.

Varying the position of free modifiers (those that can be moved from one place to another in sentences) can also be effective. Adverbs, adverb phrases and clauses, and some participial phrases and absolute phrases can be moved, giving you a choice of effects. Note, for example, the following sentences.

Struggling for a foothold, the mountain climber clung to the cliff.

The mountain climber, *struggling for a foothold,* clung to the cliff.

The mountain climber clung, *struggling for a foothold,* to the cliff.

The basic sentence pattern in English is subject-verb-object. We have already seen that opening a sentence with modifiers changes the effect of this pattern. But **inverting the pattern** can also provide variety, although you should use inversion judiciously because it often strikes readers as somewhat abnormal. You can invert the subject and the object; or you can open with a modifier, inverting the subject and verb.

These delays we would not tolerate. [object-subject-verb]

Next to the newsstand on the corner stood the police officer. [modifier-verb-subject]

Finally, **various types of sentences** can be used to create effects. Although you most often write declarative statements, an occasional question, command, or exclamation may better achieve the effect you desire. Notice how the changes in the following paragraph, from question to command to statement to exclamation to statement, lend variety and emphasis to the message:

Is it true that people will settle for trash on television? Believe it. Studies show viewers will watch almost any type of garbage as long as it isn't obscene. But if they consider a program to be pornographic, watch out! Then there is an uproar about "filth" on television.

**EXERCISE (34)-1, CHANGING SENTENCE PATTERNS AND TYPES
FOR VARIETY**

Revise each of the following sentences to begin with the listed types of constructions. Invent details as necessary to create these constructions.

Example   Ethnic actors now appear in many television programs.

(prepositional phrase) With both starring and supporting roles,
ethnic actors now appear in many television programs.

(absolute) Formerly denied work, ethnic actors now appear
in many television programs.

1. Ethnic groups have received much network attention in the last fifteen years,
    and blacks have increasingly been spotlighted.

    A. (prepositional phrase) _____

    B. (participial phrase) _____

    C. (expletive) _____

    D. (subordinate clause) _____

    E. (coordinating conjunction) _____

2. *The Jeffersons* was one of the first programs to show life in an upwardly mobile
    black family and depict the family's relations with both black and white
    neighbors.

    A. (subordinate clause) _____

    B. (expletive) _____

    C. (prepositional phrase) _____

    D. (absolute) _____

    E. (participial phrase) _____

3. For years, *Hawaii Five-O* was the only television show to offer regular work
    for Chinese-American actors.

    A. (subordinate clause) _____

    B. (participial phrase) _____

    C. (absolute) _____

    D. (expletive) _____

4. The comedies probably helped people through laughter to see the similarities as well as the differences between ethnic groups.

   A. (prepositional phrase) _____

   B. (participial phrase) _____

   C. (absolute) _____

   D. (subordinate clause) _____

5. *Star Trek* was another program that featured several ethnic characters.

   A. (subordinate clause) _____

   B. (absolute) _____

   C. (prepositional phrase) _____

   D. (coordinating conjunction) _____

Revise each of the following sentences as indicated.

Example   Ethnic actors are now common on television programs.

(Invert subject and verb.) *Now common on television programs are ethnic actors.*

6. All kinds of programs employ ethnic actors now, including police and detective dramas.

   (Reposition participial phrase.) _____

   _____

7. Television now is a medium that illustrates America's ethnic presences.

   (Invert subject and verb.) _____

   _____

EXERCISE (34)-2, SENTENCE COMBINING FOR VARIETY AND COHERENCE

On your own paper, use the techniques we have reviewed in this unit on effective sentences to revise the following paragraph. Strive for sentence variety and emphasis while achieving paragraph coherence. Your revision should contain at least one example of each of the following:

1. Short sentences combined into a complex sentence (subordinating conjunction)

2. Short sentences combined into a compound sentence (coordinating conjunction)

3. Parallel construction

4. Absolute phrase

5. Participial phrase

6. Inverted order—verb preceding subject

7. Appositive

8. Verbs in both the active and passive voices

9. Question or command

10. Effective subordination

Potatoes are not native to North America. They were exported, then imported. Finally, the potato was responsible for huge numbers of immigrants coming to America. Spanish explorers found the potato used as a food in South America. They took potatoes home to Spain. Potatoes were easy to grow. They became a cheap food source. Soon the potato became a staple in the diet of almost all northern Europeans. The potato was introduced to North America by European settlers. They brought the potato, a familiar food by that time, in their ships to the new settlements in America. The potato's spread into North America was circuitous, to say the least. Back in Europe, the Irish particularly relied on the potato. Poor Irish peasants often ate little else. In 1845 and 1846, a blight struck the Irish potato crop. The blight turned the potatoes black. It destroyed them. Thousands of poor Irish farmers starved. There was no disaster relief system in 1846. If they stayed in Ireland, these peasants would have starved to death. Nearly a million Irish people left their homes. They immigrated to America. In America they could find jobs and they could eat.

Revise each of the following sentences as indicated.

1. The influence of the potato spread quickly.

   (Reposition free adverbial modifier.) _____

   _____

2. The potato came to North America by way of Europe from South America.

   (Reposition prepositional phrase.) _____

   _____

3. Poor people greeted such a cheap food with enthusiasm, the potato being an inexpensive source of carbohydrates.

   (Invert subject and verb.) _____

   _____

   (Reposition absolute.) _____

   _____

   (Reposition prepositional phrase.) _____

   _____

4. The peasants planted the potato; the potato grew with little care; happily the peasants added the potato to their diets.

   (Reposition free adverbial modifiers.) _____

   _____

   (Invert subject and verb.) _____

   _____

   (Reposition prepositional phrases.) _____

   _____

   (Create parallel constructions.) _____

   _____

THE DICTIONARY   (36a)

Most people use a dictionary mainly for checking spelling and meaning, but a writer can use a good dictionary for aid in many other ways as well. A dictionary also records a word's pronunciation, origin (etymology), part of speech, principal parts and plurals or other forms, and frequently its synonyms, antonyms, and level of usage. Often a dictionary also includes lists of abbreviations, spelling, capitalization, and punctuation rules, biographical and geographical information, vocabularies of rhymes and given names, and a list of U.S. colleges and universities.

Rather than just using your dictionary in the usual way—to look up spelling and meaning—familiarize yourself with the whole volume. Begin by reading the **front matter.** Read the user's guide or explanatory notes, which will tell you what each part of a dictionary entry means and what special information it contains.

Then read the pronunciation guide and the explanation of the abbreviations your dictionary uses. The purpose of the various type faces, labels, abbreviations, symbols, and other conventions found in a dictionary's entries is to achieve compactness and comprehensiveness. Unless you understand their meaning and use, you will miss a great deal of the information your dictionary has to offer. Several of the exercises in this section require information from various parts of dictionary entries, so you will have to read the front matter in your dictionary before you can answer them correctly.

The **back matter** can provide a wealth of information you probably never even knew your dictionary contained. Look it over so that you will know where to find rules for capitalization, for instance, the next time you need them.

Contrary to popular belief, dictionaries do not "define" words. Rather, they record meanings of actual usage, past and present. Some dictionaries record the general, most current meaning first. Others, such as *Webster's Collegiate Dictionary*, list a word's meaning in historical order, the oldest meaning first. Check the front matter in your dictionary to see which type of order it uses.

Language constantly changes. Over time, meanings that once were current may be superseded by newer ones that have achieved wide usage and acceptance. New words enter a language, and other words disappear. For example, thirty years ago you would not have been able to find the word *astronaut* in any dictionary. Dictionaries are periodically revised to take such changes into account. Although you do not need to replace your dictionary every time a new edition is published, you will probably find that by the time you reach middle age the dictionary you used in high school or college will no longer suit your needs. The dictionary is a writer's best resource; be sure you have one that serves as a good working partner.

Practice: Using your dictionary   Read the user's guide at the front of your desk dictionary and review the index. Then answer the following questions.

1. What does the "order of definitions" or "order of senses" section say about the way meanings are listed within an entry?

2. What symbol does your dictionary use to indicate the beginning and ending of a word's etymology?

3. How many different usage labels are used in your dictionary, and what are they?

4. What does your dictionary say about cross-references?

5. What does your dictionary say about synonyms?

6. What is the zip code for Berea College?

7. What does the abbreviation CCU stand for?

8. What was Catherine Greenaway's nickname?

9. On what page can you find proofreader's marks in your dictionary?

10. In the section on style, what use is listed first for the virgule?

Title of your desk dictionary: _____

_____

EXERCISE (36a), THE DICTIONARY

A. In the blanks, identify the language from which each word was borrowed; give ony the earliest given source. Since the term *borrowing* refers to languages other than English, the answers *Middle East (ME)*, *Old English (OE)*, and *Anglo-Saxon (AS)* will not be correct.

1. clock _____	2. retort _____	3. retail _____
4. sanguine _____	5. sastruga _____	6. sidereal _____
7. sitar _____	8. stearic _____	9. tattoo _____
10. trauma _____	11. xylem _____	12. bravado _____
13. carnelian _____	14. deckle _____	15. gorgeous _____

B. In the blanks, indicate the original or etymological meaning of each word; that is, give the meaning within the brackets in the dictionary, not the meaning in the definition of the word itself. For example, the etymological meaning of the word *animism* is "soul."

1. bandana _____	2. by-law _____	3. germ _____
4. finance _____	5. arena _____	6. hypocrite _____
7. janitor _____	8. matador _____	9. memoir _____
10. tycoon _____	11. pedigree _____	12. respond _____
13. sinus _____	14. swindler _____	15. insult _____

C. All of the following words are derived from the name of a person or a place. In the blank after each word, indicate the name of the person or place from which that word is derived.

1. roentgen _____	2. Baedeker _____
3. chauvinist _____	4. Doppler effect _____
5. tarantula _____	6. jovial _____
7. camellia _____	8. jackanapes _____
9. paisley _____	10. palace _____

D. After referring to the user's guide in your dictionary, describe how it indi-
    cates the plural form of nouns.

    _____

    _____

    _____

    _____

    _____

E. Consult your dictionary and in the blanks list all the plural forms it gives
    for the following nouns.

    1. sister-in-law   _____   2. datum   _____

    3. hippopotamus   _____   4. alumna   _____

    5. sheep   _____   6. wolf   _____

    7. appendix   _____   8. focus   _____

    9. deer   _____   10. criterion _____

F. After referring to the user's guide in your dictionary, explain how it indicates
    the principal parts of verbs.

    _____

    _____

    _____

    _____

G. Consult your dictionary and in the blanks list all of the past tenses and past
    participles it gives for the following verbs.

    1. hang (suspend)   _____   2. shrink   _____

    3. lie (recline)   _____   4. swim   _____

    5. lay (place)   _____   6. bear (carry) _____

    7. rise   _____   8. bear (give
                                               birth to)   _____
    9. dive   _____
                                           10. shine   _____

INCREASING YOUR

VOCABULARY   (36b)

Just as a variety of sentence patterns or methods of paragraph development can make your writing more interesting for a reader, so a varied and appropriate use of language can improve your writing. Your choice of vocabulary can be extremely important to many aspects of your writing. Not only do the most accurate and expressive words convey your meaning best, but vocabulary choices can improve coherence within paragraphs. Synonyms, for example, can help your reader see the connections between ideas, as well as add variety to sentences.

On the other hand, you must be careful when selecting synonyms. Many words are loosely synonymous, but each word has its own connotations or shades of meaning. If you consult a thesaurus, synonym dictionary, or the synonym entries in your desk dictionary, also be sure to look up the meaning of the synonym in the dictionary. You want to be certain that the connotations of the word fit the context in which you intend to use it. Some words may not be appropriate to the tone of your paragraph, even though they are synonymous.

A word's etymology can help you decide if it is an appropriate synonym. Suppose you are looking for an alternative to the word *famous* to describe the research on pickles at Dill University. You have narrowed the synonyms down to *reputed* and *renowned*, words you found listed under *famous* in the thesaurus. The dictionary defines *repute* to mean "to assign a reputation to." Its origin is a Latin word that loosely means "to be considered." *Renowned* means "being widely honored and acclaimed." Its origin is an Old French word that means "to name again." Although the shades of meaning are subtle, you may decide that *reputed* has less positive connotations and that its etymology suggests subjective opinion, whereas *renowned* seems more forceful and carries connotations that more exactly fit your sentence's meaning.

The previous example illustrates another important point about vocabulary: Thousands of words we use regularly have been borrowed or adapted from other languages. *Renowned* can be traced to the Old French word *renomer*. As the etymology indicates, the root form of the word means "name." The prefix *re-* means "again": hence the word's meaning, "to name again."

If you study common prefixes and suffixes (attachments added to a word's beginning or ending) as well as learn to recognize common word roots, you will be able to increase your vocabulary considerably. Just by knowing the meaning of a word's parts, you can often decipher its approximate meaning even if you have never seen the word before. The following lists of prefixes, suffixes, and combining forms taken from the *Prentice-Hall Handbook for Writers,* Tenth Edition, can help you increase your vocabulary.

PREFIXES

PREFIX	MEANING	EXAMPLE
ab-	away from	absent
ad-*	to *or* for	adverb
com-*	with	combine
de-	down, away from, *or* undoing	degrade, depart, dehumanize
dis-*	separation *or* reversal	disparate, disappoint
ex-*	out of *or* former	extend, ex-president
in-*	in *or* on	input
in-*	not	inhuman
ir-	not	irrelevant
mis-	wrong	mistake
non-	not	non-Christian
ob-*	against	obtuse
pre-	before	prevent
pro-	for *or* forward	proceed
re-	back *or* again	repeat
sub-*	under	subcommittee
trans-	across	transcribe
un-	not	unclean

*The spelling of these prefixes varies, usually to make pronunciation easier. *Ad* becomes *ac* in *accuse,* *ag* in *aggregate,* *at* in *attack.* Similarly, the final consonant in the other prefixes indicated is assimilated by the initial letter of the root word: *colleague (com + league); divert (dis + vert); evict (ex + vict); illicit (in + licit); offend (ob + fend); succeed (sub + ceed).*

SUFFIXES

Noun suffixes denoting *act of, state of, quality of*

SUFFIX	EXAMPLE	MEANING
-dom	freedom	*state of* being free
-hood	manhood	*state of* being a man
-ness	dimness	*state of* being dim
-ice	cowardice	*quality of* being a coward
-ation	flirtation	*act of* flirting
-ion	intercession	*act of* interceding
-sion	scansion	*act of* scanning
-tion	corruption	*state of* being corrupt
-ment	argument	*act of* arguing
-ship	friendship	*state of* being friends
-ance	continuance	*act of* continuing
-ence	precedence	*act of* preceding
-ancy	flippancy	*state of* being flippant
-ency	currency	*state of* being current
-ism	baptism	*act of* baptizing
-ery	bravery	*quality of* being brave

Noun suffixes denoting *doer, one who*

SUFFIX	EXAMPLE	MEANING
-eer	auctioneer	*one who* auctions
-st	fascist	*one who* believes in fascism
-or	debtor	*one who* is in debt
-er	worker	*one who* works

Verb suffixes denoting *to make* or *to perform the act of*

SUFFIX	EXAMPLE	MEANING
-ate	perpetuate	*to make* perpetual
-en	soften	*to make* soft
-fy	dignify	*to make* dignified
-ize, ise	sterilize	*to make* sterile

Adjectival suffixes

SUFFIX	MEANING	EXAMPLE
-ful	full of	hateful
-ish	resembling	foolish
-ate	having	affectionate
-ic, ical	resembling	angelic
-ive	having	prospective
-ous	full of	zealous
-ulent	full of	fraudulent
-less	without	fatherless
-able, -ible	capable of	peaceable
-ed	having	spirited
-ly	resembling	womanly
-like	resembling	childlike

COMBINING FORMS (APPEARING GENERALLY, BUT NOT ALWAYS, AS PREFIXES)

COMBINING FORM	MEANING	EXAMPLE
anthropo	man	*anthropo*logy
arch	rule	*arch*duke, mon*arch*
auto	self	*auto*mobile
bene	well	*bene*ficial
eu	well	*eu*logy
graph	writing	*graph*ic, bio*graphy*
log, logue	word, speech	mono*logue*
magni	great	*magni*ficent
mal	bad	*mal*ady
mono	one	*mono*tone
multi	many	*multi*plication
neo	new	*neo*classic
omni	all	*omni*bus
pan, pant	all	*pan*hellenic
phil	loving	*phil*osophy
phono	sound	*phono*graph
poly	many	*poly*gamy
pseudo	false	*pseudo*nym
semi	half	*semi*formal
trans	across	*trans*continental

Practice A: Prefixes   Add the appropriate prefix to each of the following words to indicate a negative meaning. The answers are listed at the end of this section.

[1]entangle [2]appropriate [3]believable [4]array [5]guarded [6]resistible [7]believer [8]allow [9]edible [10]inspiring

Practice B: Suffixes   Add the appropriate suffix to each of the following words to indicate act of, state of, or quality of. Check the spelling of the new words since the addition of a suffix may change the spelling of the word. The answers are listed at the end of this section.

[1]wise [2]appear [3]father [4]clean [5]competent [6]advertise [7]administer [8]terror [9]concede [10]educate

Answers to Practice A   [1]dis- [2]in- [3]un- [4]dis- [5]un- [6]ir- [7]un- (or non-) [8]dis- [9]in- [10]un-

Answers to Practice B   [1]wisdom [2]appearance [3]fatherhood [4]cleanliness [5]competence (or competency) [6]advertisement [7]administration [8]terrorism [9]concession [10]education

EXERCISE (36b)-1, PREFIXES, SUFFIXES, AND COMBINING FORMS

Add the appropriate prefix to each of the roots below to form a word that will fit in the sentence at the right.

Example -poly   Does the library have a _____monopoly_____ on genealogical records?

1. -spect   In _____ , I realize it was foolilsh to search elsewhere.

2. -durately   A competent salesclerk will never _____ refuse to help you.

3. -tract   I'll not _____ my criticism.

4. -standard   Your work may seem _____ if you don't work harder.

5. -meate   The odor of compost seems to _____ the entire backyard.

6. -appropriated   Have the county commissioners _____ those funds for the sheriff's office?

7. -thesis   These two ideas should be combined to form a _____ _____ to guide your research.

8. -strain   You should _____ yourself until you've finished all your research.

9. -stain   I will _____ from any further criticism.

10. -jointed   But your research will seem _____ if you do not have a unifying idea.

11. -collegiate She has done nothing to promote _____ cooperation between our two schools.

12. -adjusted   Does that indicate a _____ personality?

13. -acted   The legislation will be _____ into law in June.

14. -vention   The law's _____ will be welcome in this dispute.

15. -noble   You've not acted in an _____ way, have you?

16. -sensitive We cannot be _____ to the rights of others.

17. -own   On the other hand, no one can _____ her own family and friends.

18. -ordinary   The award is in recognition of _____ service.

19. -curricular   I've been involved in a great many _____ activities while also studying hard.

20. -filtrate   Our attempts to _____ the organization were not successful.

Form verbs and adjectives by adding suffixes to the following words. Adjust spelling as necessary.

	VERB	ADJECTIVE
Example civility	_civilize_	_civil_
21. mystic	_____	_____
22. sum	_____	_____
23. false	_____	_____
24. difference	_____	_____
25. origin	_____	_____
26. type	_____	_____
27. familiarity	_____	_____
28. veneration	_____	_____
29. person	_____	_____
30. mobility	_____	_____

Write two words constructed from each of the following combining forms.

Example com	_compare_	_comparable_
31. in	_____	_____
32. pro	_____	_____
33. re	_____	_____
34. pre	_____	_____
35. ism	_____	_____
36. ate	_____	_____

37. ance _____ _____

38. ous _____ _____

39. ment _____ _____

40. dom _____ _____

On your own paper, write a sentence for each word of the pairs you constructed in items 31 through 40.

EXERCISE (36b)-2, VOCABULARY AND WORD MEANING

Circle the number of the word closest in meaning to the italicized word in each given phrase.

Example   a *ribald* story   (1) (vulgar)   (2) noble
                               (3) funny   (4) learned

1. a *surname*   (1) nickname   (2) first name
                       (3) last name   (4) rank

2. *surety*   (1) bonds   (2) stocks
                       (3) self-assurance   (4) responsibility

3. a *captious* person   (1) spacious   (2) fickle
                           (3) fault-finding   (4) slanderous

4. *libel*   (1) willing   (2) able
                       (3) to defame   (4) book

5. an *obdurate* person   (1) submissive   (2) erase
                            (3) stubborn   (4) cover

6. the *epitome* of taste   (1) letter   (2) typical
                              (3) land   (4) apex

7. *license*   (1) lust   (2) sticker
                       (3) card   (4) paper

8. *migrate*   (1) seasonal change   (2) movement
                           of location
                       (3) headache   (4) schism

9. *emigrate*   (1) movement   (2) travel
                       (3) European   (4) permanent change
                                                        of location

10. *dilatory*   (1) removes hair   (2) delaying
                       (3) fast   (4) spreading

11. a *diligent* scholar   (1) learned   (2) intelligent
                            (3) industrious   (4) licensed

12. a *digest*   (1) starfish   (2) stomach
                       (3) version   (4) synopsis

13. to *conspire*   (1) plan in secret   (2) subversive
                       (3) breathe   (4) steeple

14. *abjure*
    - (1) renounce
    - (2) servile
    - (3) displace
    - (4) agree

15. *byword*
    - (1) two words
    - (2) proverb
    - (3) class
    - (4) expletive

16. *quondam*
    - (1) former
    - (2) tenant
    - (3) share cropper
    - (4) hut

17. *subscript*
    - (1) subscribe
    - (2) written beneath
    - (3) supercilious
    - (4) signature

18. *subside*
    - (1) oppose
    - (2) sink lower
    - (3) divide
    - (4) conquer

19. *subsist*
    - (1) lower
    - (2) exist
    - (3) hose
    - (4) underwater

20. *subsequent*
    - (1) underwater
    - (2) lower
    - (3) following
    - (4) private

21. *weighty*
    - (1) fat
    - (2) waist
    - (3) momentous
    - (4) sequential

22. to *intervene*
    - (1) come between
    - (2) fight
    - (3) settle
    - (4) compromise

23. a *diurnal* cycle
    - (1) different
    - (2) daily
    - (3) circuitous
    - (4) poetic

24. the *nascent* plants
    - (1) tasteless
    - (2) final
    - (3) emerging
    - (4) vocal

25. *lucrative*
    - (1) careful
    - (2) profitable
    - (3) laughable
    - (4) gloomy

26. *corsage*
    - (1) rhyme
    - (2) bouquet
    - (3) procession
    - (4) chat

27. *conundrum*
    - (1) particles
    - (2) pipe
    - (3) puzzle
    - (4) boredom

28. a *condign* reward
    - (1) kindly
    - (2) assert
    - (3) well-deserved
    - (4) related

29. *concupiscent*
    - (1) running together
    - (2) lustful
    - (3) eccentric
    - (4) hopeless

30. *cognate* words
    - (1) related
    - (2) thoughtful
    - (3) convincing
    - (4) unlike

31. an *eclectic* decor
    - (1) specific
    - (2) military
    - (3) selective
    - (4) severe

32. a *droll* remark
    (1) amusing   (2) elf
    (3) sour   (4) waste

33. a *dolorous* face
    (1) financial   (2) sorrowful
    (3) humorous   (4) fatal

34. *disingenuous*
    (1) uncommon   (2) immature
    (3) pleasant   (4) not straightforward

35. *diffidence*
    (1) greed   (2) controversy
    (3) disguise   (4) timidity

36. *decorous*
    (1) ornamental   (2) proper
    (3) harmful   (4) old

37. *deciduous*
    (1) final   (2) decisive
    (3) leaf-shedding   (4) deadly

38. a *cursory* glance
    (1) profane   (2) superficial
    (3) greedy   (4) roomy

39. *credulous*
    (1) believable   (2) corrupt
    (3) gullible   (4) irrational

40. *craven* behavior
    (1) molded   (2) bird
    (3) cowardly   (4) profane

41. *excoriate*
    (1) denounce   (2) disembowel
    (3) atone   (4) furnish

42. to *expiate* one's guilt
    (1) explain   (2) spit
    (3) destroy   (4) atone

43. *extant*
    (1) complete   (2) existing
    (3) search   (4) praise

44. *feckless*
    (1) ineffective   (2) careless
    (3) punctual   (4) foul

45. *flagitious*
    (1) nonviolent   (2) elaborate
    (3) necessary   (4) vicious

46. *emollient*
    (1) lit   (2) soothing
    (3) timid   (4) secret

47. *envenom*
    (1) bite   (2) embitter
    (3) subjugate   (4) trap

48. *ergo*
    (1) besides   (2) therefore
    (3) scholar   (4) convent

49. *erotic*
    (1) strange   (2) extreme
    (3) amatory   (4) worn

50. *esoteric* knowledge
   (1) artistic   (2) confidential
   (3) denounced   (4) evident

51. *innocuous*
   (1) lazy   (2) harmless
   (3) foul   (4) harmful

52. *indolent*
   (1) poor   (2) lazy
   (3) energetic   (4) encouraging

53. *impotent*
   (1) all-powerful   (2) incapable
   (3) beg   (4) curse

54. *hyperbole*
   (1) exaggeration   (2) assumption
   (3) instrument   (4) platform

55. *histrionic*
   (1) historical   (2) hairy
   (3) theatrical   (4) scientific

56. *heinous*
   (1) atrocious   (2) pleasurable
   (3) wolf   (4) unorthodox

57. *gregarious*
   (1) free   (2) distorted
   (3) sociable   (4) derived

58. *gnostic*
   (1) atheist   (2) wise
   (3) glandular   (4) spiritual wisdom

59. *germane*
   (1) European   (2) verbal noun
   (3) pertinent   (4) flowery

60. *garrulous*
   (1) talkative   (2) free
   (3) greedy   (4) flowery

APPROPRIATENESS (37)

The appropriateness of your word choice directly affects the way readers respond to your writing. Inappropriate words will confuse readers and ultimately may irritate them. The words you choose set the tone of your writing; they tell the readers the attitude you are taking toward your subject and toward them as well.

What constitutes appropriate language? That depends to some extent on your topic, your purpose, and your audience. A letter to a close friend will have a much more informal style and will probably contain several slang expressions that would not be appropriate in a research report written for a college psychology class. The research report would undoubtedly contain some social-science jargon understood by people in psychology but possibly unfamiliar to the general public.

Although appropriateness is a somewhat relative matter, several guidelines do apply to all but the most informal writing:

1. Avoid **slang expressions** and **nonstandard English** unless you are recording actual conversation that uses them. Although slang is colorful and often lively, it is usually understood by a relatively small group of people. Furthermore, slang expressions quickly lose vigor. Today's slang may be meaningless to most readers in a year or two. Nonstandard English is normally associated with provincialism and lack of education; you should avoid it in your writing.

SLANG	That prof hit us with a really heavy number.
REVISION	That professor gave us a very difficult assignment.

NONSTANDARD ENGLISH	They wasn't on time, so let's don't wait for them.
REVISION	They weren't on time, so let's not wait for them.

2. Avoid **jargon** when writing for a general audience, and replace **artificial diction** with more straightforward words. Like slang, jargon is a vocabulary well known only to those in a particular group or discipline. Computer programmers, for example, are quite familiar with terms such as *byte* and *baud-rate;* general readers are not. Unless you are writing for a special audience, use jargon sparingly and define terms you think your readers might not know.

Artificial diction, on the other hand, never adds anything desirable to writing. Choose simple, direct words instead of elaborate, pompous-sounding ones. The person who writes *Males of advanced years fail to maintain their recollective faculties* gains nothing; the one who writes *Old men forget* makes an effective point.

Name _____ Date _____ Score _____

EXERCISE (37), APPROPRIATENESS: SLANG AND NONSTANDARD ENGLISH

Revise the following sentences to rid them of slang or nonstandard expressions.

Example   That new restaurant was the pits.

That new restaurant was not a place I would go to again.

1. I was really hoping it would be heavy duty.

   _____

2. It must have been a real blockhead who opened that dump.

   _____

3. I saw a coupla profs there feeding their faces.

   _____

4. That joint will bomb out within four months.

   _____

5. I don't think they're tuned in to their clients' styles.

   _____

6. The dish I ordered turned out to be really gross.

   _____

7. They shouldn't ought to have served tea in Mason jars.

   _____

8. I'd of ordered something else if I'd of known that was their plan.

   _____

9. Scarcely none of the better restaurants would follow such practice.

   _____

10. That fruitcake of a waiter almost drove me bananas.

   _____

11. Our evening was fouled up, but good.

   _____

12. I was expecting at least the real McCoy of a wine list.

   _____

13. The cook must of been just hanging out in back, instead of cooking.

   _____

14. Their other restaurant opened last year to great acclaim; it was a shoo-in to be included in the Michelin guide.

   _____

15. Maybe we shouldn't of toted in our bags of popcorn.

   _____

Revise the following sentences to correct artificial diction or jargon and any other inappropriate wording.

Example   Woody Allen's comedic style exaggerates his ethnicity to marvelous effect.

   Woody Allen's comedy exaggerates his ethnic identity in a very funny way.

16. Woody Allen's comedic style is infinitely more naturalistic than Steve Martin's.

   _____

17. Allen's persona is lent verisimilitude by that very natural style.

   _____

18. One's perceptions of Martin's characterizations are dominated by the conviction that he is merely acting out a thespian role.

   _____

19. Martin's characters seldom possess genealogy, marriage, or other relationships that typify life in the phenomenal world.

   _____

20. In _The Jerk,_ for example, the audience knows only that his character is a Caucasian foundling raised by a black family.

   _____

21. Statistically, the possibility of this happening is at a less than 0.05 probability.

   _____

22. Therefore, the audience never experiences a willing suspension of disbelief.

   _____

23. The personae adopted for the cinema by Woody Allen, on the contrary, accrue innumerable naturalistic detail.

    _____

24. Allen, né Konigsberg, always portrays a character of Jewish ethnicity and the audience possesses an awareness of the character's inner life.

    _____

25. The ethnic characteristics of Allen's characters do not allow the characters to spring at us from an existential void.

    _____

26. If you buy common stocks on margin, puts and calls are good ways of hedging.

    _____

27. If our inter-grader reliability coefficient can't be improved, we'll have to discontinue use of this instrument.

    _____

28. The superficiality of outward appearances is often incongruent with reality.

    _____

29. Preferred stocks have lower betas than do common stocks.

    _____

30. The baud rate may be impressive, but this just doesn't have the 128K I need.

    _____

EXACTNESS   (38)

If a reader is to understand what you mean, your word choice needs to be as exact as possible. Selecting correct words and appropriate synonyms, avoiding invented words and improprieties, and using concrete and specific words are ways to achieve exactness in your writing.

The previous section on vocabulary briefly discussed synonyms. Synonyms are two or more words that mean essentially, but not exactly, the same thing. Desk dictionaries discriminate between word meanings by means of **synonymies.** These explanatory passages, labeled either *Synonyms* or *Syn.,* usually follow the definition of a main-entry word. The synonymy lists a group of synonyms for the main entry and explains the difference in meaning between the words listed. The following synonymy for the word *anger* is taken from *Webster's New World Dictionary of the American Language,* Second College Edition.

> **Syn.** *anger* is broadly applicable to feelings of resentful or vengeful displeasure: *indignation* implies righteous anger aroused by what seems unjust, mean, or insulting; *rage* suggests a violent outburst of anger in which self-control is lost; *fury* implies a frenzied rage that borders on madness; *ire,* chiefly a literary word, suggests a show of great anger in acts, words, looks, etc.; *wrath* implies deep indignation expressing itself in a desire to punish or get revenge.

When you consult a dictionary to locate the synonymy for a group of words, you may not always select the entry that contains the synonymy. In such a case, the dictionary will refer to the word where the synonymy occurs. In the case shown here, for example, had you first looked up the word *indignation,* you would have found the notation *Syn. see anger.*

Exactness also requires that your word choices avoid stereotypes. Thus, you should avoid derogatory references to sex, race, ethnicity, or religion. These types of references are not only offensive, they are also inaccurate. Do not inappropriately classify occupations or activities by gender. For example, because some of the mail is delivered by women, referring to mail carriers in general as *mailmen* is inexact.

In being exact it is also important not to confuse words. Some words give trouble because of similarities in spelling or pronunciation or similarities in both respects. One such group of words is **homonyms,** words that are identical in spelling and pronunciation but that have different meanings (*butter*—a spread; *butter*—a goat in action). Another group of words, called **homographs,** are identical in spelling but have different pronunciations and meanings (*wind*—one of nature's forces; *wind*—to coil the spring of). A third group of words, called **homophones,** are pronounced the same but are spelled differently and have different meanings (*red*—a color; *read*—the past tense of the verb *read*). Still a fourth group can be called **approximate homonyms**—that is, words that are pronounced or spelled approximately the same but have different meanings (*elicit*—to bring out; *illicit*—unlawful).

The best course of action when using words of these types is to look them up in the dictionary and learn their correct spellings and meanings.

Readers usually find words used in very unexpected ways to be troublesome because they do not fit convention and their meanings are therefore likely to be unclear. You should thus use invented words and improprieties with great care and only when you are sure their meanings will be clear.

Invented words can be grouped into three categories. One group is **neologisms:** either new words or, more commonly, old words with new meanings or usages. For example, the noun *shot* originally referred to bullets or pellets for firearms. Since the invention of the camera, *shot* can also mean a photograph or single cinematic view. Another group is **coined words:** deliberately invented creations which often achieve some degree of general use. *Smog* (smoke + fog), *motel* (motor + hotel), and *flak* (antiaircraft gunfire) are examples. The third group is **noncewords,** words made up to fit special situations and generally not used more than once, as in *She committed final examicide because she didn't study for the chemistry test.*

Usually you should avoid invented words. When in doubt about whether a word is invented, consult the dictionary. If the dictionary does not list it or labels it as a substandard word, do not use the word in formal writing. In some instances in some contexts, your instructor may permit you to invent words yourself. Before doing so, however, you should determine his or her attitude toward such words.

Improprieties are legitimate words wrongly used: *The exits are signed clearly.* Sometimes you may wonder whether a word used as one part of speech can be used as another part of speech. English is fairly free in shifting words from one part of speech to another, a process called **functional shift.** For example, the noun *fire* is used as an adjective—as in *fire engine*—and as a verb—as in *fire the cannon.* However, convention dictates whether a word shifts or not. Unless a shift has generally been accepted, you would be wise to avoid it. Otherwise, the reader may find your usage inappropriate and confusing. If you are in doubt, consult the dictionary to ensure that the shift you want to use is not an impropriety.

Writing that captures the reader's interest and most effectively conveys the author's exact meaning usually relies on a high proportion of concrete and specific words to give it life and clarity. **Concrete words** name things we can perceive with our senses, things we can see, hear, touch, taste, and smell. **Abstract words,** on the other hand, name qualities, ideas, and concepts. *Honesty* is an abstraction. To say someone turned in a lost wallet at the campus police station is to show concretely what honesty means. **Specific words** refer to the individual members of a class or group. **General words** refer to all the members of a class or group. *Clothing* is general, but *shoes, shirts,* and *skirts* are specific. Using concrete and specific words in conjunction with abstract and general terms provides definition for your ideas and helps your reader to understand exactly what you mean.

Like concrete and specific words, **figurative language** can help readers understand your ideas. Fresh and appropriate figures of speech can be a very effective way of making meaning concrete. On the other hand, inappropriate figurative language will only obscure meaning. Replace **trite expressions** and **stereotyped** or **hackneyed phrases** with new or original expressions. Supply fresh figurative language instead of relying on tired clichés worn thin by constant use. But be careful not to "mix" metaphors or use figures of speech that are illogical, inept, or ludicrous.

When we read expressions such as "white as the driven snow" or "hot as the noonday sun," our reaction is likely to be "If I've heard it once, I've heard it a thousand times." As the last sentence indicates, we are apt to respond to a cliché with another cliché! Similes (comparisons introduced by the words *like, as, as if, as when*) that we have heard "a thousand times" obviously no longer stir our imaginations. Similarly, tired metaphors (implied comparisons—for example, *She riveted him to the wall with her piercing gaze.*) do not convince your readers that you have anything insightful to say about your topic. Illogical figures of speech not only fail to inform, they can be so absurd that readers may miss your point entirely or find your writing silly.

ILLOGICAL FIGURE OF SPEECH	His eyes, flashing like pools of flame, drowned me in their fire.
REVISION	His eyes, flashing like flames, seared me.

EXERCISE (38a), EXACTNESS: SYNONYMS

In your dictionary, look up the synonymy that applies to each of the following groups of words. Write sentences in which you use and differentiate in meaning, according to the synonymy, each of the words in the group. You may change tense or part of speech in making up your sentences. The synonymies in this exercise are based on the *American Heritage Dictionary,* Second College Edition. If you are using a different dictionary, it may be necesary to look up some word meanings under the base entries for those words.

Example   *misfortune* It was my misfortune to be in the wrong place.

      adversity Adversity forced me to sell my house and car.

1. *miscellaneous* ——————————————————————————

   heterogeneous ——————————————————————————

   assorted ——————————————————————————

2. *business* ——————————————————————————

   industry ——————————————————————————

   commerce ——————————————————————————

   trade ——————————————————————————

   traffic ——————————————————————————

3. *slow* ——————————————————————————

   dilatory ——————————————————————————

   leisurely ——————————————————————————

   laggard ——————————————————————————

   deliberate ——————————————————————————

4. *sly* ——————————————————————————

   cunning ——————————————————————————

   tricky ——————————————————————————

   guileful ——————————————————————————

5. *stupid* ——————————————————————————

   slow ——————————————————————————

   dull ——————————————————————————

obtuse ———————————————————————

dense ————————————————————————

crass ————————————————————————

6. *mercy* ———————————————————————

leniency ————————————————————————

clemency ———————————————————————

forbearance ———————————————————

charity ————————————————————————

7. *effort* ————————————————————————

exertion ———————————————————————

endeavor ———————————————————————

application ————————————————————

strain ————————————————————————

8. *sad* ————————————————————————

depressed ———————————————————————

dejected ———————————————————————

desolate ———————————————————————

9. *area* ————————————————————————

region ————————————————————————

district ————————————————————————

10. *decide* ———————————————————————

determine ———————————————————————

settle ————————————————————————

rule ————————————————————————

conclude ———————————————————————

resolve ————————————————————————

EXERCISE (38b), EXACTNESS: DEROGATORY STEREOTYPES

For each sentence below, provide a revision that eliminates the stereotype or derogatory term.

Examples   Every secretary has her own filing system.

Every secretary has his or her own filing system.

A deliveryman left a package on the porch while we were gone.

A deliveryperson left a package on the porch....

1. His Mexican temperament constantly gets him in trouble; he will start a fight over almost anything.

   _____

2. Most students who enroll in the video class probably hope to get jobs as cameramen after graduation.

   _____

3. My aunt has a real Scottish streak in her because she refuses to spend money on anything not absolutely necessary.

   _____

4. That commuter airplane is too small to have a stewardess on board.

   _____

5. The average fireman works a twenty-four-hour shift and then gets several days off.

   _____

6. After a beer or two, she acts like a real wild Indian.

   _____

7. A nurse who communicates well with a doctor knows she improves his treatment of the patients.

   _____

8. Some people are better than others at jewing down the salesman on the price of a new car.

   _____

9. At 8:30 A.M., the elevators are full of pinstriped Yuppies on their way to the office.

    _____

10. By 5:30 P.M., the cafeterias in town are full of geezers eating dinner and showing each other photos of their grandchildren.

    _____

EXERCISE (38c–d), EXACTNESS: SIMILAR WORDS, INVENTED WORDS, IMPROPRIETIES

Construct sentences in which each of the following words is used correctly. In the case of verbs, tense may be changed.

Example   accept *We accept the terms of the contract.*

except *I like all the colors except the blue in the carpet.*

1. *perspective* ————————————————

   prospective ————————————————

2. *conscience* ————————————————

   conscious ————————————————

3. *descent* ————————————————

   decent ————————————————

4. *your* ————————————————

   you're ————————————————

5. *precede* ————————————————

   proceed ————————————————

6. *roll* ————————————————

   role ————————————————

7. *waiver* ————————————————

   waver ————————————————

8. *affect* ————————————————

   effect ————————————————

9. *personnel* ————————————————

   personal ————————————————

10. *principle* ————————————————

    principal ————————————————

In the blanks, insert correct words for those italicized words that are substandard, invented, or improprieties. Change any derogatory sexist, racist, ethnic, or religious terms, as well. Revise the entire sentence, if need be.

Example   Many immigrants have *combated* discrimination
at first.   _fought_

11. Many ethnic people feel safer *middle-of-the-roading* it.   _____

12. Some types of businesses are *soaked* with particular
groups.   _____

13. Koreans in New York seem to have specialized
in *all-nite* grocery stores.   _____

14. The history of the United States shows that it will
except anyone.   _____

15. An immigrant can live *anywheres* he or she wants.   _____

16. Many a telephone operator has saved lives with *her*
quick thinking during emergency calls.   _____

17. I suppose a *pilot* has to live near an airport, too, so *he*
can travel more easily.   _____

18. Are you *incredible* of my analysis?   _____

19. May I *imply* from your question that you think those
remarks were sexist?   _____

20. Is it *incouth* to think that an *actress* is always a *broad*?   _____

21. Your thoughts on the subject are certainly *unregular*.   _____

22. Your last few words are *unrefutable* evidence.   _____

23. Will you continue, *irregardless* of my objections?   _____

24. The *premiere* Presley in the United States was
Andrew Presley, a blacksmith.   _____

25. His *prodigy* have spread across the United States.   _____

26. The President's *economical* plan may be well-received
by the Congress.   _____

27. They are likely to give their *ascent* to his plan.   _____

28. We *concluded* to go to the Chinese New Year festival.   _____

29. He finally *cogitated* that his position was unpopular.   _____

30. I didn't think he'd even do that, *no how*.   _____

EXERCISE (38f), EXACTNESS: SPECIFIC AND CONCRETE WORDS

Revise the following sentences, replacing nouns, verbs, and adjectives with more specific, concrete words where appropriate. Invent details as needed.

Examples   The plane left.

<u>The Cessna 110 flew out of Bush Field at noon.</u>

She read a book.

<u>She read a mystery novel.</u>

1. This is a nice room.

   _____

2. That song was a hit.

   _____

3. I painted my office.

   _____

4. The store was busy.

   _____

5. Japanese cars are very expensive.

   _____

6. The trailer is run-down.

   _____

7. Honesty always pays.

   _____

8. He's not very well.

   _____

9. I ate a lot.

   _____

10. There's a car outside.

   _____

11. Sharon is lazy.

_____

12. We laughed about that.

_____

13. I guess we were rather loud.

_____

14. We made a scene.

_____

15. I like desserts.

_____

16. Too many of you have been absent.

_____

17. I feel nervous.

_____

18. Some guy wants to see you.

_____

19. The class will write a research paper.

_____

20. Your answer was too general.

_____

21. He's nice.

_____

22. I like Mexican food.

_____

EXERCISE (38g–h), EXACTNESS: FIGURATIVE LANGUAGE, TRITENESS, CLICHES

Revise the following sentences using figures of speech that are apt and logical.

Example   Let's buckle down and rise to the occasion.
          <u>Let's buckle down, work hard, and meet this challenge.</u>

1. Let's massage this report and make sure none of our ideas drops through the cracks.
    _____

2. The hysteria was snowballing, running forward madly out of control.
    _____

3. The passenger clung to the lifeboat's rails like glue.
    _____

4. The hydroplane stuck to the water like flypaper.
    _____

5. The sailboat had a real head of steam up, feeding the flames of my lust to own one.
    _____

6. Like a lamb to the slaughter, he fell for the soft soap.
    _____

7. Defining the nature of a conspiracy is like nailing pudding to a tree.
    _____

8. This office cannot be run according to some perfect blueprint.
    _____

9. Through all his troubles he stood at the helm, peering into the future.
    _____

10. Then he lowered his sights and ran for the safety of shore.
    _____

11. He blew his stack over his advisor's fall from grace.
    _____

12. To pass this exam, you'll have to hit the deck to burn the midnight oil.

_____

13. The president's Achilles heel is his penchant for keeping his fingers in every pie.

_____

14. The committee has to stiffen their backbones or this will slip through their fingers.

_____

15. If everyone pitches in, we can keep the home fires burning.

_____

16. When the going gets rough, I'll expect you to be there for me.

_____

17. I promise I'll be cool as a cucumber.

_____

18. My testimony should come off without a hitch.

_____

19. These things can go bad on you as quick as a flash.

_____

20. I intend to be a model of decorum.

_____

21. Then you'll have to turn over a new leaf.

_____

22. Is our partnership on the rocks?

_____

23. We'll succeed if we put our shoulders to the wheel.

_____

24. But we need to keep our ears to the ground to really stay in touch with new business.

_____

25. That way, we'll know what's coming down the tracks.

_____

26. At these planning sessions, she's a ball of fire.

_____

27. She swept the competition off their feet.

_____

28. She helps us stay leaps and bounds ahead of other firms.

_____

29. And she does it all without even working up a sweat.

_____

30. She knows how to strike while the iron is hot.

_____

EXACTNESS: IDIOMS   (38e)

An **idiom** is an expression peculiar to a given language—that is, it does not follow the normal pattern of the language, or it has a total meaning different from the one suggested by its separate words. In the previous sentence, the phrase *different from* is idiomatic: it does not follow the normal pattern of English. The expression *to lose one's head* exemplifies the second type of idiom: literally, the words indicate decapitation, but native speakers of English know the expression is not meant literally. To lose one's head is to become irrational or excessively emotional.

For any writer, the most troublesome idioms are those requiring a particular preposition after a given verb or adjective. The following list can help you know which idiomatic construction to use for a given meaning.

absolved by, from	I was *absolved by* the dean *from* all blame.
accede to	He *acceded to* his children's demands.
accompany by, with	I was *accompanied by* Louise. The terms were *accompanied with* a plea for immediate peace.
acquitted of	They were *acquitted of* the crime.
adapted to, from	This machine can be *adapted to* farm work. The design was *adapted from* an Indian invention.
admit to, of	He *admitted to* the prank. The plan will *admit of* no alternative.
agree to, with, in	They *agreed to* the plan but *disagreed with* us. They *agreed* only *in* principle.

angry with, at	They are *angry with* me and *angry at* the treatment they received.
capable of	She is *capable of* great kindness.
charge for, with	He expected to be *charged for* his purchase, but he didn't expect to be *charged with* stealing something.
compare to, with	He *compared* the roundness of the baseball *to* that of the earth. He *compared* the quality of the Ford *with* that of the Volvo.
concur with, in	I *concur with* you *in* your desire to use the revised edition.
confide in, to	*Confide in* me. You *confided to* me that you had stolen the car.
conform to, with **conformity with**	The specifications *conformed to* (or *with*) my original plans. You must act in *conformity with* our demands.
connected by, with	The rooms are *connected by* a corridor. I am officially *connected with* this university.
contend for, with	Because she needed to *contend for* her principles, she found herself *contending with* her parents.
differ about, from, with	We *differ about* our taste in clothes. My clothes *differ from* yours. We *differ with* one another.
different from*	Our grading system is *different from* yours.
enter into, on, upon	She *entered into* a new agreement and thereby *entered on* (or *upon*†) a new career.
free from, of	He was *freed from* cultural assumptions by his education. He is *free of* prejudice.
identical with	Your reasons are *identical with* his.
join in, to, with	He *joined in* the fun *with* the others. He *joined* the wire cables *to* each other.
live at, in, on	She *lives at* 14 Neil Avenue *in* a Dutch Colonial house. She *lives on* Neil Avenue.
necessity for, of **need for, of**	There was no *necessity (need) for* you to lose your temper. There was no *necessity (need) of* your losing your temper.

*Different than is colloquially idiomatic when the object of the prepositional phrase is a clause:

This town looks *different from* what I had remembered. [Formal]

This town looks *different than* I had remembered it. [Colloquial]

†In many phrases, *on* and *upon* are interchangeable: *depend on* or *depend upon; enter on* or *enter upon.*

object to	I *object to* the statement in the third paragraph.
oblivious of	When he works at the computer he is *oblivious of* the passing of time.
overcome by, with	I was *overcome by* the heat. I was *overcome with* grief.
parallel between, to, with	There is a *parallel between* your attitude and his. This line is *parallel to* (or *with*) that one.
preferable to	A leisurely walk is *preferable to* violent exercise.
reason about, with	Why not *reason with* them *about* the matter?
reward by, for, with	They were *rewarded by* their employer *with* a raise *for* their work.
variance with	This conclusion is at *variance with* your facts.
vary from, in, with	The houses *vary from* one another *in* size. People's tastes *vary with* their personalities.
wait for, on	They *waited for* someone to *wait on* them.
worthy of	That candidate is not *worthy of* your trust.

EXERCISE (38e), EXACTNESS: IDIOMS

In each blank, write the preposition that forms the correct idiomatic construction.

Example   The two sites were identical __with__ each other.

1. My informant was angry _____ me.

2. Privacy is necessary _____ modern life.

3. He and I disagreed _____ many things.

4. We agreed _____ each other about the methods of anthropologists.

5. They are worthy _____ your trust.

6. The necessity _____ our interview is not in doubt.

7. You and I may differ greatly _____ our objectives.

8. The two people we will interview vary _____ each other in their backgrounds.

9. One lives _____ 112 Henry Street, on the reservation.

10. You must conform _____ the group's ways if you intend to live with them.

11. The informant confided _____ the researcher all his family's history.

12. She acceded _____ his demands for privacy.

13. The final report must conform _____ the university's style sheet.

14. That style sheet's author is oblivious _____ changing standards.

15. She was overcome _____ the deadline's being so near.

16. She is certainly capable _____ finishing her research in a year.

17. Never have two anthropologists differed _____ each other so much.

18. I think he is angry _____ the evaluation of his previous work.

19. He was not relieved _____ his responsibilities to the committee, though.

20. I may decide to enter _____ a new career.

In the following list, some expressions are idiomatically correct and some are not. Cross out incorrect prepositions and write your correction in the blank at the right, or enter *Correct* if the expression is idiomatically correct. In performing this exercise, refer either to Section 38 or to your dictionary, as necessary.

Example   My quotation was of Margaret Mead   **_from_**
                 depend upon your efforts   **_correct_**

21. different to each other   _____

22. to refrain of further interference   _____

23. antithetic with our oaths as doctors   _____

24. vary in many ways   _____

25. in regard of her wishes   _____

26. embarrassed at my bad mistake   _____

27. ashamed at my mistake   _____

28. I live over to my uncle's house.   _____

29. We'll get the money off the treasurer. _____

30. She is capable to change   _____

31. Let's compare one and the other.   _____

32. I have great confidence with you.   _____

33. Can he contend with all his problems? _____

34. the one who objected from the proposal _____

35. different than we thought   _____

36. He confided on me that he was ill.   _____

37. Your ideas are parallel on mine.   _____

38. Actually, they're identical to yours.   _____

39. I object with that conclusion.   _____

40. I waited on you nearly all morning.   _____

DIRECTNESS (39)

Your writing will be more effective if it is direct—if you use only those words that contribute to your meaning. Words and phrases that contribute nothing to meaning cause your readers to work hard at plowing through the language, but for no real payoff. Eventually readers become tired, bored, impatient, and unwilling to continue. The following guidelines can help you to remove wordiness from your writing:

1. Eliminate unnecessary nominals and weak verbs by recasting them as more vigorous and direct noun-verb combinations. A nominal is a noun formed by adding a suffix to a verb. Examples are *-ment, -tion, -ance,* or sometimes, *-ity, -ize,* or *-ness: disagreement, substitution, deliverance.* Vague, weak verbs such as *make, give,* and *take* often occur with nominals as replacements for the stronger, more energetic verbs that have been changed into nouns.

NOMINAL/WEAK VERB	The *disagreement* about taxes *took* place between Brooks and Cortini.
REVISED	Brooks and Cortini *disagreed* about taxes.
WEAK/NOMINAL VERB	The coach *made* a *substitution* of Horwich for Brown.
REVISED	The coach *substituted* Horwich for Brown.

2. Prefer the active voice to the passive voice. Section 45 explained that active voice verbs make a sentence more lively and direct. They also use fewer words because active voice sentences require neither the helping verb used in a passive verb construction nor the prepositional phrase that identifies the agent

of the action. Compare the following pair of sentences, and notice how much more economical and direct is the active voice sentence:

PASSIVE   The procedure was demonstrated by the lab technician.

ACTIVE   The lab technician demonstrated the procedure.

3. Eliminate words and phrases that do not contribute to meaning. Expressions such as *type of, in the case of, in the field of, aspect, factor, situation, I think, in my opinion* can often be cut from sentences. Expletives such as *there is, there are,* and *it is* can frequently be replaced by the true subject of the sentence to improve directness.

POOR   The best type of football team has the best quality of blockers.

IMPROVED   The best football team has the best blockers.

POOR   Pat majored in the field of engineering.

IMPROVED   Pat majored in engineering.

POOR   Another aspect of the situation that needs study, in my opinion, is the company's falling productivity.

IMPROVED   We should study the company's falling productivity.

POOR   There were four classes meeting on the third floor.

IMPROVED   Four classes met on the third floor.

4. Reduce clauses to phrases and phrases to single words when possible. Section 43 shows how economical and effective participles, appositives, and absolutes can be. These constructions frequently result from reducing whole clauses to phrase modifiers, as when *The train, which ran on time, pulled into the station.* is rewritten *The train, running on time, pulled into the station.* Phrases and clauses can sometimes be reduced to one-word modifiers for further directness.

WORDY   The slipper, which was made of glass, fit the foot of Cinderella.

REVISED   The glass slipper fit Cinderella's foot. [The clause *which was made of glass* has been reduced to the single adjective *glass;* the prepositional phrase *of Cinderella* had been reduced to the single possessive noun *Cinderella's.*]

5. Avoid ineffective repetition and redundancy. Unintentional repetition, unlike repetition intended to create emphasis and coherence, often adds unnecessary—even silly-sounding—words to a sentence.

AWKWARD REPETITION   Improved communication improved the staff's ability to satisfy top management's expectations.

REVISED   Improved communication better enabled the staff to satisfy top management's expectations.

Redundant words say the same thing twice—for example, *visible to the eyes*. Note the following list of common redundancies and their revisions:

REDUNDANT	DIRECT
advance forward	advance
continue on	continue
refer back	refer
combine together	combine
close proximity	close
circle around	circle
small in size	small
few in number	few
disappear from view	disappear
throughout the whole	throughout
basic fundamentals	fundamentals
important essentials	essentials

EXERCISE (39), DIRECTNESS: WORDINESS, REDUNDANCY, AWKWARD REPETITION

Revise the following sentences to eliminate unnecessary words and phrases or awkward repetition.

Example   Credit for the soda pop industry goes to all of five men, all of them except one from abroad.

Credit for the soda pop industry goes to five men, four of them from abroad.

1. Joseph Priestley, the inventor who invented carbonated water, was an Englishman.

   _____

2. He combined together water with the bubbles of carbonation.

   _____

3. According to many people, in their opinion water without carbonation isn't worth drinking.

   _____

4. Priestley's invention was discovered in the year 1767.

   _____

5. Three years later in 1770, a method was discovered to carbonate large quantities of soda water.

   _____

6. Torbern Bergman, a chemist in the country of Sweden, developed a commercial method of producing carbonic acid.

   _____

7. John Matthews, who was an English immigrant, opened up a soda fountain in New York City in 1832.

   _____

8. He used the scrap marble that was left over from building St. Patrick's Cathedral to make his bubbles.

   _____

9. The basic fundamental procedure was to mix the marble scrap with sulfuric acid.

   _____

10. Throughout the whole process, carbonic-acid gas is liberated.

    _____

11. But with regard to flavoring, Matthews sold his soda water plain.

    _____

12. In fact, the number of flavors available remained few in number even after they were invented.

    _____

13. To refer back in history, it was Eugene Roussel, who was a Frenchman, who first flavored soda water.

    _____

14. Roussel combined together fountain syrup and soda water to create the flavored soda in the year 1838.

    _____

15. One important essential not developed until years later was the ability to bottle the flavored soda.

    _____

16. There is some controversy about the inventor of the bottling process due to the fact that two men claim to have discovered it.

    _____

17. Benjamin Silliman, who was a chemistry professor at Yale, was the first in America to bottle soda water.

    _____

18. In my opinion, I think Asa Candler was the first to bottle soda water successfully.

    _____

19. Candler continued on with bottling as a commercial venture.

    _____

20. His efforts advanced forward until his company's name, Coca-Cola, became a household word.

    _____

21. In the case of Coca-Cola, its growth as a business must have astounded even Candler.

_____

22. In 1890, Candler closed the drugstore where he had been a pharmacist's assistant to concentrate all his efforts on marketing his bottled drink.

_____

23. In the field of soda pop there seemed to be a wide open market.

_____

24. In 1886, the drugstore had sold 25 gallons of Coke; by 1892, Candler was selling 35,360 gallons a year; by the year of 1913, he was selling almost seven million gallons a year.

_____

25. By 1919, which was when Candler sold Coca-Cola, some 280,000,000 bottles of Coke were sold in the month of July alone.

_____

SPELLING (40)

Many people, especially bad spellers, secretly believe good spellers are born, not made. There seem to be more exceptions than rules in spelling. Apart from correct pronunciation (which aids correct spelling), careful proofreading, and distinguishing between words that are similar in sound but different in meaning and spelling (such as *altar* and *alter*), the dictionary is your best resource. Learning spelling rules can also aid your spelling. Although there are exceptions to them, the following rules from the *Prentice-Hall Handbook for Writers*, Ninth Edition, provide general guidelines for correct spelling:

1. Avoid secondary and British spellings.

AMERICAN	BRITISH
encyclopedia	encyclopaedia
fetus	foetus
inquiry	enquiry
color	colour
center	centre
mold	mould
traveled	travelled
judgment	judgement

2. Distinguish between *ie* and *ei:* Write *i* before *e* except after *c* or when sounded like *a*, as in *neighbor* and *weigh*.

thief   conceive   sleigh

believe   ceiling   eight

3. Drop the final *e* before a suffix beginning with a vowel but not before a suffix beginning with a consonant.

please + ure = pleasure   sure + ly = surely

slide + ing = sliding   retire + ment = retirement

4. Change a final *y* to *i* before a suffix, unless the suffix begins with *i*.

defy + ance = defiance   cry + ing = crying

lively + hood = livelihood   rely + ing = relying

5. Double a final single consonant before a suffix beginning with a vowel when a single vowel precedes the consonant *and* the consonant ends an accented syllable or a one-syllable word. If both of these conditions do not exist, do not double the final consonant.

stop + ing = stopping   stoop + ing = stooping

admit + ed = admitted   benefit + ed = benefited

6. Usually you form the plurals of nouns ending in sounds that can be smoothly united with *-s* by adding *-s*. Form the third person singular of verbs ending in sounds that can be smoothly united with *-s* by adding *-s*.

SINGULAR	PLURAL	VERBS	
picture	pictures	blacken	blackens
radio	radios	criticize	criticizes

7. Form the plurals of nouns ending in sounds that cannot be smoothly united with *-s* by adding *-es*. Form the third person singular of verbs ending in sounds that cannot be smoothly united with *-s* by adding *-es*.

SINGULAR	PLURAL	VERBS	
porch	porches	tax	taxes
bush	bushes	collapse	collapses

8. Form the plurals of nouns ending in *y* preceded by a consonant by changing *y* to *i* and adding *-es*. Form the third person singular of verbs ending in *y* preceded by a consonant in the same way.

SINGULAR	PLURAL	VERBS	
pity	pities	deny	denies
nursery	nurseries	fly	flies

9. Form the plurals of nouns ending in *y* preceded by *a, e, o,* or *u* by adding *-s* only. Form the third person singular of verbs ending in *y* preceded by *a, e, o,* or *u* in the same way.

SINGULAR	PLURAL	VERBS	
day	days	play	plays
key	keys	employ	employs

10. Frequently you retain the plural of the original language in spelling plural nouns borrowed from French, Greek, or Latin, even though some of these nouns have been anglicized.

SINGULAR	PLURAL (foreign)	PLURAL (anglicized)
analysis	analyses	
crisis	crises	
curriculum	curricula	
datum	data	
appendix	appendices	appendixes
memorandum	memoranda	memorandums
radius	radii	radiuses

EXERCISE (40)-1, SPELLING

Some of the following words reflect preferred spellings. Others reflect British or secondary spellings. Write the preferred spelling of each word in the blank to its right.

Example   judgement   *judgment*

1.	barytone	_____	2.	grey	_____
3.	catchup	_____	4.	civilise	_____
5.	storey	_____	6.	anaesthetic	_____
7.	jeweller	_____	8.	enquiry	_____
9.	labour	_____	10.	theatre	_____
11.	gaol	_____	12.	realise	_____
13.	councillor	_____	14.	programme	_____
15.	fibre	_____	16.	cyder	_____
17.	plough	_____	18.	Pigmy	_____
19.	insure	_____	20.	reflexion	_____

Draw a line through misspelled words in the following phrases and write them correctly in the blanks at the right. Where no word is misspelled, write *Correct* in the blank.

Example   the lonelyest person around   *loneliest*

21.   loseing the case   _____

22.   a candadate's speech   _____

23.   a new devise for homeowners   _____

24.   the principle idea to be learned   _____

25.   medeival history   _____

26.   a cursury examination   _____

27.   a member of Parliment   _____

28.   an Elizabethan tradgedy   _____

29.   two paralell paths   _____

30. a priviledge you earn   _____

31. we practicly won   _____

32. spend a nickle   _____

33. you're quiet right   _____

34. lacking in judgement   _____

35. a morgage payment   _____

36. the sophmore class   _____

37. elected by acclimation   _____

38. my roll in the class play   _____

39. the high school principle   _____

40. There exercises are strenuous   _____

41. the student goverment   _____

42. the lattitude and longitude   _____

43. how's the whether   _____

44. whether they win or loose   _____

45. driving passed the street   _____

46. the capitol gains tax   _____

47. whose on first base?   _____

48. our forth game of the season   _____

49. taking seperate vacations   _____

50. the event that occured here   _____

51. a nuculear-powered submarine   _____

52. the auxilary generator   _____

53. a tempermental artist   _____

54. accidently dropped the book   _____

55. an iminent judge   _____

56. a grievous mistake   _____

57. new farm equippment   _____

58. a contemptable way to behave   _____

59. you probly will   _____

60. the read section of the orchestra   _____

To the right of each of the following sets of words, write the correct spelling of any misspelled words in the set. If no word is misspelled, write *Correct* in the space.

Example   eclectic   droll   dolerous   mournful   *dolorous*

61. circular   propheticaly   common   successful   _____

62. riches   bordom   poverty   thickness   _____

63. foul   greedyly   difficulty   loudness   _____

64. widespread   threatening   all-powerful   obvioussly   _____

65. sweet   political   noisy   oily   _____

66. closeing   baritone   joining   opening   _____

67. father   out-dated   noisy   disslike   _____

68. proud   bowing   dully   servilaty   _____

69. obece   bowing   confusion   prevention   _____

70. annoying   soothing   foul-smelling   harmfull   _____

71. congeniality   perplexed   offensive   ilogical   _____

72. wicked   knew   nerveous   hazy   _____

73. mythical   watery   sleazy   wicked   _____

74. temple   miscellaneous   dress   fraudulant   _____

75. dieing   biting   soft   sarcastic   _____

76. irons   manners   distribution   couragous   _____

77. food   plain   encounter   distributeion   _____

78. lively   heavenly   mixed   naseating   _____

79. flowing   lying   depresed   specific   _____

80. gown   comparison   mixture   voracaty   _____

81. verbal   stoppable   drowsy   concealed   _____

82. proverb   most   mosque   spirit   _____

83. imitative   belittling   adversion   abjure   _____

84. wifes   canopy   text   mold   _____

85. misuse   discomfort   satireical   generosity   _____

86. native   poor   benifical   ill-bred   _____

87. portly   cleaver   naturally   transferable   _____

88. dramaticcal   drunken   unproductive   spasm   _____

89. sharp   former   weep   fancy   _____

90. defeatted   labor   cave   preserver   _____

91. circle   modicum   exagerrate   branch   _____

92. anger   pride   proclivity   merriment   _____

93. detention   deception   vacume   conference   _____

94. steal   sieze   worship   accumulated   _____

95. lose   purify   exclude   immenent   _____

96. negate   servile   displace   poligamous   _____

97. swaying   deflection   lighten   dwelling   _____

98. divorce   rudeness   posession   legacy   _____

99. chasten   supplys   expand   polish   _____

100. adress   omniscient   heavenly   earthly   _____

EXERCISE (40)-2, SPELLING

Fill in each blank with the appropriate choice, either *ie* or *ei*. Don't guess. Use your dictionary.

1. cash__r	2. f__gn	3. n__ce	4. c__ling
5. l__sure	6. n__ghbor	7. h__r	8. f__rce
9. rec__ve	10. w__gh	11. n__ther	12. h__ght
13. f__nd	14. misch__f	15. br__f	16. hyg__ne
17. perc__ve	18. counterf__t	19. conc__t	20. sl__gh
21. bel__ve	22. w__rd	23. s__ze	24. th__ves

Write the correct spelling of each of the words formed by joining the given prefix or suffix to the given root. Remember that in some cases you will have to add, delete, or change a letter.

Examples	judge + ing	_judging_
	swim + ing	_swimming_
	busy + ness	_business_
	weight + less	_weightless_

25. run + ing _____	26. brim + ing _____
27. marriage + able _____	28. dis + taste _____
29. close + ure _____	30. beauty + ful _____
31. judge + ment _____	32. hope + less _____
33. lovely + ness _____	34. cancel + ed _____
35. continue + ance _____	36. renew + al _____
37. sever + ance _____	38. bond + age _____
39. intent + ion _____	40. disparage + ment _____
41. pit + ance _____	42. stop + er _____
43. writhe + ing _____	44. rely + ance _____
45. carry + age _____	46. pun + ing _____
47. re + arrange _____	48. debate + able _____

49. strive + ing _____ 50. pre + existing _____

51. confer + ing _____ 52. consider + able _____

53. icy + ness _____ 54. exist + ence _____

55. ninety + eth _____ 56. value + able _____

57. incidental + ly _____ 58. befit + ing _____

59. swat + ed _____ 60. petty + ness _____

61. rid + ance _____ 62. mere + ly _____

63. eighty + eth _____ 64. desire + able _____

65. label + ing _____ 66. desire + ous _____

67. succeed + ing _____ 68. tag + ing _____

69. intertwine + ing _____ 70. flab + y _____

71. mis + spell _____ 72. witty + ness _____

73. tarry + ed _____ 74. imbue + ing _____

To the right of each of the following sets of words, write the correct spelling of any misspelled word in the set. If no word in the set is misspelled, write *Correct* in the space.

Example   adjacent   textured   temparate   infectious   _temperate_

75. interested   enroll   laboratory   varous   _____

76. clumsyly   driver   elephant   defamation   _____

77. softened   generousity   extraordinary   wrong   _____

78. whirlpool   poem   mold   licenseing   _____

79. covered   grusome   authoritative   lazy   _____

80. talkative   ridiculous   sad   supplementery   _____

81. untrue   tax   prayerfull   supplement   _____

82. portraial   established   prayer   riches   _____

83. possible   text   nativaty   defamatory   _____

84. dictionary   elf   dullard   satire   _____

85. obviously   milky   briefly   cancealled   _____

86. army   trickery   vegetable   wearyness   _____

87. lewdness   fear   allowance   humorosly   _____

88. blameing   weakening   burdensome   growth   _____

89. tardiness   lewdness   fear   allowence   _____

90. briefly   tearfuly   lewdly   envious   _____

91. weariness   lazyly   tearfulness   drowsy   _____

92. circular   milky   clearence   brief   _____

93. tearing   stealling   stand   castilian   _____

94. juvenile   legalaty   confusedly   bombastic   _____

95. sinful   harmful   treacharous   carefree   _____

96. bravery   orderring   essential   firm   _____

97. turning   attacking   insertion   defendder   _____

98. healthy   weakness   envyous   angrily   _____

99. lamentation   confusion   lascivicious lacerate   _____

100. respectful   similiar   latent   humorous   _____

THE WRITING PROCESS   (41)

Sometimes when we have a writing assignment the words flow easily, and some-times we spend hours before the blank sheets of paper, struggling to produce a few lines—filling the wastebasket with rejected efforts. All writers, including professionals, face dry spells; *Writer's Digest,* a magazine for freelance writers, periodically features articles about how to overcome "writer's block."

Although the ultimate goal of every writer is to create a well-crafted, effec-tive product—whether it be an essay, a poem, a newspaper article, or a memo to the boss—that product is the result of a process. The writing process is the method a writer uses to create his or her essay, poem, or memo. When writers talk about writer's block, they are talking about ways to get the process rolling so the words will flow successfully.

We all use some process, some mental system for producing writing. One method may be more successful for you than another. Many people find that they most easily become involved in a subject if they just begin to fill pages with ideas, everything they can think of concerning their subject. Then they go back and pick and choose, order and shape, revise and edit, until they are satisfied with the result. Other people do this sort of "brainstorming" mentally and do not put words on paper until they have a fairly clear notion of what the contents and structure of the finished piece will be. Some people edit their sentences as they write them—correcting and revising as they go. Other writers edit and revise only after they have completed a first draft.

There is no one "best" or "right" writing process. You should observe your own methods and use the ones that work best for you. If your own system doesn't seem to be working, try some tactics others have found successful. One student, for example, felt dissatisfied with the "stuffy tone that just isn't 'me'" in a job application letter she had written. At her teacher's suggestion, she visualized what the letter's recipient might be like. Although she had never met the personnel officer to whom she was writing, she discovered that when she thought about her intended *audience,* a *real* reader, the tone of her letter became more forthright and better reflected her personality.

Another student found that *goals and purposes* were his stumbling block. In his application letter, he rehearsed his qualifications for the advertised job, his education and work experience, but still he felt the letter was unsatisfactory. In particular, it seemed to trail off ineffectively at the end. Once he realized that his goal in writing the letter was not just to apply for the job but also to secure an interview, the student was able to compose a strong, action ending that requested the interview.

The same assignment led another student to discover that her biggest problem was *organization.* Unhappy with the choppy, illogical structure of her letter, she decided that she needed to reorganize the paragraphs. Instead of using time order to present her education and employment experience ("first I worked here, then I went to school there"), she chose order of climax to present her skills, ending with those she believed her reader would find most important to the job she sought.

Although you may work best with a different or modified version of the writing process described next, its steps outline a method that many writers use successfully. The following sections and exercises enable you to try this method and see if it works for you.

PLANNING

1. Identify the goal(s) and purpose(s) of your writing task: What do you want to accomplish? What is your aim?

2. Select a subject appropriate to the writing task, and then brainstorm: generate a number of ideas about the subject and possible directions to go.

3. Think carefully about the kind of reader(s) to whom you are writing; the identity of the audience largely determines what you want to say and how you want to say it.

4. Begin to narrow and focus your subject to suit your purpose(s) and audience.

5. From your brainstorming list of ideas, assertions, facts, and examples that are related to your subject, develop a working outline of preliminary logical groupings.

6. Frame a specific thesis statement that will help you accomplish your writing goal(s) and purpose(s).

7. Choose those items from your preliminary list that fit your purpose(s) and support your thesis; add any new ones that are relevant. Then decide on the patterns of organization and methods of development that will best serve your purpose(s) and most effectively communicate your ideas to your readers. Now work these items into a more complete outline that you can use as a guide while you write the first draft.

WRITING AND REVISING

8. Begin writing, and keep writing until you have completed a rough draft. Don't be overly concerned about wording, phrasing, grammar, or punctuation; at this stage pursue your thoughts rather than concentrate upon correctness.

9. Try to think of an illustration, an anecdote, or an example to use as an interesting introduction for your paper. Reread each paragraph to be sure it is clearly related to your thesis. Look at your ending paragraph: it should bring your essay to a *close* and not just *quit*.

10. Go over your first draft, checking it for correct spelling, punctuation, grammar, and effective sentences. Read it again for clarity, effective organization, and sound reasoning. Revise as necessary.

11. Give your paper a "cooling-off" period. Leave it for a while. When you reread it later, you may find rough spots that escaped your notice during the first writing and that you now want to rework or polish.

12. Prepare the final copy. Don't forget to create a title for your paper that indicates the topic and catches the readers' interest.

Practice: Brainstorming about subjects   Most people love a soapbox—a chance to stand up and speak their minds about a subject. A writing assignment is a readymade soapbox: You have decided, or someone has asked you, to "sound off." List at least three subjects about which you'd like to sound off. Think about each one for a while. Then jot down some points that you think are especially important for each. Now imagine that you will be speaking from your soapbox to an audience. Compose an opening sentence for each of the subjects, a sentence you could use to begin a speech.

PLANNING: OUTLINING   (41g)

Outlining can be helpful at several stages of planning before you write your paper. As you generate ideas about the subject you have chosen, a rough or "scratch" outline can be useful for trying out various relationships among ideas and various organizational schemes. Later you may develop a more detailed outline to use as a guide while writing your paper. It is also likely that your instructor may ask you to submit a formal outline as part of a research paper assignment. The following discussion explains the conventions of **formal** outlines. If you are not yet at a stage in the process of writing a paper where a formal outline is necessary, you may want to return to this section later, after you have worked through the next several sections in this text. Alternatively, reading this section now will enable you to understand just how outlining can clarify the logical sequence and ranking of major and minor points in an essay's organization.

The two types of formal outlines generally preferred in composition classes are sentence outlines and topic outlines. In the **sentence outline,** all headings and subheadings must be sentences. In the **topic outline,** headings and subheadings are not sentences but are composed of a few words or of phrases. Each type of outline has advantages. Do not mix the two types in a single outline.

Outlines can have several levels. The first level is the main headings, designated by Roman numerals: I, II, III, etc. The second level is designated by capital letters: A, B, C, etc. The third level uses arabic numbers: 1, 2, 3, etc. The fourth and fifth levels, when used, are indicated by small letters: a, b, c, etc., and numbers in parentheses: (1), (2), (3), etc.

Remember that when a heading or subheading is divided, it is always divided into at least two parts.

```
NOT    I.                    BUT    I.
          A.                               A.
                                           B.
```

Of course, headings or subheadings may be divided into more than two parts. Insofar as possible, all headings and subheadings of the same level of importance should be written in parallel form, with the same grammatical structure. Thus, if I is a noun phrase, II and III should also be noun phrases. If A begins with a gerund, B and C should too.

Following is a *sentence outline* for the introduction of a composition "Finding a Summer Job."

I. Students can choose among several ways to spend their time during summer vacation.
   A. They may take it easy.
      1. Loafing is a lot of fun.
      2. Doing nothing requires little effort.
   B. They may get summer jobs.
      1. Working includes many worthwhile experiences.
      2. Working enables them to make money.
      3. If they desire to work during the summer they must do the following.
         a. They must consult job sources.
         b. They must write letters of application for employment.
         c. They must make good appearances at their job interviews.

THESIS
STATEMENT IN
OUTLINE FORM

If you have developed the introduction to provide for a thesis statement, you can now take the aspects of your thesis and use them for the main headings of the body of the outline.

The first aspect of the thesis statement contained in the outline on finding a summer job could be used for main heading II of the outline, which would then be developed to three levels that supply examples and details to support this aspect of the thesis.

II. They must consult job sources.
   A. They can study the newspapers.
      1. The want ad sections list many job opportunities.
      2. They can acquaint themselves with firms through their advertising.
   B. They can use the college's employment service.
      1. Many employers advertise for help through this service.
      2. They can advertise their services through this function.

Up to this point, the outline has continued to perform its basic functions:
1. It has provided details for development of this portion of the body of the composition.

347

2. Since each subheading relates to the subheading level preceding it, and level-two subheadings relate to the level-one main heading, the outline has continued to stick to the subject.

In the *topic outline* there are no sentences. Instead, each heading and subheading is followed by a noun or substantive or a phrase. You should avoid verbs in a topic outline since the resulting construction is often a sentence with an understood subject. To say *Follow the instructions carefully,* for example, is really to say *(You) follow the instructions carefully.* Also avoid constructions that are not sentences only because they lack verbs. For example, *Schools not as good as they used to be* is really only an incomplete sentence; all it needs to qualify as a sentence is the verb *are.*

CRITERIA FOR TOPIC OUTLINES

The topic outline should, of course, follow the basic requirements of all outlines: each heading and subheading, when divided, should be broken down into at least two parts, and each level should relate to the level preceding it. In addition, keep the following points in mind:

1. Use no verbs.

2. Use no expressions that would be sentences if only a verb or subject were added.

3. Strive for phrases that contain a noun (substantive) with modifiers—for example, *Progress in testing* or *Testing progress.* Generally, a noun by itself may be insufficient. Enough should be said in the outline to provide a definite guide to the writer. The outline should indicate not only the aspect, but also the particular point to be discussed concerning that aspect. *Testing,* for example, provides much less guidance to the writer than does *Progress in testing.*

EXERCISE (41g)-1, OUTLINING

Below you will find part I of a sentence outline for a paper titled "What a Teen-ager Must Know About Owning a Car." To the right of each entry of the outline, insert the appropriate letter or letters of items A–D, which describe the flaws you will find in the outline. Errors in the outline include the following:

1. Subheading is not a sentence.

2. Subheading is not broken into a minimum of two parts.

3. Subheading does not relate to the subhead level above it.

4. Subheading does not provide the basis for a thesis statement with three aspects.

I. Although owning a car can have advantages, there are also responsibilities
   A. A car brings a lot of pleasure.
      1. Entertainment is easier to find   _____
   B. Instilling of a sense of responsibility
      1. It helps a person to mature
      2. It need not cost much   _____
   C. If a teenager decides to get one
      1. He or she must pay insurance bills
      2. He or she must give it the proper maintenance   _____

Complete the following sentence outline for the introduction of a paper titled "The Advantages of Going to College." Be sure to write a complete sentence after each subheading.

I. High school students have two choices after graduation.
   A. They may go to work.

      1. _____

      2. _____
   B. They may go to college.

      1. _____

      2. _____
      3. If they go to college, they will profit in three ways.

         a. _____

         b. _____

         c. _____

Develop main headings III and IV of the outline for a paper about finding a summer job. Go to three levels, and make sure that each subheading is a full sentence. Also be sure that each subheading relates to the subheading or heading above it. The main headings, of course, relate to the other two aspects of the thesis statement. In developing III, you may wish to consider the parts of a letter of application for employment: the introductory covering statement and the resumé. You may also wish to consider what the letter will and will not do for the applicant.

III.   Students must write letters of application for employment.

     A. _____

         1. _____

         2. _____

     B. _____

         1. _____

         2. _____

In the main heading IV, you may want to consider the impression the job interviewee's appearance makes on the employer and how important appearance may be to the employer's customers.

IV.   They must make good appearances at job interviews.

     A. _____

         1. _____

         2. _____

     B. _____

         1. _____

         2. _____

Develop main heading V of the outline for the paper "Finding a Summer Job." Since this will be the conclusion of the essay, suitable development might include advice to students concerning the basis on which they would select their jobs. Be sure that each subheading is a sentence and that it relates to the outline level above it.

V.   Students should consider two factors in selecting jobs.

     A. _____

         1. _____

         2. _____

B. _____

    1. _____

    2. _____

Portions of the outline for the paper "Finding a Summer Job" are reproduced below as a topic outline. Certain parts, however, are incorrect according to the criteria we have discussed throughout the section on outlining. Study each outline heading and subheading carefully. Then, to the right of each entry, either rewrite the entry correctly or insert *Correct*. (The sentence outline form of I and II below is given in "Planning: Outlining."

I. Option of student concerning summer activity

    A. Take it easy

        1. Fun of loafing

        2. Doing nothing little effort

    B. Getting a summer job

        1. Worthwhile experiences of working

        2. Make money

II. Methods of finding a job

    A. Newspapers

        1. Job opportunities in classified ad sections

        2. Advertising of firms

    B. Utilize college's employment service

        1. Employers

        2. Advertise student's own services

Change the following portion of a sentence outline to a topic outline, using the criteria discussed in "Planning: Outlining."

II. One of the most important uses of a dictionary is looking up the meanings of words.

    A. An individual should understand the significance of the order in which meanings are given.

        1. Some dictionaries give the most common meanings first.

        2. Others give the definition with the centralized meaning first.

        3. Still others give definitions in chronological order, with the original meanings before the ones in current use.

B. The consulter should notice if the definition is labeled as a special or technical meaning.

    1. Some words have both a general and a special meaning.

    2. Some words are used only in a technical field.

II. _____

   A. _____

     1. _____

     2. _____

     3. _____

   B. _____

     1. _____

     2. _____

Using your own paper, outline a paper you have written recently. Does the outline show where you might have chosen a better ordering of ideas or where you might have included more examples or details?

EXERCISE (41g)-2, OUTLINING

Choose a subject of interest to you—possibly, for example, a subject studied in another course—and develop a three-level outline for it below. You may develop either a sentence outline or a topic outline; your instructor may specify one or the other.

Topic _____

Thesis Statement _____

_____

_____

I. _____

    A. _____

        1. _____

        2. _____

    B. _____

        1. _____

        2. _____

        3. _____

THESIS   a. _____

STATE-

MENT   b. _____

        c. _____

II. _____

    A. _____

        1. _____

        2. _____

    B. _____

        1. _____

        2. _____

III. _____

    A. _____

        1. _____

        2. _____

    B. _____

        1. _____

        2. _____

IV. _____

    A. _____

        1. _____

        2. _____

    B. _____

        1. _____

        2. _____

V. _____

    A. _____

        1. _____

        2. _____

    B. _____

        1. _____

        2. _____

PLANNING: SUBJECT BOUNDARIES AND THESIS STATEMENTS (41h)

Settling on a subject about which to write is usually not so much a matter of "finding" a topic as "creating" one. The Practice in "The Writing Process" gave you some experience with this type of activity. Whether you are assigned a subject or choose one on your own, selecting a general subject area often involves simply deciding just which aspect of the subject to use.

While you were brainstorming for the Practice, you probably "found" quite a few subjects about which you had interest and opinions. But when you listed points about those subjects and composed the opening sentences for the speeches, you also probably discovered that you needed to narrow your focus—to limit the range of the subject. You were engaged in the process of selecting an aspect of your subject, defining the subject's limits to make it interesting and effective for your audience. In other words, you were setting the boundaries of the subject so that it was manageable.

The most manageable subjects for short essays, such as those you write in English composition classes, are limited and specific. In order to do justice to a subject, you need one that is specific rather than general. Obviously, if you try to tackle freedom of speech in a short essay, you will either run out of space and time (after all, whole books have been written about it), or your treatment of the subject will be extremely superficial and loaded with unsupported generalizations. On the other hand, the high-school administrators' censorship of your student newspaper is an aspect of the subject that would enable you to discuss the principle of free speech in some detail, using concrete examples in a manageable context. You would be exploring general truths through specific applications and illustrations of them.

If you examine magazine articles by professional writers, you will see that they use the same method. For example, an author writing about good ethnic restaurants may focus on one aspect of the subject—outstanding Greek restaurants in Chicago.

In the process of setting boundaries for your subject, you are already planning what you want to say about it just by choosing which aspect you want to focus on. When you jot down a list of points and then choose the pertinent, important ones, your brainstorming produces further "invention," further creation and development of your ideas. As you arrange your points, deleting some and adding others, you are deciding in what direction you want to go with your subject. You are working out your purpose and preparing to compose the thesis statement for your paper.

The **thesis statement** presents the controlling idea you will develop in the body of your paper. Often it sets forth not only the main idea but also the important points, or **aspects,** that make up the idea. During the process of developing a thesis statement, you are thinking your subject through, determining what is relevant and what is not. You are deciding exactly what assertions you want to make and what points, examples, or illustrations you will need to support those assertions.

Usually the thesis statement can be expressed in one sentence, the grammatical subject identifying your essay's subject and the predicate making an assertion about the it:

SUBJECT
The golden years of retirement

PREDICATE
have become grim years of poverty for many senior citizens.

Mentioning the major aspects of your controlling idea will give you a good organizing statement for the development of the body of your paper and will also prepare your reader for what lies ahead:

The golden years of retirement have become grim years of poverty for many senior citizens because their fixed incomes have left them defenseless against rising prices.

Just as an essay's subject should be limited and specific, so should a thesis statement. If you are writing a 500-word essay on alcohol abuse, you know you can't say everything there is to be said about the subject, so you may decide to limit your discussion to alcohol abuse among teenagers or alcohol abuse among women. Even so, you can't say everything there is to be said about such a partially limited subject as alcohol abuse among women (causes, profile of abusers, physical and emotional effects on the drinker, effects on the family, various types of treatment and rehabilitation, recurring problems, life-long scars, etc.). So you won't want to compose a thesis that touches on all these points. Instead, you can focus in your thesis statement on one or two of them—for example, *Women who become alcoholics are often bored, lonely housewives who literally drink to "drown their sorrows."*

Notice how much more manageable this thesis statement is than *Lots of women are alcoholics.* or even *Lots of women drink because they are unhappy.* A good thesis statement restricts a subject to something you can reasonably discuss in some depth, focuses on several specific aspects of that subject, and indicates the plan you intend to use in the rest of your paper to make the case you set up in the thesis statement.

Practice A: Setting Subject Boundaries   Which of the following subjects are too broad and general as stated to be manageable in a 500-word essay? The answers are listed at the end of this section.
1. America's Ethnic History
2. The Ulster Scots and eastern Richmond County
3. Difficulties faced by Vietnamese refugees
4. How "American" food became American
5. Immigration patterns in the nineteenth century

Practice B: Focusing Thesis Statements   Which of the following thesis statements are too vague and imprecise to be effective? The answers are listed at the end of this section.
1. American culture is nonexistent.
2. In this country, anyone can be a success.
3. Of all their contributions to the history of Georgia, the political contributions of the Ulster Scots may be most important.
4. America's young people today don't want to work as hard as earlier generations did.
5. Immigration into America is now less than one-hundredth of its highest level at the turn of this century.

Answers to Practice A   1. Too general 2. Manageable 3. Manageable 4. Too general 5. Too general

Answers to Practice B   1. Too vague. 2. Too vague 3. Manageable 4. Too vague 5. Manageable

EXERCISE (41h)-1, PLANNING: SETTING SUBJECT BOUNDARIES

For each general subject below, list three examples—each one more specific than the one that precedes it.

Examples   Education

A. Humanities Courses

B. Introductory English Courses

C. Composition Courses

Politics

A. American Political Parties

B. The Republican Party

C. The Republican Party in Eisenhower's Era

1.   Television

   A. _____

   B. _____

   C. _____

2.   Automobiles

   A. _____

   B. _____

   C. _____

3.   Leisure

   A. _____

   B. _____

   C. _____

4.   Contests

   A. _____

   B. _____

   C. _____

For each general subject below, list four specific essay topics. Each topic should be more specific than the one that precedes it.

Examples   Football

A.   College football

B.   The positions on a football team

C.   How to block

D.   How to throw a "roll" block

Weapons

A.   Handguns

B.   Small-caliber handguns

C.   "Saturday Night Specials"

D.   Recent gun control legislation aimed at limiting the sale of small, cheap handguns

5.   The nuclear age

   A. _____

   B. _____

   C. _____

   D. _____

6.   Energy

   A. _____

   B. _____

   C. _____

   D. _____

7. Popular fads

A. _____

B. _____

C. _____

D. _____

8. Studying

A. _____

B. _____

C. _____

D. _____

9. Choice of a career

A. _____

B. _____

C. _____

D. _____

10. Reading

A. _____

B. _____

C. _____

D. _____

11. Neighborhoods

A. _____

B. _____

C. _____

D. _____

12. Sports

A. _____

B. _____

C. _____

D. _____

13. Music

A. _____

B. _____

C. _____

D. _____

14. Family

A. _____

B. _____

C. _____

D. _____

15. (Subject of your choice)

_____

A. _____

B. _____

C. _____

D. _____

16. (Subject of your choice)

_____

A. _____

B. _____

C. _____

D. _____

EXERCISE (41h)-2, PLANNING: EXPRESSING A CONTROLLING IDEA AS A THESIS STATEMENT

At each number below, list a general subject about which you would like to write. You may wish to use some of the subjects you listed in the previous exercise. Brainstorm for a while, and then write down the specific subject you would explore in an essay. Brainstorm some more, and then list six aspects of the subject that you might discuss in your paper.

Example   *General subject:* Television

Specific subject: Situation Comedies on Television

A. Situation comedies are currently popular.

B. Make the development of new talent possible with lower costs

C. Are frequently poorly done and trivial in content

D. Are sometimes unrealistic

E. Become repetitive in plotting

F. Take important programming time from more worthwhile topics

1. *General subject* _____

    Specific subject _____

    A. _____

    B. _____

    C. _____

    D. _____

    E. _____

    F. _____

2. *General subject* _____

    Specific subject _____

3. A. _____

    B. _____

    C. _____

    D. _____

E. _____

F. _____

4. *General subject* _____

   Specific subject _____

   A. _____

   B. _____

   C. _____

   D. _____

   E. _____

   F. _____

5. *General subject* _____

   Specific subject _____

   A. _____

   B. _____

   C. _____

   D. _____

   E. _____

   F. _____

For each of your five subjects, now select three of the aspects that would be manageable in a 500-word essay. List them. Then compose a focused thesis statement expressing the controlling idea for the essay you would write on each of the five subjects.

Example *Specific subject*: Situation Comedies on Television

A. Situation comedies are currently popular

B. Make the development of new talent possible with lower cost

C. Become repetitive in plotting

Thesis statement: Television situation comedies, although they tend to become repetitive with their plotting, are currently very popular on television, possibly because they introduce new talent at low cost to the networks.

Or Situation comedies are currently quite popular on television, often introducing new talent at lower costs than other programming, but their plots tend to become repetitive over a long series run.

1. *Specific subject* _____

   A. _____

   B. _____

   C. _____

   Thesis statement _____

   _____

   _____

   _____

2. *Specific subject* _____

   A. _____

   B. _____

   C. _____

   Thesis statement _____

   _____

   _____

   _____

3. *Specific subject* _____

   A. _____

   B. _____

   C. _____

   Thesis statement _____

   _____

   _____

   _____

4. *Specific subject* _____

   A. _____

   B. _____

   C. _____

   Thesis statement _____

   _____

   _____

_____

_____

5. *Specific subject* _____

    A. _____

    B. _____

    C. _____

    Thesis statement _____

_____

_____

_____

_____

THE WRITING PROCESS: EFFECTIVE BEGINNINGS AND ENDINGS (41j)

BEGINNINGS

Oddly enough, the best time to think about the beginning of your essay is usually after you have finished the first draft. Occasionally an interesting opening may come to mind as soon as you decide on a specific subject for your essay, or when you formulate the controlling idea. If that happens, fine. Write it down so you won't forget it. But more frequently the process of writing the paper will clarify your purpose, and composing a beginning will be easier after your first draft is completed.

Journalists and other professional writers talk about creating a "lead" or a "hook" for their stories. They want an opening that will grab the readers' interest—get them "hooked" in the opening paragraph so they will want to read the whole article. You want strong, direct, compelling openings for your own papers too.

An effective beginning attracts the readers' interests and introduces them to the subject. Although the beginning should not be too long in proportion to the rest of the paper (it is only the introduction, after all), it should be long enough to achieve some rapport with the readers and to establish a clear statement of purpose before you launch into the development of your subject's aspects. Other points to remember in beginning your paper include the following:

1. Try to get the readers' attention with a suitable anecdote, a justification of the subject, a startling statement, or a statement of the relevance of the subject to some local issue or happening.

2. Discuss briefly the general area or the subject matter, or supply background information as appropriate.

3. Indicate the purpose of the paper. A good way of doing this is to insert the thesis statement as the last sentence of the introduction.

4. Do not ramble. Make what is said in the introduction relevant either to the specific subject or to the background information.

5. Do not launch immediately into the principal topic of discussion without first providing some indication as to what the topic is going to be.

6. Do not comment upon the title without first introducing the idea in the title as a basis for discussion.

7. Do not insert material that has nothing to do with the subject.

Consider the following introduction written by a student in an English composition class:

> As we cruised down the moonlit country road, my ancient Volkswagen Beetle began to sputter. Throwing my date a worried glance, I steered to the berm, where the car finally died. "We're out of gas," I said. "Sure, sure," she replied in exasperation. "What a cheap, corny old trick. Now start this car and take me home." We really were out of gas; the fuel gauge on my VW hadn't worked in ten years, and since the car guzzled gas one minute and sipped it the next, I never knew for certain how much was in the tank. My date would not believe me. That night I learned the first of many lessons in how young women thoroughly accept stereotypes about male dating behavior.

The student's beginning paragraph accomplishes several things. First, it shows he has a sense of humor; it invites the readers to join the student as he laughs ruefully at himself and at human nature. The anecdotal opening engages the readers' interest and holds it by turning the tables on a stereotyped dating scene. Both male and female readers will identify with the characters in the anecdote and enjoy the turn of events. And finally, the student author introduces his subject—one that is quite specific. His general subject is human behavior, but he has narrowed it to dating behavior. His thesis statement focuses the subject even more tightly: women's stereotypes of their dates.

In this fairly long introduction, the author has used each sentence purposefully to get his paper on the stereotypes of dating off to a good start. He might have begun his paper in a number of other equally successful ways, but the method he chose is effective.

ENDINGS

A well-crafted paper needs an effective ending as well as good introductory and body paragraphs. Nothing detracts more from an otherwise appealing paper than to have it end abruptly or trail off into a weak or meaningless conclusion. Two things to avoid are apologizing for any weaknesses in the paper or introducing another aspect of the topic at the last moment. The first type of ending will pique readers' impatience and make them wonder why you didn't get rid of weaknesses rather than apologize for them. They will be left with a negative impression instead of a positive one. The second type of ending causes readers to feel cheated. No one likes to be left hanging at the end of an essay, wondering what you might have said if you had gone on to explore the topic's new aspect.

The ending of your paper should make the reader feel the discussion has been tied up, no loose ends, and rounded off in a satisfying way. A good ending can be compared to the bow tied on a birthday package or the icing on a cake—something good finished off with a flourish that makes the whole experience of reading your paper especially satisfying. Your reader should feel that without the conclusion the paper would have been incomplete. Some things you may do to achieve such a satisfactory ending include the following:

1. Restate briefly (not repeat word for word) the thesis statement of your paper.

2. Summarize briefly the major points of the paper.

3. Use a short anecdote or quotation that illustrates and supports your viewpoint.

4. Draw a conclusion from the discussion that shows the meaning of the facts and information you have presented.

The student who wrote the essay about dating behavior ended his paper by combining the second and fourth methods just listed.

Each of my youthful episodes contributed greatly to my understanding of female stereotypes about male dating behavior. I learned that running out of gas is always deliberate, that taking a girl to a fancy restaurant means you'll try to attack her later, and that you invite a homely girl to the prom *only* because ten other cute girls turned you down—*never* because you happen to find her more interesting to talk to. I also learned another valuable lesson: as a stereotype, I'm a complete failure.

Practice: Identifying effective beginnings and endings   Look through several popular magazines and select two or three articles that you think have especially good beginnings and/or endings. Bring them to class, ready to explain why you find them effective.

EXERCISE (41j)-1, EFFECTIVE BEGINNINGS

Questions 1–10 give the titles and introductions of compositions. In the blanks, write the letters of the characteristics listed in items *A–F* that best describe each introduction.

A. No clear purpose

B. Too short

C. Rambles

D. Discusses topic without first indicating what the topic is

E. Comments upon the title without first introducing the title into the discussion

F. Satisfactory

Example   Ethics

All around us today, we see failures in ethics and morality. Almost everyone can cite several examples. Famous people are guilty of crimes. Stockbrokers cheat their customers and trade inside information. Politicians cut their careers short because they have shady pasts.   _____

1. Minorities at the Top

Experts on organizational behavior cite several reasons for the lack of minorities at top executive levels in business. First, there are simply fewer minorities than others in management. Second, minorities are not easily accepted by majority-dominated management. Finally, many minority managers are just beginning to learn to play promotion politics.   _____

2. Nontraditional Dentists' Offices

Fully one half the population will not see one. The reason is fear. So dentists are designing offices in new ways and learning relaxation techniques. This is all to make patients less frightened.   _____

3. Gypsy Marriage Customs

Gypsy marriages are almost all arranged by parents. It's not that they don't understand romantic love. A gypsy marriage is just much more than one person marrying another person. Other things have to be considered.   _____

4. Community Watch
Community watch groups can help reduce crime. These groups can warn people and educate them about home security. Members of neighborhood watches will keep an eye on your house while you are out of town. The organization of community groups is one step toward the reduction of crime in the United States. _____

5. Recruiting Police Recruits
There are shortages of police officers in many states. If there were more police on the job, they could control and protect their jurisdictions better. Many big cities with high crime rates are understaffed and not able to enforce every law. If there were more police, they would be able to reduce the crime rate. _____

6. Lowering the Crime Rate
The crime rate in the United States is higher than that of any other industrialized nation. Crime runs rampant in the streets of America. But the problem could be solved if a little decisive action were taken. _____

7. The U.S. Crime Rate
The crime rate in the United States is about normal for a country this size. Many other countries have a much worse crime rate than ours. The United States needs to drastically change its penalties against these crimes. Otherwise, crimes against citizens will continue to soar in the United States. _____

8. Computer Mail
Computers are revolutionizing the way we receive mail. People with computers and a modem can send mail to any other computer with a modem, and send that mail instantaneously. _____

9. Status Symbols on the Job
On Friday afternoon you leave your large, carpeted office with the nice view of the park. On Monday morning you discover you've been moved to an office with no windows and with linoleum on the floor. Is the boss trying to tell you something? In many companies, office location and furnishings are clear indications of status—who is on the way up, and who is on the way down or out. _____

10. Keeping Fit
This is particularly difficult to do if you don't have a daily exercise routine. Students, working women and men with high-pressure jobs, senior citizens, almost everybody has an excuse to put it off until tomorrow, but tomorrow may be too late. _____

Below each of the following titles, write an introductory sentence or two using the specific technique for effective beginnings called for in parentheses.

11. If I Could Choose Anywhere in the World to Live

(Repeat the title.) _____

_____

_____

(Paraphrase the title.) _____

_____

_____

(Start with a statement of fact.) _____

_____

_____

(Use a startling statement or anecdote.) _____

_____

_____

12. Why Smoking Has Lost Popularity

(Repeat the title.) _____

_____

_____

(Paraphrase the title.) _____

_____

_____

(Start with a statement of fact.) _____

_____

_____

(Use a startling statement or anecdote.) _____

_____

_____

13. What Are We Getting From Research Using Animals as Subjects?

(Repeat the title.) _____

_____

_____

(Paraphrase the title.) _____

_____

_____

(Start with a statement of fact.) _____

_____

_____

(Use a startling statement or anecdote.) _____

_____

_____

14. (Title for a subject you choose) _____

(Repeat the title.) _____

_____

_____

(Paraphrase the title.) _____

_____

_____

(Start with a statement of fact.) _____

_____

_____

(Use a startling statement or anecdote.) _____

_____

_____

EXERCISE (41j)-2, EFFECTIVE ENDINGS

Using your own paper, develop thesis statements for the given composition titles. Then, for each of the approaches indicated in parentheses, write at least four sentences that would end the composition suitably.

1. Why Are So Many Americans Overweight?

   (Thesis statement)

   (Restate thesis statement.)

   (Briefly summarize major points of paper.)

   (Use supporting anecdote or quotation.)

   (Draw conclusion from paper.)

2. Why Smoking Has Lost Popularity

   (Thesis statement)

   (Restate thesis statement.)

   (Briefly summarize major points of paper.)

   (Use supporting anecdote or quotation.)

   (Draw conclusion from paper.)

3. Academic Stress

   (Thesis statement)

   (Restate thesis statement.)

   (Briefly summarize major points of paper.)

   (Use supporting anecdote or quotation.)

   (Draw conclusion from paper.)

4. Schools Fail to Educate Students—Whose Fault?

   (Thesis statement)

   (Restate thesis statement.)

   (Briefly summarize major points of paper.)

   (Use supporting anecdote or quotation.)

   (Draw conclusion from paper.)

5. (Title for the subject of your choice)

   (Thesis statement)

   (Restate thesis statement.)

   (Briefly summarize major points of paper.)

   (Use supporting anecdote or quotation.)

   (Draw conclusion from paper.)

6. (Title for a subject of your choice)

   (Thesis statement)

   (Restate thesis statement.)

   (Briefly summarize major points of paper.)

   (Use supporting anecdote or quotation.)

   (Draw conclusion from paper.)

7. What can Schools Do to Discourage Cheating?

   (Thesis statement)

   (Restate thesis statement.)

   (Briefly summarize major points of paper.)

   (Use supporting anecdote or quotation.)

   (Draw conclusion from paper.)

8. Do Extracurricular Activities Harm Students?

   (Thesis statement)

   (Restate thesis statement.)

   (Briefly summarize major points of paper.)

   (Use supporting anecdote or quotation.)

   (Draw conclusion from paper.)

9. Drunk Drivers

   (Thesis statement)

   (Restate thesis statement.)

   (Briefly summarize major points of paper.)

   (Use supporting anecdote or quotation.)

   (Draw conclusion from paper.)

10. If I Could Choose Any Job in the World

(Thesis statement)

(Restate thesis statement.)

(Briefly summarize major points of paper.)

(Use supporting anecdote or quotation.)

(Draw conclusion from paper.)

EFFECTIVE PARAGRAPHS:

PARAGRAPH UNITY   (42a)

Paragraphs are the building blocks of essays. As noted in the process outlined in "The Writing Process," every paragraph should be related to the thesis of your essay. Each paragraph furthers your purpose, supports your thesis, and explains your thinking about the subject.

The aspects of your subject thus become the paragraphs of your paper. Sometimes an aspect can be handled in a single paragraph; sometimes more than one paragraph are necessary because an aspect of your subject may contain sub-aspects that need explaining.

No matter how many paragraphs your finished essay contains, each one should be unified, coherent, and adequately developed. (The next several sections define and explain those rather abstract terms.) A good paragraph needs all three of these characteristics to be effective. A good essay needs them as well. In fact, you may find it helpful to think of a paragraph as a mini essay.

A paragraph is **unified** if it has a clear, controlling idea and if all the sentences in the paragraph relate to that idea. Most paragraphs use a **topic sentence** to state the paragraph's controlling idea. The topic sentence in a paragraph functions in the same way as the thesis statement in an essay: both express a central idea. The topic sentence of a paragraph focuses on one of the aspects or subaspects of the topic encompassed by the thesis. For example, if your thesis statement mentions three aspects (let's say, stripping, sanding, and varnishing) of a topic (refinishing furniture), then your essay will probably have three body paragraphs with corresponding topic sentences: one on stripping furniture, one on sanding it, and one on varnishing it.

The topic sentence may be the first sentence of a paragraph, it may be the last sentence of a paragraph, or it may appear in slightly different form in both places—particularly if the paragraph is long, involved, and needs summing up at the end.

Some paragraphs have implied topic sentences; but even when the topic sentence is unstated, the reader should be able to tell from the paragraph's details that a central idea is controlling the discussion. If your reader cannot formulate a topic sentence from the paragraph's discussion, then your paragraph is not controlled or unified. A paragraph that lacks a clear focus and contains irrelevant statements will cause your reader to wonder where you are headed and what the information has to do with your topic.

Practice A: Identifying topic sentences   Underline the topic sentence in each of the following paragraphs. If a paragraph has an implied topic sentence, compose your version of what the topic sentence might be. The answers are listed at the end of this section.

A.   [1]Chile con carne was not invented in Mexico, and the Mexicans don't want credit for it. [2]Food historians say that chile first appeared around 1880 in San Antonio, Texas. [3]A German from New Braunfels, Texas, invented chili powder—a spice previously unknown, of course, in Mexico or anywhere else. [4]Six years later, the inventor's canning company was turning out canned chile con carne. [5]One Mexican dictionary defines chile con carne as "detestable food with a false Mexican title."

B.   [1]Caesar salad was first served by Caesar Cardini, who owned and ran a small hotel in Tijuana. [2]Originally the salad contained only lettuce, croutons, Romano cheese, a coddled egg, lemon juice, and vinegar. [3]The anchovies were added somewhere else, as the fame of the salad spread. [4]The Caesar salad is one Mexican dish that found a home on the tables of many different cultures and on the menus of continental restaurants.

C.   [1]California is one of the largest producers of sweet potatoes in the United States today. [2]The state produces almost 800 million pounds of sweet potatoes each year. [3]John B. Avila, a native of the Portuguese Azores, planted the first twenty acres of sweet potatoes in California in 1888 and helped teach local farmers to cultivate the new crop, perfect for California's climate.

Practice B: Identifying irrelevant statements   Circle the letters of the sentences in each group that are not closely related to that group's topic sentence. The answers are listed at the end of this section.

1.   Some of the most famous department stores in America were begun by immigrants anxious to make their marks in America's economic system.
    A.   Brentano's, the bookstore chain, was founded by an Austrian immigrant.
    B.   William Filene, originally from Poland, started the stores in Boston that bear his name.
    C.   Hammacher Schlemmer, the world-famous gadget store, was started when German immigrant William Schlemmer convinced Alfred Hammacher to invest in his hardware store.

D. There is only one Hammacher Schlemmer store, on East 57th Street in New York.

E. The oldest retail store in New York is Lord and Taylor, started in 1826 by two Englishmen.

F. Rich's was begun by Morris Rich, an immigrant from Hungary.

G. Rich's has its headquarters in Atlanta and stores in most major cities in the Southeast.

2. Americans learned the custom of sending greetings on Valentine's Day from the English and French.

A. In the fourteenth century, British villagers drew the names of unmarried men and women at random and wrote love notes to their choice on February 14.

B. A Frenchman imprisoned in the Tower of London sent a love note to his wife in 1415.

C. Gradually the custom changed until notes were sent to loved ones rather than strangers, following this lead by the Duke of Orleans.

D. Valentine's Day was originally meant to honor St. Valentine, but his festival was held on the Lupercalia, the Roman fertility feast.

E. St. Valentine was an Italian priest who was martyred in 270.

Answers to Practice A   A. First sentence B. Fourth sentence C. Implied topic sentence; one possibility: *A Portuguese immigrant introduced the American West to what later became one of its major crops.*

Answers to Practice B   1. D, G   2. D, E

EXERCISE (42a), PARAGRAPH UNITY

Some sentences in the following paragraphs are irrelevant to the central ideas of the paragraphs. Write the letters of such irrelevant sentences in the blank to the right of each paragraph.

1.   (A) The number of British-Americans has decreased over the centuries. (B) This is partly explained by the American tendency to marry outside one's own ethnic group. (C) The Census officials list everyone who reports such mixed ancestry as "Other." (D) Census officials see no reason to change such a practice. (E) Ben Franklin, for example, was of British ancestry, but one of his descendants was the first American permitted to marry a native Japanese woman, in 1866. (F) Franklin's descendents are now listed as "Other."   ———————

2.   (A) Among the refugees of the Vietnam War are slightly more than 1,000 people who once earned their living fishing the South China Sea. (B) Now they are located half a world away, fishing the Gulf of Mexico off Mississippi. (C) Thirty years ago, they lived in North Vietnam but fled to the south when the Communists took over in 1954. (D) With the fall of South Vietnam in 1975, they fled again and were picked up by American ships. (E) To many of these fishing families, the whale is sacred and signifies good luck.   ———————

3.   (A) In 1798, the Federalists in Congress passed laws designed to discourage immigration after the Colonial period. (B) But the more democratic Jeffersonians welcomed the immigrants as voters. (C) Aliens were suddenly required to reside in America for fourteen years before they could apply for citizenship. (D) The President was given the power to deport or imprison undesirable immigrants. (E) Even though hundreds of revolutionaries were fleeing Europe, the laws seemed an arbitrary use of power and were never enforced.   ———————

4.   (A) New York's Fifth Avenue is perhaps the nation's most famous parade route. (B) It is the address of Tiffany's, Saks, and many other expensive, fashionable shops. (C) When the country wants to honor a hero, it schedules a parade on Fifth Avenue. (D) Astronauts, presidents, baseball teams, and returning political hostages have ridden up Fifth Avenue amid confetti and ticker tape. (E) Each year Irish, Jews, Italians, Greeks, Germans, Puerto Ricans, and Poles celebrate their ethnic heritages with parades on Fifth Avenue. (F) There is even a well-known song about Fifth Avenue's Easter Parade.   ———————

5.   (A) The Smithsonian is the world's largest museum. (B) Over 78 million items fill the shelves and storage rooms of the Smithsonian buildings, which sprawl across the entire center of Washington. (C) Even with all this room, the collection is so large that at any given time, 95 percent of the museum's collection is in storage, loaned to other museums, or in travelling exhibits. (D) No one knows why James Smithson, who had never even seen America, left his entire fortune to start this museum. (E) The collection fills thirteen huge buildings and the Washington Zoo.   _____

6.   (A) Charles Curtis was America's first Senator and Vice President to be of American Indian ancestry. (B) Curtis, who was one-eighth Kaw Indian, served as Senator from Kansas for 25 years. (C) He was also descended from French frontiersmen. (D) Under Herbert Hoover, Curtis served as Vice President. (E) During his career, Curtis helped protect the rights of Indians. (F) The Curtis Bill allowed Indians to incorporate their own towns and elect their own officials.   _____

7.   (A) Bad luck comes in many forms. (B) Japanese believe that trimming one's nails before a trip brings bad luck. (C) Ashes flying into the room from a fireplace bring bad luck, according to Greek superstition. (D) In Denmark, spilling damp salt is an evil omen. (E) Spilling dry salt brings good luck, though. (F) Sneezing while tying one's shoes is bad luck for a German. (G) Scots never mail letters on Christmas Day, February 29, or September 1—all unlucky days for letters and packages.   _____

8.   (A) A short history of one textile town in New England helps illustrate America's lure for immigrants. (B) When the mill first opened, young girls from Scotland, skilled weavers, were brought to America to teach weaving skills to local workers. (C) The Scots workers often brought their relatives over later. (D) By 1860, Irish families were becoming the basis of the work force as their work as canal builders and railroad workers led them to more New England towns. (E) By this time, over one-fourth of the town's citizens were of foreign birth. (F) German and Swedish immigrants took jobs in the mill as skilled craftsmen. (G) In the 1870s, scarce land and depleted farms in Canada sent many French-Canadians into New England mill towns in search of work, drawn by the mill's agents who travelled through Canada recruiting unskilled labor. (H) Later immigrants, particularly Greeks and Poles, arrived in smaller numbers, but the textile industry and its steady wages continued to draw immigrants as long as it was a thriving industry.   _____

9.   (A) Dr. Percy Julian was an award winning Black chemist. (B) When Julian died, he held over 130 chemical patents. (C) Julian's work with soybeans helped create low-cost foods, waterproofing

agents, fire extinguishing chemicals, and synthetic hormones. (D) Millions of arthritis sufferers can thank Percy Julian for synthetic cortisone, which made relief from pain affordable. (E) Who knows what other uses may be found for the chemicals produced by the soybean?

10.   (A) The bagel was introduced to America by Jewish immigrants. (B) Until the 1960s, the bagel was popular only in Jewish neighborhoods or in cities with large Jewish populations. (C) In 1960, there were only 40 bagel bakeries in the United States, and 30 of these were in New York. (D) Soon, however, the chewy roll caught on with Americans. (E) By 1977, there were over 360 bagel bakeries, and they were distributed all across America. (F) Bagels are first boiled, then baked. (G) This is the process that makes them so chewy. (H) The popularity that bagels suddenly enjoyed after 1963 may be traced to Harry Lender, a Polish immigrant who first opened a bagel shop in 1927, and who introduced a line of frozen bagels in 1963.

Using your own paper, write four topic sentences on subjects of your choice. Underneath each topic sentence, write four sentences related to that topic sentence. Be sure that every sentence you write directly concerns the subject matter introduced in your topic sentence.

EFFECTIVE PARAGRAPHS:
PARAGRAPH COHERENCE:
ORGANIZING IDEAS   (42b)

A paragraph is **coherent** if the sentences convey a smooth, logical flow of thought from one idea to the next. Each sentence should show an evident relationship to the one that precedes it and a clear connection to the one that follows it, as well as a bearing on the paragraph's controlling idea.

Whereas unity depends upon your selecting ideas that are relevant to the topic of your paragraph, coherence depends upon your ability to show how the ideas are relevant by presenting them in a smooth, orderly, well-knit arrangement. Smoothness in a paragraph is achieved partially by using transitional elements; these are discussed more fully in the next section. Orderliness can be achieved by using one of several organizational patterns for your sentences. The patterns you choose for your paragraphs depend upon your subject and purpose; each is a means for creating coherence in your writing.

Descriptions and examples of common organizational patterns follow. In some of the example paragraphs, transitional links are italicized.

1. **Time order (chronological order)** is the order in which events occur: one thing happens after another.

My visit to Professor Crump's office for help with an astronomy problem *at first* seemed more like a social call than a tutorial. *After* I knocked and entered the room, he invited me to be seated in one of his overstuffed chairs. We spent *the next several* minutes of our conference discussing my work in other courses, and I *began* to realize he was trying to put me at ease. *Then* he offered me a cup of tea, which he poured into china cups. *Only when* I was settled comfortably with my tea cup *did he* spread his astronomical models on the desk and ask, "*Now*, which aspect of retrograde motion would you like me to explain?"

2. **Space order (spatial order)** is sentence arrangement according to physical layout, such as top to bottom, left to right, back to front, east to west, and so forth.

> The astronomy professor's office was unlike any other faculty office in the science building. Visitors noticed first the enormous antique desk *against the far wall. On the right* were heavy, glass-fronted bookcases. *On the left* were several overstuffed chairs. The *overhead* fluorescent lights had been turned off. *Instead,* Tiffany lamps cast a warm glow through their colorful glass shades. The Victorian decor was completed by the oriental rug *underfoot.*

3. **General to particular** or **particular to general order** is a general statement followed by (1) supporting evidence and illustrations or (2) particular evidence and illustrations leading to a concluding generalization. When either of these arrangements is used, the generalization usually appears in the topic sentence— at the beginning of the paragraph in the first case, at the end of the paragraph in the second. The paragraph illustrating order of climax is also an example of particular to general order. The following paragraph shows general to particular order.

> *Sometimes* Professor Crump digressed from his class lectures on astronomy and *told anecdotes about his life. On various occasions he told about* helping to build one of the nation's first big reflecting telescopes, about his transcendental religious experience on a mountaintop in Kashmir, *about* a picnic lunch with an attractive stranger who turned out to be Mussolini's mistress. *Most of these stories* had little if anything to do with astronomy. We gradually realized, *however,* that for Dr. Crump the mysteries of the stars were just one aspect of life's rich, diverse mystery.

4. **Order of climax** is order by increasing importance: minor details lead to the main point.

> To the students on our small college campus, Professor Crump *was more than an elderly astronomer:* he *was a chunk of civilization.* At nearly eighty years of age, *he had seen* astronomy grow from relative infancy; *he had worked* with many of the century's greatest scientists. *He had witnessed* two world wars, *taught* at five colleges and universities, *and led* a full—even exotic—life. *Yet he chose* to end his long career with us. We were flattered.

5. **Comparison** and **contrast** are natural methods of organization for many topics. Comparison stresses similarities between items. Contrast explains their differences. Sometimes you will develop an entire paragraph using just one method or just the other; sometimes you will want both to compare and to contrast in the same paragraph. The following paragraph principally uses contrast to develop its controlling idea. Notice how the transitional words provide the reader with clear connections between ideas.

> *Except for* the fact that dogs and cats are both four-legged, furry mammals, they are distinctly different types of pets. Dogs are very loyal and subservient to their mas-

ters. Cats, *on the other hand,* never totally commit their allegiance to anyone, *but instead* maintain their independence. Cats are relatively self-sufficient and can be left alone if their owners go away for the weekend. All they need is a supply of food and fresh water and a clean litter box. Dogs, *however,* wolf all their food immediately and have to be taken out every few hours. Woe to owners whose dogs get lonely while they are gone; upon returning they will find chewed shoes, hats, gloves, and furniture.

6. **Analysis** and **classification** take things apart and put them together again. When you **analyze** something, you break it down into its various parts and look at the characteristics of those parts and at how they fit together to comprise the whole. For example, if you analyze the time you spend doing homework, you are likely to find you spend so many minutes on getting your books and cup of coffee; so many minutes on daydreaming, petting the dog, and rereading the assignment; and so many minutes actually studying productively.

When you **classify,** you put items into groups according to their common characteristics. Suppose you want to classify fruit. First you have to establish a basis for classification: natural fruits. Once you have established this basis, you must be sure that the classifications are mutually exclusive, that the items being classified are comparable, and that you do not shift the basis of classification (an error known as **cross-classification**). These points are illustrated here:

BASIS OF CLASSIFICATION
FRUITS IN THEIR NATURAL STATE

(1)	(2)	(3)	(4)	(5)
citrus fruit	oranges	oranges	oranges	oranges
noncitrus fruit	apples	apples	winesaps	apples
	grapefruit	grapefruit	grapefruit	grapefruit
	pears	winesaps	pears	potatoes
	peaches	peaches	peaches	peaches

In list (1) are broad groupings of fruit. In (2) are listed various species of fruit. Both (1) and (2) classify fruit in accordance with the stated basis of classification. In (3), however, both apples and winesaps are listed. This classification is not **mutually exclusive**—that is, it lists a subcategory as a separate aspect of discussion. If the subcategory is to be discussed, it must be discussed under the category of which it is a member. In (4), by contrast, winesaps, a subcategory of apples, are listed as being comparable to the categories oranges, grapefruit, pears, and peaches. Hence, the classification is not **comparable** because the subcategory is classified at the same level as the main category. Finally, list (5) departs altogether from the basis of classification, which was fruits, by listing potatoes, which are, of course, vegetables. The result is a **cross-classification.**

PARAGRAPH USING CLASSIFICATION AND ANALYSIS

We can communicate in three basic ways. Each way has its advantages. One way is by speaking. When we speak we have a chance to judge our audience's reactions. If they don't understand, we can reword as necessary to make our points. We can also invite additional questions and clarify additional aspects for our listeners. Another way of communicating is by writing. When we write, we have more time. We can think our subject through thoroughly. We can modify our development and polish our phraseology until we get it the way we want it. The third way of communicating is nonverbal. Communication of this type can involve such actions as a look, a nod of the head, or a shake of the hand. Nonverbal communication can be quite effective in a very noisy atmosphere or when we don't want to dignify a response with actual words.

The preceding paragraph establishes as the basis for classification the ways of communication. Its classification is mutually exclusive since it analyzes sub-aspects of speaking, writing, and nonverbal communication only under the aspects to which they pertain. The aspects in its classification are comparable, and no cross-classification occurs since speaking, writing, and nonverbal communication are all methods of communication.

7. **Definition** is useful for clarifying terms or concepts the reader may not know or understand in just the way you want them understood. Sometimes you need not go into much detail as you define. In this case, you will be employing an informal definition, which can involve as little as a word or a phrase.

The eosin (dye) was smeared all over the page.

The kibitzer (an onlooker who offers advice) infuriated the card players.

At other times, though, you may choose or need to be more detailed or explicit when you define. Then you may employ a **formal definition,** which consists of a term to be defined; a genus (class), which is a general category in which the term can logically be included; and differentia, which is a statement of the way the term differs from other members of the genus. The following is a formal definition:

TERM TO BE DEFINED	GENUS (CLASS)	DIFFERENTIA
Introductory Composition is a	communicative process	in which students convey their thoughts in writing, often in compositions about 500 words long.

Often a formal definition will be expanded into an **extended definition.** The extended definition may use examples, comparison and contrast, and any of the other forms of organization and development to explain its subject more fully.

A door is a movable structure contained within a framework that separates two areas by covering an opening and whose principal purpose is to facilitate entrances and exits. There are all kinds of doors. There are hanging doors, swinging doors, overhead doors, trap doors, and sliding doors. As a matter of fact, even strings of beads or sheets of canvas or leather have been used as doors. Doors come in all sizes and shapes. Although they can be made of beads or canvas, they more customarily are made of wood, steel, aluminum, or glass. However we describe them, we have to conclude that they are pretty handy devices. Without them, our living wouldn't be nearly as comfortable or as secure as it is.

8. **Organization** by **cause** and **effect** works in one of two ways. You can list the effect, condition, or result first and then discuss the causes or reasons why the effect has come about. Or you can reverse the process, first investigating the causes or reasons and then discussing what effects, conditions, or results they have produced. Like comparisons and contrasts, causes and effects may be handled in the same paragraph, or you may want to divide them among several paragraphs—one or more on causes, one or more on effects—depending on the nature and complexity of your topic. The following paragraphs first detail effects and then explore the causes of those effects.

My mother could not understand why her left arm was swollen, itching, and covered with a red rash. When the rash turned to blisters that broke and suppurated, and when the itching kept her awake at night, she went to the doctor. His diagnosis was poison ivy.

She protested that she had not come in contact with any poison ivy plants, although the salve the doctor gave her healed the blisters. A few days later my father mentioned that the highway department had sprayed the poison ivy along our road. The mystery of the rash was solved. While driving with her arm out the car window, my mother had come in contact with the oily fumes of the dying poison ivy plants.

EXERCISE (42b), PARAGRAPH COHERENCE: ORGANIZING IDEAS

In the blank following each set of sentences, write the numbers of the sentences in the order that would develop a coherent paragraph.

A. 1. At fifteen, King entered Morehouse College in Atlanta, where he was a high ranking student.

      2. It was in his work with the Council that King first came into contact with whites on a regular basis.

      3. Martin Luther King studied at two high schools, University High and Booker Washington High, and graduated in two years.

      4. At Morehouse, he worked with the City Intercollegiate Council, a group of students from all the colleges in Atlanta who worked on college social problems.

      5. "As I got to see more of white people," King later said, "my resentment softened and a spirit of cooperation took its place."

_____

B. 1. Nevertheless, he was impressed by the way the students all worked closely together.

      2. In Gandhi, King discovered a man, a member of an oppressed group, who had met that oppression with a new weapon, nonviolent resistance.

      3. King attended Crozier Theological Seminary in Chester, Pennsylvania.

      4. Most of all, King admired the writings of Gandhi.

      5. He worked as hard as the rest, reading all the works of the great social philosophers.

      6. This was King's first experience in an integrated school and his first time in the North.

      7. In reading Gandhi and the other philosophers, King thought he saw a way to ease racial tension and begin a struggle for civil rights.

      8. At Crozier, he was one of only six blacks in a group of a hundred graduate students.

_____

C. 1. He was the first to link scientifically certain diseases such as rickets, pellagra, and scurvy with nutritional deficiencies.

      2. Vitamins were discovered by Casimir Funk in Warsaw, Poland.

3. When it was later determined that not all vitamins contained an amino group, the *e* was dropped from the word.

4. Three years before he immigrated to the United States in 1915, Funk published his research findings on the connection between disease and the lack of what he dubbed *vitamines*.

5. He created the word *vitamine* from *vita,* meaning life, and *amino.*

6. Hence the word became *vitamin,* as we spell it today.

7. *Amino* stood for the nitrogen group he thought was a chemical component of all *vitamines*.

8. Sailors long ago discovered that citrus fruits such as oranges prevent and cure scurvy.

9. It took a Polish-American scientist to learn the reason and give it a name.

D. 1. If sweets weren't enough, pushcarts sold dill pickles and pickled tomatoes.

2. But the favorite of all, according to Harry Golden, who has written about this fantastic open-air market, was the good old hot dog with mustard.

3. The best of all the old candies were halvah or "buckser" from Palestine.

4. In the old immigrant neighborhoods in New York, pushcart vendors and other sidewalk salesmen sold every kind of ethnic food imaginable.

5. Imagine being sent out onto those teeming streets with a whole dime!

6. First there were all sorts of confections.

7. A schoolboy or schoolgirl could sample candy from Turkey, the Orient, or from eastern Europe.

8. Baked sweet potatoes, nuts, hot corn-on-the-cob, and hot chick-peas were among the more substantial foods offered for sale.

9. Other vendors sold all sorts of fruits, exotic and common, as the seasons allowed.

10. In those days, according to Golden, a hot dog was three cents and the accompanying drink was two cents.

Using your own paper, first list six different paragraph topics. You may want to choose some of the topics you developed in earlier exercises. Then write a coherent paragraph for each topic, using a different organizational pattern each time. Choose from the following patterns: *chronological order, spatial order, general-to-particular order, particular-to-general order, order of climax, comparison and/or contrast, analysis and classification, definition, cause and effect.*

EFFECTIVE PARAGRAPHS: PARAGRAPH COHERENCE: CONNECTING IDEAS/CONNECTING LANGUAGE (42c–d)

Sentence arrangement helps to achieve coherence in paragraphs, but to establish the relationships between ideas clearly, you need to guide your reader smoothly from one thought to the next. Doing so involves the effective use of transitional elements. These are: (1) a consistent point of view; (2) parallel grammatical structure; (3) repeated words and phrases, synonyms, or repeated ideas; and (4) transitional words and phrases.

1. **Consistent point of view** is maintained if you avoid unnecessary shifts in person, verb tense, or number within a paragraph (see the section "Shifts in Point of View"). The following paragraph shows how such unnecessary shifts can ruin continuity and confuse the reader:

> Many fanciful beliefs have surrounded the moon. People at one time or another believed the moon was a goddess, it is a man's face, or it was thought to be the cause of various diseases. You know, strange creatures even had been thought to live on the moon. After decades of space flights, we find the moon much less mysterious.

Notice how much smoother the revision is:

> People have believed many fanciful things about the moon. At one time or another they have believed the moon to be a goddess, a man's face, or the cause of various diseases. People have even thought strange creatures lived on the moon. After decades of space flights, the moon has become much less mysterious.

2. **Repeated key words or phrases, synonyms, or repeated ideas** indicate to the reader that relationships exist between thoughts in a paragraph. Something

as simple as using a pronoun to refer to a clearly established antecedent or inserting a synonym can provide coherence for a paragraph. The preceding example paragraph not only uses parallel structure but also repeats words and phrases to cement relationships between ideas and to provide a smooth flow. The three crucial repetitions in that paragraph are *it is, believed in,* and *life of.* The pronouns *his* and *he,* referring to Professor Crump, remind the reader that the same individual is the subject throughout the paragraph. The following paragraph relies even more heavily on repetition to achieve coherence:

> His gentle presence will be sorely missed from this campus. *It is clear that he loved* the college and its students deeply, and *it is a challenge to live* up to his high standards of character and academic excellence. *Clifford Crump believed in the life of the mind; he believed in the life of the spirit,* and his own life proved that the two can be one in daily practice.

3. **Parallel grammatical structure in successive sentences** emphasizes the relationship between them and the relationship between them and the relationship to the paragraph's main idea. The sentences in the general-to-particular paragraph in the previous use parallel structure to reinforce their relationship. Notice that the subject-verb arrangement of the clauses beginning *he had seen, he had worked, he had witnessed ... taught ... and led* echo the structure and support with examples the controlling idea in the topic sentence *He was a chunk of civilization.* In the following paragraph, written by the college president after the death of the astronomy professor described in the previous paragraph, the parallel grammatical structures are italicized.

> *Star gazing* on a winter night *is not necessarily a romantic pastime.* Even when *your* boyfriend is the instructor, *learning constellations* for *your* astronomy midterm *is not necessarily* a *heart-warming experience. All you* can think about is *your cold* feet, *your cold* hands, *your cold* nose. *All you* want to do is *get someplace* warm, and *get there* as quickly as possible.

4. **Transitional words and phrases** that appear at or near the beginning of a sentence indicate a relationship between that sentence and the one preceding it. Coordinating conjunctions such as *and, but, or, nor, so,* and *yet* are often used in informal writing to provide bridges between sentences. However, you can use many other words and phrases to establish connections in more formal writing. A number of them are listed here:

ADDITION	again, also, and, and then, besides, equally important, finally, first, furthermore, in addition, last, likewise, moreover, next, second, third, too
CAUSE AND EFFECT	accordingly, as a result, because, consequently, hence, otherwise, since, so, then, therefore, thus
COMPARISON	by the same token, in a like manner, likewise, similarly
CONCESSION	after all, at the same time, even though, of course

CONTRAST	although, at the same time, but, by contrast, for all that, however, in spite of, nevertheless, on the contrary, on the other hand, still, yet
EXAMPLE OR ILLUSTRATIONS	for example, for instance, in fact, in other words, specifically, such as, that is, to illustrate
SUMMARY	in brief, in conclusion, in essence, in short, on the whole, to conclude, to sum up
TIME RELATIONS	after, afterwards, as long as, as soon as, at last, at that time, before, immediately, in the meantime, later, meanwhile, next, presently, soon, then, thereafter, thereupon, until, when, while

Use transitional elements appropriately. Remember what these words mean, and do not simply throw them into your sentences without regard for sense.

Be aware, too, that transitional words can become extremely tiresome if they are overused. If every sentence in a paragraph begins with one of these words, the paragraph can become very choppy, as the following example shows:

> Many of the constellations were named by the Greeks. *However,* the Greeks were not the first people to name configurations of stars. *In fact,* 5,000 years ago the Mesopotamians saw patterns or pictures in the stars and named them after animals and occupations. *Moreover,* today we still use many of the ancient names for constellations. *For example,* the constellation containing the Big Dipper is called Ursa Major, the Great Bear. *Furthermore,* we call the constellation that looked to some ancients like a bowman, Sagittarius, the Archer.

Learn to use a variety of means to show relationships between your ideas. Notice how much smoother the revision of the preceding example paragraph becomes when several types of transitions are used to replace some of the transitional words at the beginnings of sentences. Also notice how combining some of the sentences smooths the flow of ideas.

> Although the Greeks named many of the constellations, they were not the first people to name configurations of stars. In fact, 5,000 years ago the Mesopotamians saw patterns or pictures in the stars and named them for animals and occupations. Today we see the same heavenly patterns and call them by many of the same ancient names: Ursa Major, the Great Bear, the constellation containing the Big Dipper; Sagittarius, the Archer, the constellation that looks like a bowman.

EXERCISE (42c–d), PARAGRAPH COHERENCE: CONNECTING IDEAS/CONNECTING LANGUAGE

Using your own paper, revise the following paragraphs, eliminating unnecessary shifts in point of view and providing transitional elements where they are needed. You may combine or rearrange sentences to achieve a smooth, coherent paragraph.

1. Friday and the 13th have bad reputations as days of bad luck. Fridays were reserved for hangings and public executions. Many evil events in the Bible, such as the temptation of Eve, occurred on Friday. According to superstition, thirteen guests at a party is a bad omen. Thirteen people were present at the last supper in the New Testament. When Loki, the Norse god of mischief, showed up at a banquet for 12 other gods, the result was the death of Baldur, one of the favored gods.

2. American history and Scandinavian folklore show no such fear of the number 13 or of Fridays. There were thirteen original American colonies. The Revolutionary Army was taken over by Washington on Friday the 13th. On Friday the 13th construction began on the White House. The American dollar has 13 stars. They have 13 arrows. There are 13 leaves and 13 olives in the eagle's right claw. Each pyramid has one side with 13 rows of building blocks. Scandinavians consider Friday a lucky day. People born on the 13th are considered lucky. Friday the 13th is their lucky day.

3. The government of England once decided to prove that all the superstitions associated with Friday were simply superstitions. A naval yard began construction of a new ship on Friday. The ship was named on a Friday. As its name, it bore *HMS Friday*. On a Friday, the ship was launched. Its maiden voyage began on a Friday. They have never been seen or heard from again.

4. Some of the most common superstitions are "immigrants" from other countries. The Dutch were the first to knock on wood for good luck. He has to knock on unpainted wood for it to work, so we knock on the unvarnished underside of a table. A Dane believes that breaking a mirror can bring either good or bad luck for seven years. Unfortunately, they can't predict which it will be. An American tied shoes to the car of a couple going on a honeymoon in imitation of an Irish custom of throwing shoes after a person starting on a long journey. Many cultures preserved the custom of throwing rice, salt, or flowers at a newlywed couple. These objects all represented fertility and prosperity in many European cultures.

5. The Romans believed June was the best month for marriage. The bridal veil was introduced by the Romans. Veils shielded the bride from evil spirits. A wedding cake was prepared and served to assure prosperity. The French

introduced the custom of throwing the bride's bouquet to her maids. Ancient Hebrews considered blue the color of love and purity. He urges a bride to wear "something blue." Egyptians first used the ring as a symbol of eternity for weddings. Romans and early Christians made the rings the size of fingers. The custom of wearing wedding bands was introduced to America by early German settlers.

6. Various cultures set the entry into adulthood at different times. A Jewish boy enters adulthood on his 13th birthday. A traditional ceremony, Bar Mitzvah, marks the passage. Japanese celebrated the passage into adulthood at the age of fifteen or sixteen. A ceremony in which the boy is given an adult's cap, marks the change to adult ways of dressing. "Sweet 16" parties or debutante balls celebrate the fact that an American girl was ready to enter society or to start dating. The *quince* is a celebration of a girl's fifteenth birthday. A *quince* was the Hispanic equivalent of a debutante ball. *Quinces* can be very elaborate and expensive; it signified not only that the young girl was ready to begin dating, but also that she was ready to start dating seriously.

Using your own paper, write paragraphs at least four sentences long that illustrate the use of the transitional elements called for in items 7 through 10. Underline and label the transitional elements you use.

Example   comparison, contrast, concession, example, summary

A sentence outline and a topic outline are alike in some respects. The sentence outline uses headings and subheadings. The topic outline proceeds *similarly* in this respect. *Likewise,* both outlines, if they are properly developed, will be unified; *that is,* all subheadings will relate to the subheadings or headings above them. *In turn,* the main headings will pertain to the subject of the paper. The two papers differ, *on the other hand,* in that whereas the sentence outline contains only sentences, the topic outline has none. *Of course,* both outlines are good. *In essence,* the one should be used which best fits the needs of the occasion.

7. comparison, contrast, examples, parallel structure

8. cause and effect, addition, summary, synonyms

9. time relations, concession, contrast, summary

10. word repetition, addition, examples

EFFECTIVE PARAGRAPHS: PARAGRAPH DEVELOPMENT (42e–f)

A paragraph is adequately **developed** if it has enough evidence, examples, supporting facts, details, and reasons for your readers to understand your topic sentence fully and be persuaded of its validity. Just as all the paragraphs in your essay should explain and support your thesis statement, so the sentences in your paragraphs should clarify and support the topic sentences.

Details, examples, and illustrations are the most common types of support for a paragraph's controlling idea. In fact, most methods of development rely on details and examples. Details are a catalog of particulars, usually presented without much explanation. Examples, on the other hand, require some explanation to show their relevance to the paragraph's main topic. Development by illustration is the same as development by example, except that instead of using several examples to support the main point, you use one example that you explain at considerable length. The following paragraph is developed with details. It makes use of a chronological arrangement to ensure the coherence of these details. The second paragraph is developed with examples.

PARAGRAPH DEVELOPED WITH DETAILS

Getting ready to write a composition is quite an ordeal. First, you have to find a quiet place where you can concentrate. Then you have to make sure you have a good pen, plenty of paper, a dictionary, a handbook, and plenty of hot coffee. When you are finally settled and ready to go, you next have to think of a subject, construct a thesis statement, and make up an outline with the right number of headings and subheadings. If you are still with it after having done all of the preceding, then you write a rough draft. The next to the last step is to revise the composition, making sure that it is coherent, unified, properly developed with good sentences and paragraphs, and that there are no errors in spelling, mechanics, punctuation, and diction. The last step is to endorse it, say a short prayer, and collapse on your bed. As you do, you hope you will have no nightmares in which English instructors are chasing you with gigantic red pens and waving papers you have written which have more red marks on them than anything else.

PARAGRAPH DEVELOPED WITH EXAMPLES

One can meet all kinds of drivers on the road. First, there is Obnoxious Oscar. Oscar careens down the street with the throttle wide open, poisoning the atmosphere with noxious smoke, waking up everyone within miles with his noisy muffler, and honking insistently at anyone who happens to be driving ahead of him. Second, there is Cautious Chauncey. Chauncey putters along at only ten miles per hour. He slows down to two miles per hour at each driveway and displays massive indifference to the immense traffic jam behind him. Third, there is Slippery Sam. Sam writhes in and out of traffic like an eel among coral. Nothing ever seems to happen to him, but such is not true of the other drivers who have been around him. Most of them are basket cases with thoroughly jangled nerves and with hips that have been hopelessly dislocated by jamming down on the brakes in trying to avoid him.

How much paragraph development is enough? That is a hard question to answer. Only your readers know for sure. If readers are not given enough examples or explanations to understand or accept your topic sentence, your paragraph is not sufficiently developed and, hence, one of the aspects of your thesis will be weakened.

Put yourself in the readers' position. If you were seeing the essay for the first time, would you find enough information in the body paragraphs to follow the author's ideas and understand the essay's generalizations and conclusions?

EXERCISE (42e–f), PARAGRAPH DEVELOPMENT

Read the following paragraphs and decide if they are sufficiently developed with supporting evidence. If a paragraph is sufficiently developed, write *Yes* in the upper blank at the right; if it is not, write *No*. Then decide which principal method of development is being used (details, examples, illustration, comparison, contrast, definition, cause and effect, analysis, classification), and write the method in the lower blank.

Example   Professors actually face many of the same pressures faced by students. Both have many strict deadlines to meet.

no

comp.

1. Hollywood has always been a boom town for talented Americans, but it sometimes seems that ethnic Americans have found that Hollywood especially rewarded their talents. Frank Capra, the famous director of many classic films, was born in Palermo, Sicily. John Cassavetes, actor and director, is the son of Greek immigrants. Francis Ford Coppola is the son of a Neapolitan musician who moved to New York to conduct at the Radio City Music Hall. Even Alfred Hitchcock started as a director in his native London in the 1920s. The Warner brothers were four Jewish immigrants from Ontario; Jack, Harry, Albert, and Sam were originally the Eichelbaum brothers. Like many ethnic Americans who found success in Hollywood, they "Americanized" their names.

2. Warner Brothers made its reputation and its fortune by use of every technological advance available. They made some of the first "talkies," including the first full-length sound picture, *The Jazz Singer*.

3. Elia Kazan, the famous director, remembers that his Greek grandmother was proud that the first thing she did in her new home in America was to make yogurt "in the Greek way." To do this she heated milk until it was almost boiling.

4. David O. Selznick learned the craft of filmmaking from his father, a pioneer film producer born in the Ukraine. The elder Selznick advertised his films with the slogan, "Selznick pictures make happy hours." Unlike his father, David made his reputation with brooding, tragic, and sentimental films like *Gone with the Wind*, *Rebecca*, *Intermezzo*, *Portrait of Jenny*, and *A Farewell to Arms*.

5. Before deciding to pursue a career in the theater or in
   film, one should carefully consider training and experience. The type of training one has received will usually
   determine the kinds of jobs one can do. In addition, recognizing this limitation will prevent disappointments later
   on.

   _____

   _____

Choose a topic, and then, using your own paper, write a paragraph developed
by the method called for in each of items 6 through 11. Be sure to write a topic
heading above each paragraph.

6. Choose a topic and then use details about the topic to develop a paragraph
   of at least four sentences.

7. Choose a topic and then use examples and explanatory remarks concerning
   those examples to develop a paragraph of at least four sentences.

8. Choose a topic and develop a paragraph of at least four sentences. Start
   the paragraph with a formal definition and then extend the definition using
   examples, comparison and contrast, and any other forms of development
   you find suitable.

9. Choose a topic and develop a paragraph of at least four sentences in which
   you explain an effect or result in terms of its causes.

10. Choose a topic and write a paragraph containing at least four sentences
    using comparison and contrast as the method of development. Be sure that
    you have at least one comparison and at least one contrast in the paragraph.

11. Choose a topic and then develop it in a paragraph of at least four sentences
    using classification and analysis. Be sure to indicate your basis of classifi-
    cation. Also be sure that the aspects in your classification are mutually ex-
    clusive, comparable, and do not result in cross-classification.

EFFECTIVE PARAGRAPHS: PARAGRAPH CONSISTENCY: TONE (42g)

A paragraph is **consistent** if its tone does not change unexpectedly for no apparent reason. The tone of your writing should be appropriate—both for your assumed audience and for your purpose and subject matter. Readers are unlikely to find your ideas and point of view credible if the language is sarcastic in one sentence, light and humorous in the next, and very solemn in the next. They will not trust you if the tone keeps shifting, because tone is an indication of attitude.

That is not to say that an essay may not shift among lighter moments and more serious ones; good writing often does that deliberately, to further the purpose and achieve desired effects. But unnecessary changes in tone will disconcert the reader, an experience you have probably had yourself. Imagine reading a paragraph that has a fairly serious tone when suddenly the author seems to find the subject very funny. You may become uncomfortable, even rather embarrassed, and begin to wonder if you've somehow overlooked the punch line or missed the point.

Tone is a cue to readers about the attitude you are taking toward the subject—and the attitude you want them to take. It is also a cue about your attitude toward the readers. If the level or type of vocabulary is inappropriate and inconsistent, not only will readers be confused and unsettled, they are likely to become irritated or even insulted.

The type and level of vocabulary used in a paragraph give it its tone. Notice how the tone of the following two paragraphs differs, although the subject is the same in both:

Last night I had a blind date with one of the most attractive but least popular women in the class. She has a very superior attitude and makes men feel that they are not good enough for her. In view of her attitude toward the opposite sex, few men date her twice.

Last night I was set up with one of our class's real losers. She's a knockout as far as looks go, but as for personality—a drag for sure. Talk about stuck up! She made it plain that on a scale of one to ten, I was a minus two. No wonder none of the guys are beating down her door.

The tone in each paragraph is consistent. In the first paragraph it is fairly formal, impersonal, and unemotional. The tone in the second paragraph is very informal. The use of slang emphasizes the writer's intensely personal feelings. The word choice conveys a sarcastic, somewhat angry attitude.

The tone of the second paragraph would be appropriate for a letter written to one of the author's close friends. The tone of the first paragraph is appropriate for a broader, more general audience. Imagine how inappropriate the second paragraph would be for that audience. Furthermore, imagine how inappropriate a mixture of the two tones would be.

Last night I had a blind date with a real knockout as far as looks go, but she is one of the least popular women in the class. A real drag for sure, she has a very superior attitude and makes men feel like a minus two. In view of her attitude toward the opposite sex, none of the guys are beating down her door for dates.

Tone is one way of telling the reader how you want the meaning of a paragraph to be understood. If the tone is inconsistent, readers may dismiss your writing as amateurish, uncontrolled, and immature.

EXERCISE (42g), PARAGRAPH CONSISTENCY: TONE

Revise the following paragraphs so they reflect a tone appropriate for a thoughtful, college-level audience.

Christo is a Bulgarian-born artist who gets a lot of media attention for the kind of stuff he likes to call out. This guy makes millions of bucks for doing the most bizarre things you can imagine. He blew two million bucks on 2,000 panels of white nylon to put up "Running Fence," a curtain that ran for 24 miles in northern California. If that's not wierd enough, "Wrapped Walk Ways" covered three miles of Kansas City park trails with orange nylon, and "Valley Curtain" was a 400-foot curtain hung in Colorado. I mean, if you think that's art, you must be more than a little ignorant; you couldn't even get his stuff in a museum.

———————————————————————————————

———————————————————————————————

———————————————————————————————

———————————————————————————————

———————————————————————————————

———————————————————————————————

———————————————————————————————

———————————————————————————————

———————————————————————————————

———————————————————————————————

———————————————————————————————

I'm just absolutely insane about Alfred Hitchcock's movies. His movies alternately fascinate me with their technical mastery and then scare the pooey out of me. In the 1920s, well before he left England for Hollywood, he was making spy and crime movies that had incredibly spooky lighting and camera angles. He later got serious and started cranking out psychological thrillers like *The Birds, North by Northwest,* and *Psycho.* Boy, I still can't take a shower when I'm alone in the house, and I sure couldn't take a shower in some isolated motel. When I'm driving, I won't even look at a motel unless it's one of the big chains. Hitchcock made more than fifty motion pictures—he worked for five decades, after all—and his movies made over $200 million. I'm crazy about his stuff.

PERSUASIVE WRITING (43d)

To be effective, writing must not only be unified, coherent, developed, and consistent, it must also be persuasive. An essay with a clear, manageable thesis that is sufficiently supported with well-organized, well-developed paragraphs will not be successful unless the reasoning used in the paragraphs is logical and fair.

That means that the generalizations presented in the thesis statement, topic sentences, and conclusions should not be so broad or overstated that they cannot be supported adequately by evidence. Judgments should be fair and soundly based in facts, not emotions or prejudices. The reasoning used to draw conclusions about the topic and to show the truth of a point of view should be logical, not filled with fallacies and errors. If you want to convince your readers, your writing must be credible. Credibility is built on supportable generalizations, fair judgments, and sound reasoning.

An unqualified **generalization** asserts that what is sometimes true is always true.

> I know two members of the varsity football team and they are very poor students. It's too bad that football players are so stupid.

In this example, a sweeping statement has been made based upon very limited evidence. Checking the scholastic records of all members of the team, however, very likely would have shown that on an overall basis, football players make about the same grades as other students. Some may be poor students, but others are good students and the majority, like the majority of all students, are probably average in their studies.

The point is, of course, that generalizations should be based upon a scrutiny of representative samples of actual, verifiable evidence. If, for example, the scholastic records of an entire football team were examined and it was determined that the scholastic average of these players was below average, it could be stated with authority, in this particular instance, at that particular school, that football players were below-average performers in the classroom. But to go further and state that all football players are below average would be making a generalization that had not been substantiated.

Unless you are certain about the absolute truth of a generalization and certain your readers are aware of its truth, you need to qualify the generalization to conform to the evidence. For example, the assertion about football players would have been more accurate and acceptable if the author had written, "It's too bad some football players are so stupid." If the reader can think of exceptions to the "rule" asserted in your generalization, then the generalization is "hasty." It is too broad, and making it weakens the credibility of your argument.

Fair judgments, like generalizations, must be based on facts. Making a judgment on what you want to believe is rarely as good as making a judgment on what you know. You should be particularly careful to avoid prejudice. Prejudiced statements can be not only those based on your own prejudices but those that appeal to the prejudices of others. Another tactic you should avoid is making your argument against an individual instead of against the issue; this type of argument is known as *argumentum ad hominem*, "argument to the man."

For example, one politician may say of an opponent, "Candidate Robbins will not represent working people's interests in the legislature. He inherited all his money. What could he know about the problems of average, working people?" This argument attacks Robbins personally because he has inherited wealth. It does not deal with the issue of his abilities as a state legislator. Robbins certainly does not necessarily have to be poor or even middle class to understand his constituents' problems or to speak on their behalf.

If a judgment cannot be supported by hard evidence, no amount of name calling or appealing to readers' personal biases will make it legitimate. Even if your prejudices are shared by readers, you are still responsible for presenting a fair and truthful point of view. Besides, thoughtful, questioning readers, unlikely to be fooled by prejudicial judgments derived from sketchy, loaded, or manipulated evidence, will respond negatively to arguments so constructed.

Various forms of unsound reasoning are known as **logical fallacies.** Some of the more common types of fallacious reasoning can be broadly categorized as fallacies of oversimplification or fallacies of distortion. Two fallacies have already been mentioned: *hasty, broad generalization*, a fallacy of **oversimplification**; and *"argument to the man,"* a fallacy of **distortion.** Following is a discussion of some other fallacies included in these two categories.

FALLACIES OF OVERSIMPLIFICATION

1. *Post hoc, ergo propter hoc* ("after this, therefore because of this") is an inappropriate assumption that a cause-and-effect relationship exists.

> I knew when that black cat crossed my path last week I would have some bad luck. Sure enough, today I broke my leg. [It's very doubtful the cat was a contributing cause.]

2. *False analogy* occurs when the arguer assumes that because two things are alike in some respects, they are alike in all respects.

> Children are like fragile spring flowers. To be properly raised, both need lots of tender, loving care and plenty of protection from life's cold winds. [Children and flowers do benefit from loving care, but as many parents will testify, children are also resilient and suffer if they are overprotected from learning to deal with life's disappointments.]

3. *Either/or* (also known as *"all or nothing"*) *fallacy* is a statement that assumes only two alternatives when more than two are involved. This fallacy is sometimes called a "false dilemma."

> I know she isn't a Republican so she must be a Democrat. [The woman may be an Independent, a Communist, a Libertarian, unaffiliated, and so on.]

FALLACIES OF DISTORTION

4. *Argumentum ad verecundiam* (transfer fallacy) is an attempt to transfer characteristics, knowledge, or authority from one area of expertise to an unrelated area. This fallacy is commonly used in political campaigns and consumer advertisements such as endorsements by celebrities.

> Indianapolis 500-winner Ralph Racer says Super-Slick Oil is best. I'd better get some for my car. [There aren't many similarities between a race car and the family station wagon; Ralph's testimony may be less "expert" than it is being made to seem.]

5. *Argumentum ad populum* ("argument to the people") is an appeal to readers' emotions and biases, usually playing on beliefs that are widely held to be sacred (such as family values or patriotism) or on deeply ingrained distrust and fear (such as threats of Communist invasion or nuclear war). A related fallacy is known as *"bandwagon"*; it appeals to people's instincts to "join the crowd."

> Every right-thinking citizen believes the federal government interferes too much in Americans' lives—except for Nicholas, but then he's an admitted socialist. [The "glitter" words "right-thinking citizen" and the "scare" word "socialist" play upon the crowd's desire to belong to an in-group.]

6. *Non sequitur* ("it does not follow") is a wrong inference instead of a logically sound conclusion, usually a leap in logic that omits proof.

> He is the person the class voted to be most successful. He is bound to be a company president. [Success has many definitions, and it's a long way to the executive suite.]

7. *Begging the question* is an assumption of the truth of a statement when, in fact, the truth has to be proven.

> Since she's rich, she must have done something illegal to get all that money. [Wealth is assumed to be evil or at least the result of evil doings. The writer assumes but does not prove that wealth cannot be acquired honestly. The fact is, many fortunes are built on honest labor and sound, legal investments.]

8. *Red herring* is a false "scent" or "trail," an attempt to distract the reader from the real issue needing proof by changing the subject to something else. A red herring often introduces an emotional subject intended to divert the reader's attention.

> I didn't deserve a D on the French test. Besides, the instructor doesn't like me. [Personal dislike, whether true or not, is beside the point. The issue is the quality of the student's work.]

Practice: Identifying Unqualified Generalizations   Some of the following statements contain qualifying words that make them acceptable generalizations. Others do not contain qualifiers, are too sweeping, and thus are unacceptable generalizations. Underline the qualifying words in the acceptable generalizations. Write *Unacceptable* after those generalizations that are unqualified and too sweeping. The answers are listed at the end of the section.

> [1]Anyone who doesn't watch television is uninformed about the world he or she lives in. [2]Anyone who doesn't watch television is more cultured than the rest of us. [3]People who are proud that they don't watch television may think they're proving that they're intelligent and cultured. [4]Handsome men are really self-centered, aren't they? [5]Conservatives will oppose his candidacy. His voting record in Congress is a liberal's dream. [6]A person who has taken three writing courses will generally write better than a person who has taken none. [7]Some Italians talk very fast and wave their hands while they talk. [8]Swedes are all big and blonde. [9]Because the South once had a history of racial prejudice, some people are concerned that Blacks occasionally cannot get a square deal in parts of the South. [10]Orientals sometimes have trouble learning English because the linguistic systems of the Indo-European languages and Oriental languages are so different.

Answers to the Practice   [1]Unacceptable [*anybody who doesn't watch television* is too sweeping and all-inclusive] [2]Unacceptable [3]*May* [4]Unacceptable [*Handsome men* is too all-inclusive] [5]Unacceptable [*Conservatives* and *liberal's* are too imprecise and all-inclusive] [6]*generally* [7]*Some* [8]Unacceptable [*Swedes* and *all* are too all-inclusive] [9]*once, some, occasionally, parts* [10]*Sometimes*

EXERCISE (43)-1, PERSUASIVE WRITING: GENERALIZATIONS AND FAIRNESS

For each of the following statements, insert an *X* in the blank at the right if the statement is a faulty generalization; if the statement is not faulty, write *OK*.

Examples   Fat people don't care about their looks or they'd lose weight.   *X*

It seldom rains in Southern California.   *OK*

1. All doctors are rich. _____

2. Dr. Jones is a well-liked instructor. In student evaluations, over 90 percent of her students give her the highest possible rating. _____

3. When the barometer drops sharply, it indicates that rain or some kind of inclement weather is probable. _____

4. College graduates are more intelligent than high school graduates. _____

5. If you go out with wet hair, you are bound to catch a cold. _____

6. Women make poor business managers; they're too emotional. _____

7. Swedes are a cold and reserved people, as a rule. _____

8. We sold twice as many Lee jeans in our store as all other brands combines. Our customers obviously prefer them to other brands. _____

9. Sales in district A have dropped. We need a new district manager who can shake things up. _____

10. Statistics show that over 50,000 people die and over 2 million others are injured in automobile accidents every year in the U.S.A. You take your life in your hands every time you get into a car. _____

11. Less than half the people in the 18–21 age group voted last year. Obviously, young people don't care about their country's future. _____

12. O'Malley flunked biology, chemistry, anatomy, and physiology. I think she should give up trying to be a doctor. _____

13. Some high school students should not go on to college. _____

14. Because nobody obeyed the 55-miles-per-hour speed limit, the legislature changed it. _____

15. He voted against the school bond issue. I wonder why he is against providing our children the best education possible. _____

16. Hemingway is regarded as one of the great writers of this century. Everyone who reads him likes him. _____

17. On our campus, engineering students take only one semester of English composition. Obviously, they are good writers and don't need a second writing course. _____

18. You can't play basketball well unless you're over six feet tall. _____

19. All of Professor Simpkin's students get A's and B's. This proves he is a good teacher. _____

20. Every time I go to the doctor, he finds something wrong with me. Doctors are certainly out after the money. _____

21. Capital punishment involves the destruction of a human being. Consequently, everyone who favors it is a murderer at heart. _____

22. College entrance scores have gone down considerably over the past ten years. This proves that young people are not as smart as they used to be. _____

23. Grades are bad because they give some students an inferiority complex. Consequently, we should do away with grades. _____

24. We know we have a good coach because our team has won the championship six years in a row. _____

25. Prices at the grocery keep going up. Farmers must be making a nice profit. _____

For each of the following statements, insert an *X* in the blank to the right if the statement is unfair, unethical, prejudiced, or based on apparent wishful thinking rather than on a straightforward examination of the evidence. If the statement is correct, write *OK*.

Example   My neighbor Jack says Ann Jones hates children; no wonder she's a lousy teacher.   X

26. They made their money in the liquor business, so they are obviously an immoral lot. _____

27. I know that they have a much better record than we do, but our team has spirit and will win. _____

28. Hudson County would vote for the Devil himself if he were on the Democratic ticket. _____

29. My son says he saw the minister's daughter shoplifting at the discount store. He must have been mistaken. _____

30. He has been convicted twice for graft. I can't vote for him for county treasurer. _____

31. There must be something wrong with their merchandise since the prices are so low. ____

32. College professors are smart in the classroom, but they don't have enough common sense to walk across the street. ____

33. Teenagers pay more for insurance because statistics show that a greater percentage of that age group is involved in accidents than are other groups. ____

EXERCISE (43)-2, PERSUASIVE WRITING: FALLACIES

For each of the following statements, write an *X* in the blank to the right if the statement contains any of the fallacies discussed in "Persuasive Writing." If the statement is logical, write *OK*.

Example   The rich are not lazy; it they were, they wouldn't be rich.   ___X___

1. All twentieth-century U.S. wars were started under Democratic administrations. So if you want war, vote Democratic.   _____

2. If *The New York Times* says so, I wouldn't believe it.   _____

3. Senator Millstrom says the Russians will never attack us, so let's do away with our land-based missiles.   _____

4. They pull their pants on one leg at a time just as we do, so they can't be any better than we are.   _____

5. The rain came because the Indians staged their rain dance.   _____

6. I'm sure she isn't Catholic, so she must be a Protestant.   _____

7. I have had trouble with botany, so I'll probably have trouble with zoology.   _____

8. Since he was a Heisman Trophy winner, his chances of being a starter for the Cowboys are good.   _____

9. Professor Stillwell kicked the demonstrators out of his class. He certainly doesn't believe in free speech.   _____

10. Sue worked twenty hours a week this term and flunked out. It just goes to prove you can't go to school and work at the same time.   _____

11. He is a very inconsistent person because he does one thing one time and just the opposite the next.   _____

12. Flu shots work only about three-fourths of the time. But it's still a good idea to take them if a flu epidemic is expected.   _____

13. They won the national championship last year and have most of their personnel back. So they're bound to win it again this year.   _____

14. Twenty movie stars have endorsed this new automobile. If it's good enough for them, it's good enough for you.   _____

15. American auto workers have sabotaged several cars still on the production lines. You're better off buying a foreign car.   _____

16. If you have insomnia, you can either toss and turn or take a sleeping pill. _____

17. Since he received nothing but A's in accounting, he should be a good accountant. _____

18. To become a successful person, one must be successful in everything one ever attempts. _____

19. Buying stock in our company is a good investment. We are planning to expand our market and the value of your shares will skyrocket. _____

20. Professor Jones is one of the top psychologists in the country, so when she says that nuclear power is dangerous, we should listen to her. _____

21. Cleenzo must be the best detergent or it wouldn't be the leading brand. _____

22. I said you're too young to drive 400 miles to your grandmother's by yourself. Since I'm your parent, I know what's best. _____

23. Television programs that portray violence are a threat to the mental health of viewers. _____

24. A prison can be a lot like a pressure cooker. If the prisoners' anger and frustration reach the boiling point and find no safe release, the lid can blow off. _____

25. After Marcia dyed her hair green, she had many more dates. It is not true that blondes have more fun. _____

BUSINESS CORRESPONDENCE   (48)

All the skills you have practiced throughout this workbook are applicable to the writing tasks you will face on the job. Both academic and business writing require attention to the same elements of composition: purpose, audience, tone, style, grammar, spelling, punctuation, and organization. If anything, your business associates will be *less* tolerant of poor writing than your college teachers have been. The purpose of business correspondence is to get things done. Consequently, good business writing does not waste a reader's time. It is clear, straightforward, and, above all, efficient.

When you compare business correspondence with academic writing such as essays or term papers, you first might think of the visual differences. College papers are usually composed of uninterrupted paragraphs headed by a title. They also tend to run for a number of pages, frequently three or more. On the other hand, business correspondence uses various kinds of headings, routing instructions, and visual cues to assist the reader. With the exception of reports, most business correspondence is much shorter than college papers: letters are usually no more than a page or two, memos rarely more than three pages long.

Visual cues are important in business correspondence. Paragraphs tend to be shorter than in an essay, research paper, or novel. Lists are sometimes presented vertically, and series may include bullets (dots, asterisks, or dashes preceding listed items) or numbers that would be omitted in an essay.

These stylistic differences between academic and business writing have to do with the way business letters and memos are used. As part of its function of getting a job done, business correspondence often serves as a reference document. Consequently, the reader must be able to find items quickly. By dividing the discussion more frequently into subtopics and by providing more visual cues, the writer aids not only the reader's understanding but also provides a fast, easy reference to specific portions of the document. (For a full discussion of business correspondence types and formats, see Section 48 of the *Prentice-Hall Handbook for Writers,* Tenth Edition.)

The following examples illustrate how the same topic might be treated in the opening paragraphs of a college essay and in a business memo. Notice the differences in the looks of the two examples.

Those Vital Volunteers

ESSAY

Volunteers comprise a vital part of the staff behind a city's efforts to help its disadvantaged citizens. Volunteers assist the professional personnel in many social service agencies by answering telephones, providing transportation, raising funds, and meeting clients when appropriate. Locally, volunteers serve many programs such as Legal Advocates for the Poor, Crisis Hot-Line, the Job Training Center, and the Battered Wives and Children Shelter. In recent years, the number of volunteers has decreased. Our city's Chamber of Commerce is developing a Leadership Program to attract and train large numbers of volunteers for this important work.

MEMO

To: Barbara Swift, Mayor
From: Stan Cox, Councilman
Date: July 26, 198___
Subject: Local Volunteer Leadership

The Chamber of Commerce on July 22 approved a plan for a Leadership Program. The purpose of the program would be to train leaders for local volunteer work. Having attended that meeting, I recommend that the City Council endorse the Chamber's plan.

Program Priorities

The Chamber members believe our city must enlarge its dwindling corps of volunteers to assist local social service agencies. A recent Chamber survey shows that programs in great need include

- Legal Advocates for the Poor
- Crisis Hot-Line
- Job Training Center
- Battered Wives and Children Shelter

Besides using routing instructions—usual in the memo format—and short paragraphs, a list with bullets, and a heading, this memo shows two other features common to effective business correspondence: a **summary beginning** and **streamlined sentences.**

The section "Effective Beginnings and Endings" discusses various types of beginnings for essays. Although any of these may occasionally be effective in business correspondence, most businesspeople prefer an opening that gets right to the point—as Stan Cox does when he states his recommendation in the first paragraph. Remember, recipients of business correspondence are not reading for pleasure or for edification. They are reading because they need information to make decisions, to take action. If your letter or memo takes too long to get to the point, you will have wasted your reader's time and tried his or her patience. As a result, you are less likely to achieve the response you want from the reader.

This same principle of efficiency should be carried out in the sentence structure you use. Try to give your readers the greatest amount of necessary information in the fewest number of words. For instance, compare

> The Chamber members believe our city must enlarge its dwindling corps of volunteers to assist local social service agencies.

> It is believed by the members of the Chamber of Commerce that the corps of volunteers, whose numbers have decreased in recent years, needs to be enlarged by our city so that they can give assistance to social service agencies in the local area.

Obviously, the second example is much more long-winded than the first. The extra words are caused by unnecessary nominals, weak verbs, passive voice verbs, expletives, and phrases. Although none of these are grammatically incorrect, they can be time wasters in business correspondence.

Nominals are nouns formed from verbs: *assistance* from *assist; opposition* from *oppose; statement* from *state.* Common suffixes added to verbs in forming nominals are *-ment, -tion, -ance,* and sometimes *-ity, -ize, -ness.*

Weak verbs such as *give, make,* or *take* often appear with nominals because strong verbs have been changed into nouns, so that new verbs must be found for the sentences. The previous sample contains just such a combination of nominal and weak verb: "so that they can *give assistance.*" Notice how restoring a strong verb adds power and brevity to the sentence: "so that they can *assist.*"

Passive voice verbs tend to drain energy from sentences while adding extra words. (Passive constructions are discussed thoroughly in the sections "Verbs: Active and Passive Voice" and "Emphasis.") For instance, the phrases "It *is believed* by the members" and "the corps . . . *needs to be enlarged* by our city" become more forceful when revised: "The members *believe*" and "our city *needs to enlarge* the corps. . . ."

Expletives (*it is, there were,* etc.) can also be great time wasters. The previous example shows that "It is" adds nothing important to its sentence. An expletive often occurs with a relative pronoun clause containing a sentence's real subject: "*It is* clear *that we* need volunteers." Replacing the expletive with the subject of the relative pronoun clause streamlines the sentence: "Clearly, *we* need volunteers."

Unnecessary phrases can clog writing, too. Frequently, relative pronouns can be "understood" and thus dropped from a sentence: "The Chamber of Commerce believes (*that*) our city must . . . ." Often a prepositional phrase can be rewritten as a single-word modifier: "social service agencies *in the local area*" becomes "*local* social service agencies"; "the members *of the Chamber of Commerce*" becomes "the *Chamber* members." Using the *'s* possessive form can sometimes eliminate a phrase: instead of "the decision *of the mayor*" write "the *mayor's* decision." Verbals (root verb + *ing*) can also be substituted for prepositional phrases into one short, smooth verbal phrase: *with regard to the meeting on Tuesday* becomes *regarding Tuesday's meeting.*

Nominals, passive voice verbs, expletives, relative pronoun and prepositional phrases all have their place in good writing, including good business writing. The point is, we often use more of them than we need; as a result, we use more words than we need or our readers want. Besides lengthening sentences, these constructions can add a ponderous, pompous tone to writing, creating stuffy-sounding business correspondence.

Letters and memos should sound cordial and natural. You don't want a chummy, overly casual tone, but neither do you want to sound like a stuffed shirt. Avoid **business jargon:** rather than creating a businesslike tone, it simply makes your writing sound stiff and old-fashioned, even cold and unfriendly. Instead of "as per your request" say "as you requested"; instead of "at the time of this writing" say "now" or "today." The following list contrasts jargon phrases to more natural, often shorter equivalents preferred in modern business correspondence:

JARGON	PREFERRED
at all times	always
due to the fact that	because
in the amount of [referring to money]	for
in the event that	if
please find enclosed	enclosed is
pursuant to	concerning

Much business correspondence wastes a reader's time because its subject, purpose, and main point are unclear or buried in a mass of detail. Furthermore, the ending of a business letter or memo should not leave the reader wondering what happens next. The writer should supply an **"action ending"** that clearly indicates the action the writer desires from the reader or indicates what will happen next.

EXERCISE (48)-1, BUSINESS CORRESPONDENCE: SUMMARY BEGINNINGS AND ACTION ENDINGS

Read the following memo, paying careful attention to its organization as well as to its contents. Then write a subject line that more accurately and specifically identifies what you believe to be the memo's true topic. Second, write a new opening paragraph that clearly expresses what you believe to be the memo's main point and purpose. Finally, write a concluding paragraph that contains an action ending.

To: Sondra P. Williams, Vice President of Operations
From: Velmer Johnson, Procurement Office
Date: May 14, 19___
Subject: Company Cars

I've talked to most of the auto dealers for major manufacturers in Atlanta, so I just thought I'd let you know what I've found out so far. The information is just about what we expected.

An average case will illustrate my findings. If we buy a fleet of mid-sized automobiles, say a group of Pontiac Grand Ams, the payments will be approximately $285.00 per month for each car, for 48 months. However, if we lease these cars, the lease payment will be $240.00 per month. If we lease the same car for a 50-month contract, a current special offer will allow us payments of $199.00 per month.

While leasing means that we have no equity in the cars when the lease period is over, leasing also requires no down payment on our part. And in the past our maintenance schedules have allowed us to use each fleet car for at least five years. In those five years we average 124,000 miles on each vehicle, so our trade-in values at the end of our extended use of these cars have generally been less than the original amount of the down payment.

I think you can see which course of action is best. By the way, the Grand Am would be a good choice for us, too. It's mid-sized, economical, and roomy. The prices quoted above include the usual power options and air conditioning, but no radios.

To: Sondra P. Williams
From: Velmer Johnson
Date: May 14, 19___

Subject:_____

Opening paragraph _____

_____

_____

_____

_____

_____

_____

_____

Concluding paragraph _____

_____

_____

_____

_____

_____

_____

_____

_____

_____

_____

EXERCISE (48)-2, BUSINESS CORRESPONDENCE: STREAMLINING SENTENCES AND ELIMINATING JARGON

The following application letter is set out in correct business form and is well organized. However, its style is poor. The letter contains long-winded sentences and stuffy business jargon that give it an impersonal, unpleasant tone sure to create a negative impression of the job applicant. Revise the letter, eliminating nominals, weak verbs, passive voice verbs, expletives, and unnecessary phrases where doing so improves the letter's tone and readability. Substitute more cordial, natural-sounding expressions for the jargon.

> 3412 Cannongate Drive
> Augusta, Georgia
> May 14, 19___

Ms. Natasha Hill
Personnel Director
Capitol Press Services
244 Washington Street
Atlanta, Georgia 30334

Dear Ms. Hill:

Pursuant to your notice which was posted in the college placement office at my school, I see you have an opening available with Capitol Press Services. It is my hope that you will give consideration to this, my application for that opening.

My qualifications include a four-year course of study which leads to a bachelor's degree in journalism which will be received on June 15 from East Georgia College. Last summer I gained further experience by working as a reporter for the Burke County *Bugle*, a local weekly paper in this area. This year I was also given employment on a part-time basis with the college newspaper at East Georgia College where I was responsible for the editing of all news stories. I was chosen over four other editors who were majoring in journalism who applied for the job to be news editor.

In accordance with your request, please find enclosed a resume, which gives further details of my educational and work experience. You will see that my initiative and reliability are evidenced by the fact that most of my college education has been paid for by myself.

Due to the fact that I will be making a visit to the home of my parents soon, I would like to pay Capitol Press Services a visit and discuss your job opening with you. You will get a call from me early next week to make arrangements for an interview. In the event that you have questions in the meantime, please do not hesitate to contact me.

Sincerely,

Dale Allen

_____

_____

_____

_____

_____

_____

_____

_____

_____

_____

_____

_____

_____

_____

Using your own paper, write an application letter for a job you would like. Further discussion of employment letters and resumes can be found in Section 48 of the *Prentice-Hall Handbook for Writers,* Tenth Edition.

PRENTICE-HALL DIAGNOSTIC TEST REVIEW I

Name _____ Date _____ Score _____

The purpose of this section and the next one is to provide practice for the *Prentice-Hall Diagnostic Test for Writers.* The instructions are similar to those on the diagnostic test. This section reviews punctuation, basic grammar, and sentence recognition.

Some of the following sentences require additional punctuation. Decide if any punctuation is needed immediately *before* the italicized word, and then write the corresponding number in the blank at the right.

1. The sentence needs a comma.

2. The sentence needs a semicolon.

3. The sentence needs a colon.

4. The sentence is correctly punctuated.

Example The book had been ordered *however* it had not arrived.   <u>2</u>

1. In his book about immigrants *Julian* L. Simon discusses myths about immigrants.   ____

2. As a matter of fact *Nine Myths About Immigration* is the title of Simon's book.   ____

3. When immigrant families and native families are matched by age and education *neither* category tends to use welfare services more than the other. _____

4. The average immigrant family is younger *than* the average native family. _____

5. Because immigrant families are younger and tend to have younger children *they* do in fact spend more money on education. _____

6. When a family spends money on public education *the* government is also paying to provide that service. _____

7. The higher education cost is offset *however,* by lower payments from Social Security, Medicare, and Medicaid. _____

8. In 1975 *the* base year used for Simon's study, the average native family received more money from these sources than did immigrant families. _____

9. The average native family received $922 from these sources *the* average immigrant family received only one-tenth this amount. _____

10. There are studies which show that *even* illegal immigrants do not place excessive burdens on the country's social agencies. _____

11. Only four percent of illegal immigrants go to school free *and* only one percent receive food stamps or welfare payments. _____

12. Seventy-seven percent of all illegal immigrants pay Social Security taxes *but* almost none of them receives these funds back from Social Security. _____

13. Within three to five years after legal entry into the United States *immigrant* family earnings are higher than those of native families. _____

14. Immigrant wage earners are, of course, subject to the same income taxes, sales taxes *and* excise taxes everyone else pays. _____

15. Clearly, immigrants continue to *improve* the tax base in the United States. _____

Read the following sentences carefully for errors in standard English. Circle any errors, and then revise the sentences specifically to correct the errors you have circled.

Example   Do immigrants actually take jobs away from native workers who wants work?

Do immigrants actually take jobs away from native workers who want work?

16. That immigrants actually increase unemployment are one of the most common myths.

   _____

17. In a few cases these charge may be true.

   _____

18. There have been a large influx of foreign physicians into the United States.

   _____

19. Native physician may earn less since this influx has increase the number of available physicians.

   _____

20. However, in the restaurant, agriculture, and hotel industries immigrants take jobs that they won't take.

   _____

21. A study in San Diego concluded that recent immigrants often take jobs that "were not appealing to the local residents."

   _____

22. The wages was too low, the hours was too long, and the work was too difficult.

   _____

23. Four out of five legal immigrants under the age of forty.

   _____

24. Immigrants starts their own businesses more rapidly than do natives.

   _____

25. The image of immigrants as a burden on the country are in sharp contrast with the economic reality.

   _____

PRENTICE-HALL DIAGNOSTIC

TEST REVIEW II

Name ———————————————— Date ————————— Score ————————

This section reviews sentence, paragraph, and composition elements in a manner similar to the *Prentice-Hall Diagnostic Test for Writers.*

Each of the following three groups contains four sentences expressing the same general thought. Select the most precise, clear, and effective one and write its number in the blank at the right.

A. 1. Immigrants are not a burden on the economy, and are often blamed for it.

    2. Immigrants are people who are not a burden on the economy and blamed for it.

    3. Immigrants are not a burden on the economy and are people who are blamed for being so.

    4. Although they are not a burden on the economy, immigrants are sometimes blamed for being so.　　　　————

B. 1. In the modern world of today we desire the world of tomorrow with impatience, but looking back from tomorrow, we may want today back again.

    2. Today we await the future impatiently, but tomorrow we may long for the past.

3. We may be impatient for the future, but tomorrow we may long for the past.

4. Today impatient, the past may be longed for by us tomorrow. _____

C. 1. Immigrants as a whole contain uneducated and educated.

2. The entire population of immigrants has some dummies and some really sharp types.

3. With respect to the attainment of various levels of education, the immigrant population exhibits a remarkably high standard deviation.

4. The immigrant population in this country includes a high percentage of unskilled workers, but it also includes a very high percentage of highly skilled, highly educated professionals. _____

Each of the following two groups contains a topic sentence for a paragraph and five supporting sentences. Read the sentences and then decide how the supporting sentences would best form a well-organized paragraph. You may decide to omit some sentences entirely. In the blank following each exercise, list the number of the supporting sentences in the order you believe they should appear in the paragraph.

A. Topic Sentence: Eric Weiss, later known as Harry Houdini, became the most famous magician and escape artist who ever lived.

1. It wasn't until he discovered a "secret" of performing that Houdini became a success.

2. He learned to play up the drama by sweating, straining, and struggling to escape.

3. Houdini started out as a midway performer, escaping from chains, boxes, and handcuffs.

4. In his early performances, his error was to escape as quickly and effortlessly as possible.

5. Weiss may have been born in Budapest, but the records are unclear.

6. He changed his name to Houdini, a name he took from one of his magician idols.

7. Weiss was the fifth son of a Hungarian rabbi. _____

B. Topic Sentence: There are logical explanations for all of Houdini's famous tricks.

1. Safes were made to keep people out, not in; removable plates on the inside give access to the locks.

2. As the tricks grew more complex, so did the props.

3. Houdini's theme song was always played loudly enough to cover the hammering noises.

4. First of all, nearly every pair of handcuffs made before 1920 could be opened with the same key.

5. Houdini had crates nailed together with small nails so an end of the crate could be pulled off and nailed back on quickly.

6. Most importantly, Houdini could swallow keys and lock picks and other devices and then spit them up at will.

7. This talent—called "retroperistalsis"—made him "the world's greatest escape artist." _____

The following two groups list ideas that might be used for a 500-word essay. Read each essay assignment and choose the answer you think would be the most suitable. Write its number in the blank at the right of the exercise.

A. For an assignment requiring a 500-word essay on *popular music,* which of the following topics has the best focus?

1. The influence of Scots Border Ballads on American Country Music

2. The Modern Symphony

3. The Appeal of Black Gospel Songs

4. Protest Music and the 1960s. _____

B. For a 500-word essay on *recent immigrants,* which of the following topics has the best focus?

1. Recent Immigrants

2. Recent Immigrants to the United States

3. Problems Faced by Recent Vietnamese Immigrants to the United States

4. Immigrants: Myths and Realities _____

INDEX

shift from indirect to direct (shift of discourse), 133